WITHDRAWAL

The Eighteenth Century

Donald F. Bond

**Goldentree Bibliographies
in Language & Literature**

$3.95

The Eighteenth Century

GOLDENTREE BIBLIOGRAPHIES

In Language and Literature
under the series editorship of
O. B. Hardison, Jr.

The Eighteenth Century

compiled by

Donald F. Bond

The University of Chicago

/\H/

AHM Publishing Corporation
Northbrook, Illinois 60062

ISBN: 0–88295–547–0

Library of Congress Card Number: 74–28590

Contents

CONTENTS

CONTENTS

CONTENTS

CONTENTS

Preface

Like the other volumes in this series, the present bibliography is selective, and attempts to steer a middle course between the brief lists provided by the average textbook and the exhaustive references in the professional bibliographies. The proliferation in our own time of editions, biographies, and interpretative studies of the eighteenth century and its writers, both major and minor, has been so extensive that only a selection is possible within the limits of the present series. Pope, Swift, and Johnson, who have attracted most research during the present century, have each been the subject of recent book-length bibliographies, and the space given them here represents of course only a fraction of the critical discussion which they have inspired. No attempt has been made to give a full or historical view of research on eighteenth-century topics or writers. The aim, rather, has been to provide a useful guide to books and articles, generally of more recent date, which illustrate the variety of research most helpful to the graduate and advanced undergraduate student specializing in the eighteenth century.

Another bibliography in this series, by Professors Kolb and Booth, is in preparation on the eighteenth-century novel; consequently such authors as Defoe, Fielding, and Smollett are not represented here, though they wrote not only fiction but poetry, plays, and miscellaneous prose. All their work, as well as that of the other writers of fiction in the century, will be found in the volume devoted to the novel. As for Blake, who appears in many histories of eighteenth-century literature, he is to be taken, along with Wordsworth and Coleridge (who also began writing before 1800), as a figure of the Romantic period and has been given a place in the Goldentree Bibliography *Romantic Poets and Prose Writers,* by Professor Fogle. Finally, a number of books and articles which cover both the Restoration and the eighteenth century aryincluded in the Goldentree Bibliography *The Age of Dryden,* by the present writer. It has not seemed desirable to increase the size of this bibliography by repeating these items.

Items are numbered consecutively throughout the book, and the two indexes—one of subjects and one of modern scholars—refer always to numbered items, not pages. Items with material on more than one subject are generally listed but once; and instead of cross-references all material is included in the subject index. Thus an article on "Johnson and Goldsmith" may be entered under Goldsmith, without a cross-reference to Johnson, but it will be found in the subject index under both heads. Consequently *the index should be constantly consulted.*

In the college or university library, the student specializing in eighteenth-century studies will have access to such standard reference works as Watt's *Bibliotheca Britannica* and the *Dictionary of National Biography* as well as the *New Cambridge Bibliography of English Literature,* of which Volume 2 covers the Restoration and the eighteenth century. For current scholarship the student will use the three annual bibliographies which cover the entire field of English literature and philology—*The Year's Work in English Studies,* the MHRA *Annual Bibliography,* and the *MLA International Bibliography.*

The student of this period is particularly fortunate in having available the series of critical bibliographies founded by R. S. Crane ("English Literature, 1660–1800: A Current Bibliography") which have appeared annually since 1926 in the *Philological Quarterly.* These have been reprinted, with indexes, by Princeton University Press—the issues for 1926–50 in 1950–52, 2 vols.; those for 1951–60 in 1962, 2 vols.; and those for 1961–70 in 1972, 2 vols. (Since 1971 the series has been under the auspices of the American Society for Eighteenth-Century Studies, with an extension of the field to foreign literatures [including Slavic and American] and greater selectivity in the coverage of English.)

In addition there are several valuable newsletters and journals devoted exclusively to eighteenth-century studies. These not only provide specialized bibliographies but also contain articles and reviews, critical discussions, and all kinds of up-to-date news regarding regional meetings, dissertations, work in progress, with notes and queries and other items of interest to the specialist in this field:

1. *Johnsonian News Letter* (1940–). Edited by James L. Clifford (its founder) and John H. Middendorf at Columbia University. Although its main concern is Johnson and his circle, it covers every aspect of English literature from 1660 to 1800 and has been a major instrument in stimulating research in the period.

2. *Restoration and 18th Century Theatre Research* (1962–). Founded by David G. Spencer and Carl J. Stratman at Loyola University, Chicago. It contains news, reports of work in progress, lists of dissertations, and bibliographies.

3. *Eighteenth-Century Studies* (1967–). A quarterly, founded by Robert H. Hopkins and Arthur E. McGuinness at the University of California at Davis. Now "interdisciplinary" in coverage and since 1970 the official journal of the American Society for Eighteenth-Century Studies.

4. *Studies in Burke and His Time* (1967–). Originally "The Burke Newsletter," edited by Peter J. Stanlis and C. P. Ives, in *Modern Age* (1959–61), and as a quarterly (1961–67) at the University of Detroit. From 1967 (as Vol. 9) it has been issued under the title *Studies in Burke and his Time*. Now published three times yearly at Alfred University, it covers the later eighteenth century generally.

5. *The Scriblerian and the Kit-Cats* (1968–). Published twice yearly at Temple University and edited by Peter A. Tasch, Arthur J. Weitzman, and Roy S. Wolper. Originally entitled *The Scriblerian: A Newsletter devoted to Pope, Swift and Their Circle*, it has enlarged its scope to include other early eighteenth-century writers and also Dryden. A special feature is the summaries of foreign books and articles.

Attention is called to the following features in the present bibliography:

1. Extra margin on each page allows for listing of library call numbers of often-used items.

2. Space at the bottom of the page permits inclusion of additional entries.

3. Blank pages for notes follow the final entry.

4. There are two indexes, one of subjects and one of authors.

An asterisk (*) following an entry indicates a work of unusual importance or interest. A dagger (†) indicates a paperback edition.

Donald F. Bond

Abbreviations

Symbols follow the standard forms used in the *MLA International Bibliography*.

ARS	Augustan Reprint Society
BC	Book Collector
BJA	British Journal of Aesthetics
BJRL	Bulletin of the John Rylands Library
BNYPL	Bulletin of the New York Public Library
CCC	College Composition and Communication
CL	Comparative Literature
DUJ	Durham University Journal
EA	Etudes Anglaises
E&S	Essays & Studies by Members of the English Association
ECS	Eighteenth-Century Studies
EHR	English Historical Review
EIC	Essays in Criticism
EL	Everyman's Library
ELH	ELH: A Journal of English Literary History
ELN	English Language Notes
ES	English Studies
ETJ	Educational Theatre Journal
GRM	Germanisch-romanische Monatsschrift
HLB	Harvard Library Bulletin
HLQ	Huntington Library Quarterly
HSNPL	Harvard Studies & Notes in Philology & Literature
IJES	Indian Journal of English Studies
JAAC	Journal of Aesthetics and Art Criticism
JBS	Journal of British Studies
JEGP	Journal of English and Germanic Philology
JHI	Journal of the History of Ideas
JWCI	Journal of the Warburg and Courtauld Institute
ML	Modern Library
MLN	Modern Language Notes
MLQ	Modern Language Quarterly
MLR	Modern Language Review
MP	Modern Philology

ABBREVIATIONS

NM	Neuphilologische Mitteilungen
N&Q	Notes & Queries
PBA	Proceedings of the British Academy
PBSA	Papers of the Bibliographical Society of America
PLL	Papers on Language and Literature
PMASAL	Papers of the Michigan Academy of Science, Arts and Letters
PMLA	Publications of the Modern Language Association of America
PQ	Philological Quarterly
QJS	Quarterly Journal of Speech
RECTR	Restoration and 18th Century Theatre Research
RES	Review of English Studies
RLC	Revue de Littérature Comparée
RMS	Renaissance & Modern Studies
RS	Research Studies (Washington State University)
SAQ	South Atlantic Quarterly
SB	Studies in Bibliography
SBHT	Studies in Burke and His Time
SEL	Studies in English Literature 1500–1900
SF&R	Scholars' Facsimiles & Reprints
SM	Speech Monographs
SN	Studia Neophilologica
SP	Studies in Philology
SQ	Shakespeare Quarterly
SR	Sewanee Review
SSL	Studies in Scottish Literature
SVEC	Studies on Voltaire and the Eighteenth Century
TCBL	Transactions of the Cambridge Bibliographical Society
TEAS	Twayne's English Author Series
TLS	Times Literary Supplement
TN	Theatre Notebook
TSL	Tennessee Studies in Literature
TSLL	Texas Studies in Literature and Language
TWA	Transactions of the Wisconsin Academy of Sciences, Arts, and Letters
UTQ	University of Toronto Quarterly
WC	World's Classics
WTW	Writers and Their Work

NOTE: The publisher and compiler invite suggestions for additions to future editions of the bibliography.

Part One
General Topics

Bibliographies and Surveys of Scholarship

1   *The Ashley Library: A Catalogue of Printed Books, Manuscripts and Autograph Letters Collected by Thomas James Wise.* 11 vols. London, 1922–36.

2   BOND, Donald F. *A Reference Guide to English Studies.* 2d ed. Chicago, 1971. Pp. 76–83: "English Literature, 1660–1800."†

3   CLIFFORD, James L. "The Eighteenth Century." *Contemporary Literary Scholarship: A Critical Review,* ed. Lewis Leary (New York, 1958), pp. 83–108.

4   CLIFFORD, James L. "The Eighteenth Century." *MLQ,* 26 (1965), 111–34.

5   DYSON, H. V. D., and John BUTT. *Augustans and Romantics, 1689–1830.* 3d ed. London, 1961.

6   FOXON, David. *Libertine Literature in England, 1660–1745.* New York, 1965.

7   *Johnsonian News Letter.* See Preface, p. xi.

8   METZDORF, Robert F. *The Tinker Library: A Bibliographical Catalogue of the Books and Manuscripts Collected by Chauncey B. Tinker.* New Haven, Conn., 1959.

9   MORGAN, William T., and Chloe S. MORGAN. *A Bibliography of British History (1700–1715), with Special Reference to the Reign of Queen Anne.* 5 vols. Bloomington, Ind., 1934–42. Of equal value to the student of literature Vol. 3 (correspondence, autobiographies, and diaries; periodicals; plays); Vol. 4 (unpublished manuscripts); and Vol. 5 (supplement and subject index).

10 *Philological Quarterly.* For the annual bibliography founded by R. S. Crane see Preface, p. xi.

11 *Restoration and 18th Century Theatre Research.* See Preface, p. xi.

12 *The Rothschild Library: A Catalogue of the Collection of Eighteenth-Century Printed Books and Manuscripts Formed by Lord Rothschild.* 2 vols. Cambridge, Eng., 1954.

13 *The New Cambridge Bibliography of English Literature.* Vol. 2: *1660–1800.* Ed. George Watson. Cambridge, Eng., 1971.*

14 SCHULZ, H. C. "English Literary Manuscripts in the Huntington Library." *HLQ,* 31 (1968), 251–302.

15 *The Scriblerian and the Kit-Cats.* See Preface, p. xi.

16 *Studies in English Literature 1500–1900.* The summer issue contains an annual bibliographical survey, "Recent Studies in the Restoration and Eighteenth Century."

17 TOBIN, James E. *Eighteenth Century English Literature and Its Cultural Background: A Bibliography.* New York, 1939.

18 TODD, William B. *New Adventures Among Old Books: An Essay in Eighteenth-Century Bibliography.* Lawrence, Kans., 1958.

19 TONELLI, Giorgio. *A Short-Title List of Subject Dictionaries of the Sixteenth, Seventeenth, and Eighteenth Centuries as Aids to the History of Ideas.* (Warburg Institute Surveys, IV) London, 1971.

20 WILES, Roy M. *Serial Publication in England Before 1750.* Cambridge, Eng., 1957.

Collected Studies

21 ANDERSON, Howard, and John S. SHEA, eds. *Studies in Criticism and Aesthetics, 1660–1800: Essays in Honor of Samuel Holt Monk.* Minneapolis, Minn., 1967.

22 BOND, W. H., ed. *Eighteenth-Century Studies in Honor of Donald F. Hyde.* New York, 1970.

23 BOYS, Richard C., ed. *Studies in the Literature of the Augustan Age: Essays Collected in Honor of Arthur Ellicott Case.* Ann Arbor, Mich., 1952.

24 BRADY, Frank, John PALMER, and Martin PRICE, eds. *Literary Theory and Structure: Essays in Honor of William K. Wimsatt.* New Haven, Conn., 1973.

25 BRISSENDEN, R. F., ed. *Studies in the Eighteenth Century: Papers Presented at the David Nichol Smith Memorial Seminar, Canberra, 1966.* Canberra, Australia, 1968.

26 BUTT, John, ed. *Of Books and Humankind: Essays and Poems Presented to Bonamy Dobrée.* London, 1964.

27 CAMDEN, Carroll, ed. *Restoration and Eighteenth-Century Literature: Essays in Honor of Alan Dugald McKillop.* Chicago, 1963.

28 CLIFFORD, James L., and Louis A. LANDA, eds. *Pope and His Contemporaries: Essays Presented to George Sherburn.* Oxford, 1949.

29 CLIFFORD, James L., ed. *Eighteenth-Century English Literature: Modern Essays in Criticism.* New York, 1959.†

30 DAVIES, Hugh Sykes, and George WATSON, eds. *The English Mind: Studies in the British Moralists Presented to Basil Willey.* Cambridge, Eng., 1964.

31 *Essays on the Eighteenth Century Presented to David Nichol Smith in Honour of His Seventieth Birthday.* Oxford, 1945.

32 FRITZ, Paul, and David WILLIAMS, eds. *The Triumph of Culture: Eighteenth-Century Perspectives.* Toronto, 1972.

33 GAY, Peter, ed. *Eighteenth-Century Studies Presented to Arthur M. Wilson.* Hanover, N.H., 1972.

34 HIBBARD, George R., ed. *Renaissance and Modern Essays, Presented to Vivian de Sola Pinto in Celebration of His Seventieth Birthday.* 1966.

35 HILLES, Frederick W., and Harold BLOOM, eds. *From Sensibility to Romanticism: Essays Presented to Frederick A. Pottle.* New York, 1965.

COLLECTED STUDIES

36 HUGHES, Peter, and David WILLIAMS, eds. *The Varied Pattern: Studies in the 18th Century.* Toronto, 1971.

37 JONES, Richard Foster, and Others Writing in His Honor. *The Seventeenth Century: Studies in the History of English Thought and Literature from Bacon to Pope.* Stanford, Cal., 1951.

38 KORSHIN, Paul J., ed. *Proceedings of the Modern Language Association Neoclassicism Conferences 1967–1968.* New York, 1970.

39 KORSHIN, Paul J., ed. *Studies in Change and Revolution: Aspects of English Intellectual History, 1640–1800.* Menston, Yorkshire, 1972.

40 LEWIS, Wilmarth S., ed. *The Age of Johnson: Essays Presented to Chauncey Brewster Tinker.* New Haven, Conn., 1949.

41 MacLURE, Millar, and F. W. WATT, eds. *Essays in English Literature from the Renaissance to the Victorian Age Presented to A. S. P. Woodhouse.* Toronto, 1964.

42 MAZZEO, J. A., ed. *Reason and the Imagination: Studies in the History of Ideas, 1600–1800.* [*Festschrift* for Marjorie H. Nicolson.] New York, 1962.

43 MIDDENDORF, John H., ed. *English Writers of the Eighteenth Century. Essays in Honor of James Lowry Clifford Presented by His Students.* New York, 1971.

44 MILIC, Louis T., ed. *The Modernity of the Eighteenth Century. Studies in Eighteenth-Century Culture,* Vol. 1. Cleveland, 1971.

45 MILLER, Henry K., Eric ROTHSTEIN, and George S. ROUSSEAU, eds. *The Augustan Milieu: Essays Presented to Louis A. Landa.* Oxford, 1970.

46 MINER, Earl, ed. *Stuart and Georgian Moments: Clark Library Seminar Papers on Seventeenth- and Eighteenth-Century English Literature.* Berkeley, Cal., 1972.

47 PAGLIARO, Harold, ed. *Irrationalism in the Eighteenth Century.* (Studies in Eighteenth-Century Culture, Vol. 2.) Cleveland, 1972.

48 PAGLIARO, Harold, ed. *Racism in the Eighteenth Century.* (Studies in Eighteenth-Century Culture, Vol. 3.) Cleveland, 1973. These two volumes edited by Mr. Pagliaro (nos. 47 and 48) and the one above edited by Mr. Milic (no. 44) are publications of the American Society for Eighteenth-Century Studies.

49 PATTERSON, Daniel W., and Albrecht B. STRAUSS, eds. *Essays in English Literature of the Classical Period Presented to Dougald MacMillan.* Chapel Hill, N.C., 1967.

50 SCHILLING, Bernard N., ed. *Essential Articles: For the Study of English Augustan Backgrounds.* Hamden, Conn., 1961.

51 SWEDENBERG, H. T., Jr., ed. *England in the Restoration and Early Eighteenth Century: Essays on Culture and Society.* Berkeley, Cal., 1972.

52 WASSERMAN, Earl R., ed. *Aspects of the Eighteenth Century.* Baltimore, 1965.

53 WATT, Ian, ed. *The Augustan Age: Approaches to its Literature, Life, and Thought.* Greenwich, Conn., 1968.

54 WILLIAMS, Kathleen. *Backgrounds to 18th Century Literature.* Scranton, Pa., 1971.[†]

Histories and General Studies

Histories of Literature

55 BREDVOLD, Louis I. "The Literature of the Restoration and the Eighteenth Century, 1660–1798." Book 3 of *A History of English Literature*, ed. Hardin Craig (New York, 1950).†

56 BUTT, John. *The Augustan Age*. 3d ed. New York, 1966.†

57 *Cambridge History of English Literature*. Ed. A. W. Ward and A. R. Waller. Cambridge, Eng., and New York, 1907–16. 15 vols. Vol. 9: *From Steele and Addison to Pope and Swift*, 1912. Vol. 10: *The Age of Johnson*, 1913.

58 CAZAMIAN, Louis. "Le Classicisme (1702–1740)," "La Survivance du Classicisme (1740–1770)," "La Période Pré-Romantique (1770–1798)." Books 7–9 of Emile LEGOUIS and Louis CAZAMIAN, *Histoire de la littérature anglaise* (Paris, 1924). Eng. trans. by W. D. MacInness and the author (New York, 1927, and later editions).*

59 CHURCHILL, R. C. *English Literature of the Eighteenth Century*. London, 1953.

60 DOBRÉE, Bonamy. *English Literature in the Early Eighteenth Century, 1700–1740. Oxford History of English Literature*, Vol. 7. Oxford, 1959. Rev. by Donald F. Bond in *MP*, 60 (1962), 138–41.

61 ELTON, Oliver. *A Survey of English Literature, 1730–1780*. 2 vols. London and New York, 1928.

62 FORD, Boris, ed. *Pelican Guide to English Literature*. Vol. 4: *From Dryden to Johnson*. London, 1957.†

63 LONSDALE, Roger, ed. *Dryden to Johnson*. (Sphere History of Literature in the English Language, Vol. 4.) London, 1971.

64 McCUTCHEON, Roger P. *Eighteenth-Century English Literature*. London, 1950.

65 McKILLOP, Alan D. *English Literature from Dryden to Burns*. New York, 1948.

66 MINTO, William. *The Literature of the Georgian Era*. Ed. William Knight. Edinburgh, 1894; New York, 1895.*

67 SAINTSBURY, George. *The Peace of the Augustans: A Survey of Eighteenth Century Literature as a Place of Rest and Refreshment*. London, 1916. Rpt. *(WC)*, 1946.

68 SHERBURN, George. "The Restoration and Eighteenth Century (1660–1789)." Book 3 of *A Literary History of England*, ed. Albert C. Baugh. New York, 1948. Rev. ed. by Donald F. Bond, New York, 1967.*†

General Studies

69 BREDVOLD, Louis I. "Some Basic Issues of the Eighteenth Century." *Michigan Alumni Quarterly Rev.*, 64 (1957), 45–54.

70 DOBSON, Austin. *Eighteenth Century Vignettes.* 3 series. 1892–1896. 3 vols. Rpt. *(WC),* London, 1923.

71 EHRENPREIS, Irvin. "Personae." In 27, pp. 25–37.

72 FUSSELL, Paul, Jr. *The Rhetorical World of Augustan Humanism: Ethics and Imagery from Swift to Burke.* Oxford, 1965.[†]

73 HIGHET, Gilbert. *The Classical Tradition: Greek and Roman Influences on Western Literature.* New York, 1949.[†]

74 LUCAS, F. L. *The Search for Good Sense: Four Eighteenth-Century Characters: Johnson, Chesterfield, Boswell, Goldsmith.* London, 1958.

75 LUCAS, F. L. *The Art of Living: Four Eighteenth-Century Minds: Hume, Horace Walpole, Burke, Benjamin Franklin.* London, 1959.

76 MacLEAN, Kenneth. *Agrarian Age: A Background for Wordsworth.* New Haven, Conn., 1950.

77 PRICE, Martin. *To the Palace of Wisdom: Studies in Order and Energy from Dryden to Blake.* Garden City, N.Y., 1964.[†]

78 TILLOTSON, Geoffrey. "The Nineteenth Century and the Eighteenth." In 22, pp. 383–400.

79 WATKINS, W. B. C. *Perilous Balance: The Tragic Genius of Swift, Johnson, and Sterne.* Princeton, N.J., 1939.

The Question of Nomenclature

80 BOAS, George. "In Search of the Age of Reason." In 52, pp. 1–19. Rpt. in 54.

81 BRONSON, B. H. "When Was Neoclassicism?" In 21, pp. 13–35. Rpt. in 54.

82 BURGUM, E. B. "The Neo-Classical Period in English Literature: A Psychological Definition." *SR,* 52 (1944), 247–65.

83 CRUTTWELL, Patrick. "The Eighteenth Century: A Classical Age?" *Arion,* 7 (1967), 110–32.

84 ERSKINE-HILL, Howard. "Augustans on Augustanism: England, 1655–1759." *RMS,* 11 (1967), 55–83.[*]

85 FORD, Franklin L. "The Enlightenment: Towards a Useful Redefinition." In 25, pp. 17–29.

86 GREENE, Donald. "Augustinianism and Empiricism: A Note on Eighteenth-Century English Intellectual History." *ECS,* 1 (1967), 33–68. Comment by Vivian de S. Pinto, "Augustan or Augustinian? More Demythologizing Needed?" *Ibid.,* 2 (1969), 286–93, and reply by Greene, pp. 293–300.

87 HATZFELD, Helmut. "Use and Misuse of 'Baroque' as a Critical Term in Literary History." *UTQ,* 31 (1962), 180–200.

88 JOHNSON, James W. "The Meaning of 'Augustan.'" *JHI,* 19 (1958), 507–22.

89 JOHNSON, James W. *The Formation of English Neo-Classical Thought.* Princeton, N.J., 1967.

90 JOHNSON, James W. "What *Was* Neo-Classicism?" *JBS,* 9 (1969), 49–70. See also Donald Greene, "What Indeed Was Neo-Classicism?" *Ibid.,* 10 (1970), 69–79.

91 MILLER, Henry K. "The 'Whig Interpretation' of Literary History." *ECS,* 6 (1972), 80–84.

92 SECRETAN, Dominique. *Classicism.* London, 1973.[†]

93 TRICKETT, Rachel. "The Difficulties of Defining and Categorizing in the Augustan Period." *New Literary History,* 1 (1970), 163–79.

94 WATT, Ian. "Three Aspects of the Augustan Tradition." *The Listener,* 77 (1967), 454–57, 489–91, 553–55.

95 WELLEK, René. "The Term and Concept of 'Classicism' in Literary History." In 52, pp. 105–28.*

Backgrounds

Historical Background

Bibliography

96 FURBER, Elizabeth C., ed. *Changing Views on British History: Essays on Historical Writing Since 1939.* Cambridge, Mass., 1966. Contains "Early Hanoverian England (1714–1760): Some Recent Writings," by William A. Bultmann (pp. 181–205); "The Reign of George III in Recent Historiography," by J. Jean Hecht (pp. 206–33).

97 HANSON, L. W. *Contemporary Printed Sources for British and Irish Economic History, 1701–1750.* Cambridge, Eng., 1963.

98 MAXWELL, L. F. *A Bibliography of English Law from 1651 to 1800.* London, 1931.

99 PARGELLIS, Stanley, and D. J. MEDLEY. *Bibliography of British History, 1714–1789.* Oxford, 1951.*

100 WILLIAMS, Judith B. *A Guide to the Printed Materials for English Social and Economic History, 1750–1850.* New York, 1925.

Historical Studies

101 ASHTON, Thomas S. *An Economic History of England: The Eighteenth Century.* London, 1955.[†]

102 ASHTON, Thomas S. *The Industrial Revolution, 1760–1830.* 2d ed. London, 1968.

103 CARSWELL, John. *The South Sea Bubble.* London, 1960.

104 CHURCHILL, Winston S. *Marlborough: His Life and Times.* 4 vols. London, 1933–38.[†]

105 CLIFFORD, James L., ed. *Man Versus Society in Eighteenth-Century Britain: Six Points of View.* Cambridge, Eng., 1968.[†]

106 *English Historical Documents.* Vol. 10: *1714–1783.* Eds. D. B. Horn and Mary Ransome (1957). Vol. 11: *1783–1832.* Eds. A. Aspinall and E. Anthony Smith London, 1959.

107 FEILING, Keith G. *The Second Tory Party, 1714–1832.* Oxford, 1938.

108 HERVEY, John, Lord. *Some Materials Towards Memoirs of the Reign of King George II.* Ed. Romney Sedgwick. 3 vols. London, 1931.

109 HOLMES, Geoffrey. *British Politics in the Age of Anne.* London, 1967.*

110 LAMBERT, Sheila. *Bills and Acts: Legislative Procedure in Eighteenth-Century England.* Cambridge, Eng., 1971.

111 LAPRADE, William T. *Public Opinion and Politics in Eighteenth Century England to the Fall of Walpole.* New York, 1936.

112 NAMIER, Lewis. *The Structure of Politics at the Accession of George III.* London, 1929. 2d ed., 1957.*

113 NAMIER, Lewis, and John BROOKE, eds. *The History of Parliament: The House of Commons, 1754–1790.* London, 1964. 3 vols.

114 OWEN, John B. *The Rise of the Pelhams.* London, 1957.

115 PLUMB, J. H. *England in the Eighteenth Century, 1714–1815.* (Penguin) London, 1950.†

116 PLUMB, J. H. *Sir Robert Walpole.* 2 vols. London, 1956–60.*

117 RADZINOWICZ, Leon. *A History of English Criminal Law and Its Administration from 1750.* 4 vols. London, 1948–69.

118 ROBBINS, Caroline. *The Eighteenth-Century Commonwealthmen.* New York, 1968.†

119 SEDGWICK, Romney. *The House of Commons, 1715–1754.* 2 vols. London, 1970.

120 SMELLIE, K. B. *Great Britain Since 1688.* Ann Arbor, Mich., 1962.

121 SUTHERLAND, Lucy S. *The East India Company in Eighteenth Century Politics.* Oxford, 1952.

122 TREVELYAN, George Macaulay. *England Under Queen Anne.* 3 vols. London, 1930–34.*

123 WALCOTT, Robert, Jr. *English Politics in the Early Eighteenth Century.* Oxford, 1956. Rev. by J. H. Plumb in *EHR,* 72 (1957), 126–29.

124 WATSON, J. Steven. *The Reign of George III, 1760–1815.* Oxford, 1960.*

125 WHITE, R. J. *The Age of George III.* London, 1968.

126 WIGGIN, Lewis M. *The Faction of Cousins: A Political Account of the Grenvilles, 1733–1763.* New Haven, Conn., 1958.

127 WILLIAMS, Basil. *The Whig Supremacy, 1714–1760.* Oxford, 1939. 2d ed., rev. by Charles H. Stuart. Oxford, 1962.*

128 WILLIAMS, Basil. *Carteret and Newcastle: A Contrast in Contemporaries.* Cambridge, 1943.

Social and Cultural Background

129 ALLEN, Robert J. *The Clubs of Augustan London.* Cambridge, Mass., 1933.

130 ASHTON, John. *Chap-Books of the Eighteenth Century.* London, 1882. Rpt., with Introduction by Victor Neuberg. London, 1970.†

131 ASHTON, John. *Social Life in the Reign of Queen Anne.* London, 1882, 1883. 2 vols. Rpt., with Introduction by Leslie Shephard. Detroit, Mich., 1968.

132 BAYNE-POWELL, Rosamond. *Eighteenth-Century London Life.* London, 1937.

133 BAYNE-POWELL, Rosamond. *English Country Life in the Eighteenth Century.* London, 1935.

134 BEATTIE, John M. *The English Court in the Reign of George I.* London, 1967.

135 BURTON, Elizabeth. *The Georgians at Home, 1714–1830.* London, 1967.

136 CUNNINGTON, Cecil W., and Phillis CUNNINGTON. *Handbook of English Costume in the Eighteenth Century.* London, 1957.

137 DICKINSON, H. T. "The October Club." *HLQ,* 33 (1970): 155–73.

138 FUSSELL, G. E. *Village Life in the Eighteenth Century.* Worcester, Eng., 1947.

139 GEORGE, M. Dorothy. *English Social Life in the Eighteenth Century. Illustrated from Contemporary Sources.* London, 1923.

140 HECHT, J. Jean. *The Domestic Servant Class in Eighteenth-Century England.* London, 1956.

141 HUMPHREYS, A. R. *The Augustan World: Life and Letters in Eighteenth-Century England.* London, 1954. Rpt. New York, 1963.

142 IRVING, William H. *John Gay's London.* Cambridge, Mass., 1928.

143 JONES, Louis C. *The Clubs of the Georgian Rakes.* New York, 1942.

144 JONES, M[ary] G. *The Charity School Movement: A Study of Eighteenth-Century Puritanism in Action.* Cambridge, Eng., 1938.

145 LILLYWHITE, Bryant. *London Coffee-Houses: A Reference Book.* London, 1963.

146 McELROY, Davis D. *Scotland's Age of Improvement: A Survey of Eighteenth-Century Literary Clubs and Societies.* Pullman, Wash., 1969.

147 MALCOLMSON, Robert W. *Popular Recreations in English Society, 1700–1850.* Cambridge, Eng., 1973.

148 MARSHALL, Dorothy. *Eighteenth Century England.* 1962.

149 MARSHALL, Dorothy. *Doctor Johnson's London.* London, 1968.

150 QUINLAN, Maurice J. *Victorian Prelude: A History of English Manners, 1700–1830.* New York, 1941.

151 RICHARDSON, Albert E. *Georgian England: A Survey of Social Life, Trades, Industries and Art from 1700 to 1820.* London, 1931.

152 RODGERS, Betsy. *Cloak of Charity: Studies in Eighteenth-Century Philanthropy.* London, 1949.

153 ROGERS, Pat. *Grub Street: Studies in a Subculture.* London, 1972.

154 RUDÉ, George. *Hanoverian London, 1714–1808.* Berkeley, Cal., 1971.

155 SOUTHWORTH, James G. *Vauxhall Gardens: A Chapter in the Social History of England.* New York, 1941.

156 TINKER, Chauncey B. *The Salon and English Letters.* Chapters on the Interrelations of Literature and Society in the Age of Johnson. New York, 1915.

157 TREVELYAN, George M. *Illustrated English Social History.* Vol. 3: *The Eighteenth Century.* London, 1951.†

158 TURBERVILLE, A. S. *English Men and Manners in the Eighteenth Century: An Illustrated Narrative.* 2d ed. Oxford, 1929.

159 TURBERVILLE, A. S. *Johnson's England: An Account of the Life and Manners of His Age.* 2 vols. Oxford, 1933. Rev. ed., 1952.*

160 WILLIAMS, E. Neville. *Life in Georgian England.* London, 1962.

161/2 WOODFORDE, James. *The Diary of a Country Parson.* Ed. John Beresford. 5 vols. Oxford, 1924–31. Rpt. 1968.

163 WRIGHT, Thomas. *Caricature History of the Georges.* London, 1868. Originally published as *England Under the House of Hanover* (1848), 2 vols.

Intellectual Background

164 ARMSTRONG, Robert L. *Metaphysics and British Empiricism.* Lincoln, Neb., 1970.

165 BECKER, Carl L. *The Heavenly City of the Eighteenth-Century Philosophers.* New Haven, Conn., 1932. See *Carl Becker's "Heavenly City" Revisited,* ed. Raymond O. Rockwood (Ithaca, N.Y., 1858), and Peter Gay, below.†

166 BREDVOLD, Louis I. *The Brave New World of the Enlightenment.* Ann Arbor, Mich., 1961.

167 BROWN, Robert, ed. *Between Hume and Mill: An Anthology of British Philosophy, 1749–1843: Selected Readings from Hartley to Ferrier.* New York, 1970.

168 BRYSON, Gladys. *Man and Society: The Scottish Inquiry of the Eighteenth Century.* Princeton, N.J., 1945.

169 CASSIRER, Ernst. *The Philosophy of the Enlightenment.* Trans. F. C. A. Koelln and J. P. Pettegrove. Princeton, N.J., 1951.*

170 COBBAN, Alfred. *In Search of Humanity: The Role of the Enlightenment in Modern History.* London, 1960.

171 CRANE, R. S. "The Humanities and Themes of Education in the Eighteenth Century." In his *The Idea of the Humanities* (Chicago, 1967), I, 89–121.

172 GAY, Peter. *The Enlightenment: An Interpretation.* 2 vols. New York, 1966–69.* See also Roger Emerson, "Peter Gay and the Heavenly City," *JHI,* 28 (1967), 383–402, and James R. Leith, "Peter Gay's Enlightenment," *ECS,* 5 (1971), 157–71.

173 GRAVE, S. A. *The Scottish Philosophy of Common Sense.* Oxford, 1960.

174 HARRIS, R. W. *Reason and Nature in the Eighteenth Century, 1714–1780.* London, 1968.

175 HAZARD, Paul. *La Pensée européenne au XVIII* siècle: de Montesquieu à Lessing.* 3 vols. Paris, 1946. Eng. trans. by J. Lewis May, London and New Haven, 1954.

176 HAMPSON, Norman. *The Enlightenment.* (Penguin) London, 1968.†

177 HUMPHREYS, A. R. "The Eternal Fitness of Things: An Aspect of Eighteenth-Century Thought." *MLR,* 42 (1947) 188–98.

178 LOVEJOY, Arthur O. *The Great Chain of Being: A Study of the History of an Idea.* Cambridge, Mass., 1936.*† For discussion of Lovejoy's method see Louis O. Mink in *ECS,* 2 (1968), 7–25, with comment by Philip P. Wiener, *Ibid.,* 2 (1969), 311–17, and reply by Mink, pp. 318–20.

179 MANUEL, Frank E. *The Eighteenth Century Confronts the Gods.* Cambridge, Mass., 1959.†

180 PASSMORE, J. A. "The Malleability of Man in Eighteenth-Century Thought." In 52, pp. 21–46.

181 RAPHAEL, D. Daiches, ed. *British Moralists, 1650–1800.* 2 vols. Oxford, 1969.†

182 ROBERTS, T. A. *The Concept of Benevolence: Aspects of Eighteenth Century Moral Philosophy.* London, 1973. Hutcheson, Butler, and Hume.

183 RØSTVIG, Maren-Sofie. *The Happy Man: Studies in the Metamorphosis of a Classical Ideal.* 2 vols. Oslo, Oxford, and New York, 1954–58. 2d ed., 1962–71.

184 RØSTVIG, Maren-Sofie. *The Background of English Neo-Classicism: With Some Comments on Swift and Pope.* Oslo, 1961.

185 SCHILLING, Bernard N. *Conservative England and the Case against Voltaire.* New York, 1950.

186 SCHOFIELD, Robert E. *Mechanism and Materialism: British Natural Philosophy in an Age of Reason.* Princeton, N.J., 1970.

187 SMITH, Preserved. *A History of Modern Culture.* Vol. 2: *The Enlightenment, 1687–1776.* New York and London, 1934.†

188 STEPHEN, Leslie. *History of English Thought in the Eighteenth Century.* 3d ed., New York, 1949.†

189 SUCKLING, Norman. "The Unfulfilled Renaissance: An Essay on the Fortunes of Enlightened Humanism in the 18th Century." *SVEC.* 86 (1971), 25–136.

190 TRAWICK, Leonard M., ed. *Backgrounds of Romanticism: English Philosophical Prose of the Eighteenth Century.* Bloomington, Ind. 1967.†

191 VEREKER, Charles H. *Eighteenth-Century Optimism: A Study of the Interrelations of Moral and Social Theory in English and French Thought Between 1689 and 1789.* Liverpool, 1967.

192 WILLEY, Basil. *The Eighteenth-Century Background: Studies on the Idea of Nature in the Thought of the Period.* London, 1940; New York, 1941.†

Religion

193 ALDRIDGE, Alfred Owen. "Polygamy and Deism." *JEGP,* 48 (1949) 343–60.

194 BARLOW, Richard B. *Citizenship and Conscience: A Study in the Theory and Practice of Religious Toleration in England During the Eighteenth Century.* Philadelphia, 1962.

BACKGROUNDS

195 BENNETT, Gareth V. *White Kennett, 1660–1728, Bishop of Peterborough: A Study in the Political and Ecclesiastical History of the Early Eighteenth Century.* London, 1957.

196 CARPENTER, Edward. *Thomas Sherlock, 1678–1761.* London, 1936.

197 CARPENTER, Edward. *Thomas Tenison, Archbishop of Canterbury: His Life and Times.* London, 1948.

198 COLIE, Rosalie L. "Spinoza and the Early English Deists." *JHI,* 20 (1959), 23–46.

199 CRAGG, Gerald R. *The Church and the Age of Reason, 1648–1789.* (Penguin) London, 1960.†

200 CRAGG, Gerald R. *Reason and Authority in the Eighteenth Century.* Cambridge, Eng., 1964.

201 CRANE, Ronald S. "Anglican Apologetics and the Idea of Progress, 1699–1745." *MP,* 31 (1934), 273–306, 349–82. Rpt. in his *The Idea of the Humanities* (Chicago, 1967), I, 214–87.

202 CREED, J. M., and J. S. B. SMITH. *Religious Thought in the Eighteenth Century, Illustrated from Writers of the Period.* Cambridge, 1934.

203 DALLIMORE, Arnold A. *George Whitefield: The Life and Times of the Great Evangelist of the Eighteenth-Century Revival.* Vol. I. London, 1970.

204 DAVIES, Horton. *Worship and Theology in England from Watts and Wesley to Maurice, 1690–1850.* Princeton, N.J., 1961.

205 DAVIES, Paul C. "The Debate on Eternal Punishment in Late Seventeenth- and Eighteenth-Century English Literature." *ECS,* 4 (1971), 257–76. Comment by Donald Greene, *ibid.,* 5 (1972), 436–63, and reply by Davies, 464–66.

206 DAVIES, Rupert, and Gordon RUPP, eds. *A History of the Methodist Church in Great Britain.* Vol. I. London, 1965.

207 DAVIS, Joe Lee. "Mystical Versus Enthusiastic Sensibility." *JHI,* 4 (1943), 301–19.

208 DOWNEY, James. *The Eighteenth-Century Pulpit: A Study of the Sermons of Butler, Berkeley, Secker, Sterne, Whitefield and Wesley.* Oxford, 1969.*

209 GILL, F. C. *Charles Wesley.* London, 1964.

210 GREENE, Donald J. "The Via Media in an Age of Revolution: Anglicanism in the 18th Century." In 36, pp. 297–320.

211 HART, A. Tindal. *The Life and Times of John Sharp, Archbishop of York.* London, 1949.

212 HOLMES, Geoffrey. *The Trial of Doctor Sacheverell.* London, 1973.*

213 HOYLES, John. *The Edges of Augustanism: The Aesthetics of Spirituality in Thomas Ken, John Byrom, and William Law.* The Hague, 1972.

214 LINCOLN, Anthony. *Some Political and Social Ideas of English Dissent, 1763–1800.* Cambridge, Eng., 1938.

215 LOANE, Marcus L. *Cambridge and the Evangelical Succession.* London, 1952.

216 LYLES, Albert M. *Methodism Mocked: The Satiric Reaction to Methodism in the Eighteenth Century.* London, 1960.

217 MARTIN, Bernard. *John Newton,* London, 1950.

218 MORAIS, Herbert M. *Deism in Eighteenth-Century America.* New York, 1934.

219 OVERTON, John H., and F. RELTON. *The English Church from the Accession of George I to the End of the Eighteenth Century (1714–1800).* London, 1906.

220 ROSENBLATT, Paul. *John Woolman.* New York, 1969.

221 SMYTH, Charles. *Simeon and Church Order: A Study of the Origins of the Evangelical Revival in Cambridge in the Eighteenth Century.* Cambridge, Eng., 1940.

222 STROMBERG, Roland N. *Religious Liberalism in Eighteenth-Century England.* London, 1954.

223 SYKES, Norman. *Edmund Gibson, Bishop of London: A Study of Politics and Religion in the Eighteenth Century.* Oxford, 1926.

224 SYKES, Norman. *Church and State in the Eighteenth Century.* Cambridge, Eng., 1934.*

225 SYKES, Norman. *William Wake: Archbishop of Canterbury, 1657–1737.* 2 vols. Cambridge, Eng., 1957.*

226 TOWLSON, Clifford W. *Moravian and Methodist: Relationships and Influences in the Eighteenth Century.* London, 1957.

227 TUCKER, Susie I. *Enthusiasm: A Study in Semantic Change.* Cambridge, Eng., 1972.

228 VANN, Richard T. *The Social Development of English Quakerism, 1655–1755.* Cambridge, Mass., 1969.

229 WINNETT, A. R. "Were the Deists 'Deists'?" *Church Quarterly Rev.,* 161 (1960), 70–77.

230 WOOLMAN, John. *Journal and Major Essays.* Ed. Phillips P. Moulton. London, 1971.

Fine Arts

Painting, Sculpture, Architecture

231 APPLETON, William W. *A Cycle of Cathay: The Chinese Vogue in England During the Seventeenth and Eighteenth Centuries.* New York, 1951.

232 BUCHWALD, Emilie. "Gainsborough's 'Prospect, Animated Prospect.'" In 21, pp. 358–79.

233 BURKE, Joseph. "Hogarth, Handel and Roubiliac: A Note on the Interrelationships of the Arts in England, c. 1730 to 1760." *ECS,* 3 (1969), 157–74.

234 CLARK, Kenneth. *The Gothic Revival, an Essay in the History of Taste.* London, 1928.*†

235 DALE, Antony. *James Wyatt.* Oxford, 1957.

236 DE BEER, E. S. "Gothic: Origin and Diffusion of the Term: The Idea of Style in Architecture." *JWCI,* 11 (1948), 142–62.

237 DOWNES, Kerry. *Hawksmoor.* London, 1959.

238 DOWNES, Kerry. *English Baroque Architecture.* London, 1966.

BACKGROUNDS

239 DOWNES, Kerry. *Christopher Wren.* London, 1971.

240 FALK, Bernard. *Thomas Rowlandson, His Life and Art: A Documentary Record.* London, 1950.

241 FLEMING, John. *Robert Adam and His Circle in Edinburgh and Rome.* London, 1962.

242 FOSS, Michael. *The Age of Patronage: The Arts in England, 1660–1750.* Ithaca, N.Y., 1971.

243 FRY, Roger, *et al. Georgian Art (1760–1820).* London, 1929.

244 GAINSBOROUGH, Thomas. *Letters.* Ed. Mary Woodall. Ipswich, 1963.†

245 GAUNT, William. *The Great Century of British Painting, Hogarth to Turner.* London, 1971.

246 GEORGE, M. Dorothy. *English Political Caricature: A Study of Opinion and Propaganda.* 2 vols. Oxford, 1959.*

247 GEORGE, M. Dorothy: *Hogarth to Cruikshank: Social Change in Graphic Satire.* London, 1967.

248 GREEN, David. *Grinling Gibbons: His Work as Carver and Statuary, 1648–1721.* London, 1964.

249 GRUNDY, C. Reginald. *English Art in the XVIIIth Century.* London, 1928, 1934.

250 HARDIE, Martin. *Water-Colour Painting in Britain.* Vol. 1: *The Eighteenth Century.* Ed. DUDLEY SNELGROVE. London, 1966.

251 HARRIS, John, *Sir William Chambers, Knight of the Polar Star.* London, 1970.

252 HAYES, John. *The Drawings of Thomas Gainsborough.* New Haven, Conn., 1971. Rev. by Ronald Paulson in *ECS,* 6 (1972), 106–17.

253 HERSEY, G. L. "Associationism and Sensibility in Eighteenth-Century Architecture." *ECS,* 4 (1970), 71–89.

254 HUSSEY, Christopher. *English Country Houses: Early Georgian, 1715–1760; Mid-Georgian, 1760–1800.* 2 vols. London, 1955–56.

255 HUTCHINSON, Sidney C. *The History of the Royal Academy, 1768–1968.* London, 1968.

256 LEES-MILNE, James. *The Age of Adam.* London, 1948.*

257 LEES-MILNE, James. *Baroque, 1685–1715.* London, 1970.

258 LESLIE, C. R. *Memoirs of the Life of John Constable.* London, 1951.

259 LIPKING, Lawrence. *The Ordering of the Arts in Eighteenth-Century England.* Princeton, N.J., 1970.*

260 LITTLE, Bryan. *The Life and Work of James Gibbs, 1682–1754.* London, 1955.

261 NICOLSON, Benedict. *Joseph Wright of Derby, Painter of Light.* 2 vols. London, 1968.

262 PAULSON, Ronald. "Zoffany and Wright of Derby: Contexts of English Art in the Late Eighteenth Century." *ECS,* 3 (1969), 278–95.

263 PAULSON, Ronald. "The Pictorial Circuit and Related Structures in 18th-Century England." In 36, pp. 165–87.

264 PAULSON, Ronald. *Rowlandson: A New Interpretation.* London, 1972.*

265 RICHARDSON, Albert E. *An Introduction to Georgian Architecture.* London, 1949.

266 RITCHIE, Andrew C. *English Painters, Hogarth to Constable.* Baltimore, Md., 1942.

267 ROSCOE, S. *Thomas Bewick: A Bibliography Raisonné . . .* London, 1953.

268 ROSENBLUM, Robert. "The Dawn of British Romantic Painting, 1760–1780." In 36, pp. 189–210.

269 SUMMERSON, John. *Georgian London.* Rev. ed. London, 1970.

270 TAYLOR, Basil. *Stubbs.* New York, 1971.

271 TINKER, Chauncey B. *Painter and Poet: Studies in the Literary Relations of English Painting.* Cambridge, Mass., 1938.

272 WATERHOUSE, Ellis. *Gainsborough.* London, 1958.

273 WEBB, M. I. *Michael Rysbrack, Sculptor.* London, 1954.

274 WEEKLEY, Montague. *Thomas Bewick.* London, 1953.

275 WHINNEY, Margaret. *Christopher Wren.* London, 1971.

276 WHITLEY, William T. *Artists and Their Friends in England, from 1700 to 1799.* 2 vols. London, 1928. Rpt. New York, 1968.*

277 WITTKOWER, Rudolf. *Palladio and Palladianism.* London, 1973.

278 WOODALL, Mary. *Thomas Gainsborough: His Life and Work.* London, 1949.†

Gardening

279 BALD, R. C. "Sir William Chambers and the Chinese Garden." *JHI,* 11 (1950), 287–320.

280 GREEN, David. *Gardener to Queen Anne: Henry Wise (1653–1738) and the Formal Garden.* London, 1956.†

281 HUNT, John Dixon. "Emblem and Expressionism in the Eighteenth-Century Landscape Garden." *ECS,* 4 (1971), 294–317.

282 HUSSEY, Christopher. *English Gardens and Landscapes, 1700–1750.* London, 1967.

283 HYAMS, Edward. *Capability Brown and Humphry Repton.* London, 1971.

284 JOURDAIN, Margaret. *The Work of William Kent: Artist, Painter, Designer and Landscape Gardener.* London, 1948.

285 MALINS, Edward. *English Landscaping and Literature, 1660–1840.* Oxford, 1966.

286 SIRÉN, Osvald. *China and the Gardens of Europe in the Eighteenth Century.* New York, 1950.

287 STROUD, Dorothy. *Capability Brown.* London, 1950. Rev. ed., 1957.

288 STROUD, Dorothy. *Humphry Repton.* London, 1962.

289 WILLIS, Peter. "Jacques Rigaud's Drawings of Stowe in the Metropolitan Museum of Art." *ECS,* 6 (1972), 85–98.

290 WOODBRIDGE, Kenneth. *Landscape and Antiquity: Aspects of English Culture at Stourhead, 1718–1838.* Oxford, 1970.

Music

291 CARSE, Adam. *The Orchestra in the XVIIIth Century.* Cambridge, Eng., 1940.

292 HUMPHRIES, Charles, and William C. SMITH. *Music Publishing in the British Isles . . . A Dictionary of Engravers, Printers, Publishers and Music Sellers. . . .* 2d ed., with Supplement. Oxford, 1970.

293 LANG, Paul Henry. "The Enlightenment and Music." *ECS,* 1 (1967), 93–108.

294 LANGLEY, Hubert. *Doctor Arne.* Cambridge, 1938.

295 LOWINSKY, Edward E. "Taste, Style, and Ideology in Eighteenth-Century Music." In 52, pp. 163–205.

296 McGUINESS, Rosamond. *English Court Odes, 1660–1800.* Oxford, 1971.

297 SIMONDS, Bruce. "Music in Johnson's London." In 40, pp. 411–20.

298 SMITH, William C., and Charles HUMPHRIES. *A Bibliography of the Musical Works Published by the Firm of John Walsh During the Years 1721–1766.* London, 1968.

299 WELLESZ, Egon, and F. W. STERNFELD, eds. *New Oxford History of Music.* Vol. 7: *The Age of Enlightenment.* Oxford, 1973.*

Handel

300 *Letters and Writings.* Ed. Eric H. Müller. London, 1935.

301 BELL, A. Craig. *A Chronological Catalogue of Handel's Works.* Greenock, Eng., 1969.

302 DEAN, Winton. *Handel's Dramatic Oratorios and Masques.* London, 1959.

303 DEAN, Winton. *Handel and the "Opera Seria."* London, 1970.

304 DEUTSCH, Otto Erich. *Handel: A Documentary Biography.* London, 1955.

305 FLOWER, Newman. *George Frideric Handel: His Personality and his Times.* Rev. ed., London, 1947.

306 LANG, Paul Henry. *George Frideric Handel.* New York, 1966.*

307 LARSEN, Jens Peter. *Handel's "Messiah": Origins, Composition, Sources.* London, 1957.†

308 SQUIRE, W. Barclay. *Catalogue of the King's Music Library.* Part 1: *The Handel Manuscripts.* London, 1927.

309 YOUNG, Percy M. *The Oratorios of Handel.* London, 1949.

Science

Bibliography

310 DUDLEY, Fred A. *The Relations of Literature and Science: A Selected Bibliography, 1930–1967.* Ann Arbor, Mich., 1968.

311 WHITROW, Magda. *Isis Cumulative Bibliography: A Bibliography of the History of Science Formed from Isis Critical Bibliographies 1–90, 1913–1965.* 2 vols. London, 1971.

General Studies

312 BAILEY, E. B. *James Hutton, the Founder of Modern Geology.* Amsterdam, 1967.

313 COPEMAN, W. S. C. *A Short History of the Gout.* Berkeley, Cal., 1964.

314 DAUMAS, Maurice. *Scientific Instruments of the Seventeenth and Eighteenth Centuries.* Trans. and ed. Mary Holbrook. New York, 1972.

315 DOBSON, Jessie. *John Hunter.* Edinburgh, 1969.

316 FOUCAULT, Michel. *Madness and Civilization: A History of Insanity in the Age of Reason.* Trans. Richard Howard. New York, 1965.[†]

317 FRENCH, Roger. *Robert Whytt, the Soul, and Medicine.* London, 1969.

318 GUERLAC, Henry. "Where the Statue Stood: Divergent Loyalties to Newton in the Eighteenth Century." In 21, pp. 317–34.

319 HILL, John. *Hypochondriasis: A Practical Treatise* (1766). Ed. G. S. Rousseau. (*ARS.*) Los Angeles, 1969.

320 JONES, R. F. "The Background of the Attack on Science in the Age of Pope." In 28, pp. 96–113. Rpt. in 29.

321 JONES, William Powell. *The Rhetoric of Science: A Study of Scientific Ideas and Imagery in Eighteenth-Century English Poetry.* London and Berkeley, 1966.

322 KING, Lester S. *The Medical World of the Eighteenth Century.* Chicago, 1958.

323 MACALPINE, Ida, and Richard HUNTER. *George III and the Mad Business.* London, 1969.

324 NICOLSON, Marjorie. "Ward's 'Pill and Drop' and Men of Letters." *JHI,* 29 (1968). 177–96.

325 RATHER, L. J. *Mind and Body in Eighteenth-Century Medicine: A Study Based on Jerome Gaub's De Regimine Mentis.* London and Berkeley, 1965.

326 RICHMOND, William K. *The English Disease: A Study in Despondency.* London, 1958.

327 ROUSSEAU, G. S. "Science and the Discovery of the Imagination in Enlightened England." *ECS,* 3 (1968), 108–35.

328 SARTON, George. *Introduction to the History of Science.* 3 vols. in 4. Baltimore, 1927–48.

329 SINGER, Charles, *et al.,* eds. *A History of Technology.* Vol. 4: *The Industrial Revolution, c. 1750 to c. 1850.* London, 1958.

330 SYPHER, Wylie. *Literature and Technology: The Alien Vision.* New York, 1968.[†]

331 THACKRAY, Arnold. *Atoms and Powers: An Essay on Newtonian Matter-Theory and the Development of Chemistry.* Cambridge, Mass., 1970.

332 VEITH, Ilza. *Hysteria: The History of a Disease.* Chicago. 1965.[†]

333 WILLEY, Basil. "The Touch of Cold Philosophy." In 37, pp. 369–76.

Romanticism and Related Ideas

Romanticism

334 ABRAMS, M. H. *The Mirror and the Lamp: Romantic Theory and the Critical Tradition.* New York, 1953, 1958.[*†]

335 BARZUN, Jacques. *Romanticism and the Modern Ego.* Boston, 1943. See also Norman Suckling, "A Further Contribution to the Classic-Romantic Debate." *DUJ,* 39 (1946), 20–26.

336 BERNBAUM, Ernest. *Guide Through the Romantic Movement.* New York, 1930.

337 DE MAAR, Harko G. *A History of Modern English Romanticism. I. Elizabethan and Modern Romanticism in the Eighteenth Century.* London, 1924.

338 FURST, Lillian R. *Romanticism in Perspective: A Comparative Study of Aspects of the Romantic Movements in England, France, and Germany.* London, 1969.

339 HAVENS, Raymond D. "Discontinuity in Literary Development: The Case of English Romanticism." *SP,* 47 (1950), 102–11.

340 IMMERWAHR, Raymond. "The First Romantic Aesthetics." *MLQ,* 21 (1960), 3–26.

341 JOHNSTON, Arthur. *Enchanted Ground: The Study of Medieval Romance in the Eighteenth Century.* London, 1964.

342 KAUFMAN, Paul. "Defining Romanticism: A Survey and a Program." *MLN,* 40 (1925), 193–204.

343 KUHN, Albert J. "English Deism and the Development of Romantic Mythological Syncretism." *PMLA,* 62 (1956), 1094–1116.

344 LOVEJOY, Arthur O. *Essays in the History of Ideas.* Baltimore, 1948. Reprints most of Lovejoy's studies of the beginnings of romanticism in Germany, France, and England.[†]

345 MARTIN, Roland. " 'Sensibility,' 'Neoclassicism,' or 'Preromanticism'?" In 33, pp. 153–63.

346 PARKS, George B. "The Turn to the Romantic in the Travel Literature of the Eighteenth Century." *MLQ,* 25 (1964), 22–33.

347 ROSTON, Murray. *Prophet and Poet: The Bible and the Growth of Romanticism.* Evanston, Ill., 1965.

348 SNYDER, Edward D. *The Celtic Revival in English Literature, 1760–1800.* Cambridge, Mass., 1923.

349 STERN, Bernard H. *The Rise of Romantic Hellenism in English Literature, 1732–1786.* Menasha, Wis., 1940.

350 VAN TIEGHEM, Paul. *Le Préromantisme: Etudes d'Histoire Littéraire Européanne.* 3 vols. Paris, 1924–47.*

351 WELLEK, René. "The Concept of 'Romanticism' in Literary Theory. I. The Term 'Romantic' and Its Derivatives. II. The Unity of European Romanticism." *CL,* 1 (1949), 1–23, 147–72.* Rpt. in his *Concepts of Criticism* (New Haven, Conn., 1963). Rev. by R. S. Crane in *PQ,* 29 (1950), 257–59.

Primitivism

352 BISSELL, Benjamin. *The American Indian in English Literature of the Eighteenth Century.* New Haven, Conn., 1925.

353 CRANE, R. S. "An Early Eighteenth-Century Enthusiast for Primitive Poetry: John Husbands." *MLN,* 37 (1922), 27–36.

354 FAIRCHILD, Hoxie N. *The Noble Savage: A Study in Romantic Naturalism.* New York, 1928.

355 FITZGERALD, Margaret M. *First Follow Nature: Primitivism in English Poetry, 1725–1750.* New York, 1947.

356 FOERSTER, Donald M. "Scottish Primitivism and the Historical Approach." *PQ,* 29 (1950), 307–23.

357 FRANTZ, Ray W. *The English Traveller and the Movement of Ideas, 1660–1732.* Lincoln, Neb., 1934.

358 HUSE, W. A. "A Noble Savage on the Stage." *MP,* 33 (1936), 303–16.

359 LOVEJOY, A. O., and George BOAS. *Primitivism and Related Ideas in Antiquity.* Baltimore, 1935.

360 PEARCE, Roy H. "The Eighteenth-Century Scottish Primitivists: Some Reconsiderations." *ELH,* 12 (1945), 203–20.

361 TINKER, Chauncey B. *Nature's Simple Plan: A Phase of Radical Thought in the Mid-Eighteenth Century.* Princeton, N.J., 1922. Rev. by R. S. Crane in *MLN,* 39 (1924), 291–97.

362 WHITNEY, Lois. *Primitivism and the Idea of Progress in English Popular Literature of the Eighteenth Century.* Baltimore, 1934.

Sentimentalism

363 ALDRIDGE, A. O. "The Pleasures of Pity." *ELH,* 16 (1949), 76–87.

364 ALLEN, B. Sprague. "The Dates of *Sentimental* and Its Derivatives." *PMLA,* 48 (1933), 303–7.

365 BABCOCK, R. W. "Benevolence, Sensibility, and Sentiment in Some Eighteenth-Century Periodicals." *MLN,* 62 (1947), 394–97.

366 BREDVOLD, Louis I. *The Natural History of Sensibility.* Detroit, 1962.

367 BRISSENDEN, R. F. " 'Sentiment': Some Uses of the Word in the Writings of David Hume." In 25, pp. 89–107.

368 CRANE, R. S. "Suggestions toward a Genealogy of the 'Man of Feeling.' " *ELH,* 1 (1934), 205–30. Rpt. in his *The Idea of the Humanities* (Chicago, 1967), I, 188–213; in 23; and in 54.

369 ERÄMETSÄ, Erik. *A Study of the Word 'Sentimental' and of Other Linguistic Characteristics of Eighteenth-Century Sentimentalism in England.* Helsinki, 1951.

370 FRIEDMAN, Arthur. "Aspects of Sentimentalism in Eighteenth-Century Literature." In 45, pp. 247–61.

371 FRYE, Northrop. "Towards Defining an Age of Sensibility." *ELH,* 23 (1956), 144–52. Rpt. in 29 and 54.

372 HUMPHREYS, A. R. " 'The Friend of Mankind' (1700–60)—An Aspect of Eighteenth-Century Sensibility." *RES,* 24 (1949), 203–18.

373 JONES, W. Powell. "The Captive Linnet: A Footnote on Eighteenth-Century Sentiment." *PQ,* 33 (1954), 330–37.

374 SOLOMON, Stanley J. "Conflicting Sensibility in Death Poetry: 1740 to the Romantic Age." *Enlightenment Essays* 2 (1971), 67–81.

375 WARNER, James H. " 'Education of the Heart': Observations on the Eighteenth-Century English Sentimental Movement." *PMASAL,* 29 (1943), 553–60.

376 WHITFORD, Robert C. "Satire's Views of Sentimentalism in the Days of George the Third." *JEGP,* 18 (1919), 155–204.

377 WHITNEY, Edward A. "Humanitarianism and Romanticism." *HLQ,* 2 (1939), 159–78.

The Literature of Melancholy

378 DOUGHTY, Oswald. "The English Malady of the Eighteenth Century." *RES,* 2 (1926), 257–69.

379 DRAPER, John W. *The Funeral Elegy and the Rise of English Romanticism.* New York, 1929. Rpt. 1967. Rev. by R. S. Crane in *PQ,* 9 (1930), 173–76.

380 McKILLOP, Alan D. "Nature and Science in the Works of James Hervey." *Texas Studies in English,* 28 (1949), 124–38.

381 MOORE, C. A. "The English Malady." *Backgrounds of English Literature, 1700–1760* (Minneapolis, 1953).

382 REED, Amy L. *The Background of Gray's Elegy: A Study in the Taste for Melancholy Poetry, 1700–1751.* New York, 1924.

383 SENA, John F. *A Bibliography of Melancholy, 1660–1800.* London, 1970.

384 SICKELS, Eleanor M. *The Gloomy Egoist: Moods and Themes of Melancholy from Gray to Keats.* New York, 1932.

Poetry

Bibliography

385 BOYS, Richard C. "A Finding List of English Poetical Miscellanies 1700–48 in Selected American Libraries." *ELH,* 7 (1940), 144–62.

386 CASE, Arthur E. *A Bibliography of English Poetical Miscellanies, 1521–1750.* Oxford, 1935.

387 CRUM, Margaret. *First-Line Index of English Poetry, 1500–1800 in Manuscripts of the Bodleian Library, Oxford.* 2 vols. Oxford and New York, 1969.

388 EDDY, Donald D. "Dodsley's *Collection of Poems by Several Hands* (Six Volumes), 1758: Index of Authors." *PBSA,* 60 (1966), 9–30.

389 OSBORNE, Mary T. *Advice-to-a-Painter Poems, 1633–1856: An Annotated Finding-List.* Austin, Tex., 1949.

General Studies

390 BALLIET, Conrad A. "The History and Rhetoric of the Triplet." *PMLA,* 80 (1965), 528–34.

391 BATE, William J. *The Burden of the Past and the English Poet.* Cambridge, Mass., 1970.

392 BOND, Richmond P. *English Burlesque Poetry, 1700–1750.* Cambridge, Mass., 1932. Additions by A. J. Sambrook, *SB,* 23 (1970), 176–79; by A. B. England, *Ibid.,* 27 (1974), 236–40.

393 BRADNER, Leicester. *Musae Anglicanae: A History of Anglo-Latin Poetry, 1500–1925.* New York, 1940. Supplementary List in *The Library,* 5th ser., 22 (1967), 93–103.

394 BRONSON, Bertrand. "The Pre-Romantic or Post-Augustan Mode [in English Poetry]." *ELH,* 20 (1953), 15–28.

395 BROWN, Wallace Cable. *The Triumph of Form: A Study of the Later Masters of the Heroic Couplet.* Chapel Hill, N.C., 1948.

396 BUDICK, Sanford. *Poetry of Civilization: Mythopoeic Displacement in the Verse of Milton, Dryden, Pope, and Johnson.* New Haven, Conn., 1974.

397 BUTT, John. "Science and Man in Eighteenth-Century Poetry." *DUJ,* 39 (1947), 79–88. Rpt. in his *Pope, Dickens, and Others: Essays and Addresses,* Edinburgh, 1969, pp. 91–110.

398 BUTT, John. "The Imitation of Horace in English Poetry," in *Pope, Dickens, and Others* (Edinburgh, 1969), pp. 73–90.

399 CHAPIN, Chester F. *Personification in Eighteenth-Century English Poetry.* New York, 1955.

400 COHEN, Ralph. "The Augustan Mode in English Poetry." *ECS,* 1 (1967), 3–32. Rpt. in 25.

401 CRAWFORD, Thomas. "Scottish Popular Ballads and Lyrics of the Eighteenth and Early Nineteenth Centuries: Some Preliminary Conclusions." *SSL,* 1 (1963), 49–63.

402 DRAPER, John W. "The Metrical Tale in XVIII-Century England." *PMLA,* 52 (1937), 390–97.

403 EDWARDS, Thomas R. *Imagination and Power: A Study of Poetry on Public Themes.* New York, 1971.

404 FAIRCHILD, Hoxie N. *Religious Trends in English Poetry.* 5 vols. Vol. 1: *1700–1740: Protestantism and the Cult of Sentiment* (1939). Vol. 2: *1740–1780: Religious Sentimentalism in the Age of Johnson* (1942). Vol. 3: *1780–1830: Romantic Faith* (1949). New York, 1939–62.

405 FRIEDMAN, Albert B. *The Ballad Revival: Studies in the Influence of Popular on Sophisticated Poetry.* Chicago, 1961.

406 FROST, William, "English Persius: The Golden Age." *ECS,* 2 (1968), 77–101.

407 FUSSELL, Paul, Jr. *Theory of Prosody in Eighteenth-Century England.* New London, Conn., 1954.

408 GREENE, Donald J. " 'Logical Structure' in Eighteenth-Century Poetry." *PQ,* 31 (1952), 315–36.

409 HAVENS, Raymond D. "The Poetic Diction of the English Classicists." *Kittredge Anniversary Papers* (Boston, 1913), pp. 435–44.

410 HAVENS, Raymond D. *The Influence of Milton on English Poetry.* Cambridge, Mass., 1922.* Contains (chap. 19) "A History of the Sonnet in the eighteenth and early nineteenth centuries." See also R. P. McCutcheon in *MLN,* 40 (1925), 513–14; R. D. Havens, *ibid.,* 45 (1930), 77–84; Robert A. Aubin, *ibid.,* 49 (1934), 507–9.

411 HAVENS, Raymond D. "Assumed Personality, Insanity, and Poetry." *RES,* N.S. 4 (1953), 26–37.

412 HEATH-STUBBS, John. *The Ode.* London, 1969.

413 HORNING, Sister Mary Eulogia. *Evidences of Romantic Treatment of Religious Elements in Late Eighteenth-Century Minor Poetry, 1771–1800.* New York, 1972.

414 KOVACEVICH, Ivanka. "The Mechanical Muse: The Impact of Technical Inventions on Eighteenth-Century Neo-Classical Poetry." *HLQ,* 28 (1965), 263–81.

415 LEVINE, Jay A. "The Status of the Verse Epistle before Pope." *SP,* 59 (1962), 658–84.

416 McKILLOP, Alan D. "Local Attachment and Cosmopolitanism: The Eighteenth-Century Pattern." In 35, pp. 191–218.

417 MILES, Josephine. *Eras and Modes in English Poetry.* Berkeley, Cal., 1957.

418 MINER, Earl. "From 'Narrative' to 'Description' and 'Sense' in Eighteenth-Century Poetry." *SEL,* 9 (1969), 471–87.

419 MOORE, C. A. "Whig Panegyric Verse, 1700–1760: A Phase of Sentimentalism." *PMLA,* 41 (1926): 362–401. Rpt. in his *Backgrounds of English Literature, 1700–1760* (Minneapolis, 1953).

420 MORRIS, David B. *The Religious Sublime: Christian Poetry and Critical Tradition in Eighteenth-Century England.* Lexington, Ky., 1972.

421 PIPER, William B. *The Heroic Couplet.* Cleveland, 1969.

422 RENWICK, W. L. "Notes on Some Lesser Poets of the Eighteenth Century." In 31, pp. 130–46.

423 RICHARDS, Edward Ames. *Hudibras in the Burlesque Tradition.* New York, 1937.

424 SAMPSON, H. Grant. *The Anglican Tradition in Eighteenth-Century Verse.* The Hague, 1971.†

425 SHUSTER, George N. *The English Ode from Milton to Keats.* New York, 1940.

426 SMITH, David Nichol. *Some Observations on Eighteenth-Century Poetry.* London, 1937. 2d ed., 1964.†

427 SPACKS, Patricia M. *The Insistence of Horror: Aspects of the Supernatural in Eighteenth-Century Poetry.* Cambridge, Mass., 1962.

428 SPACKS, Patricia M. *The Poetry of Vision: Five Eighteenth-Century Poets.* Cambridge, Mass., 1967. Collins, Cowper, Gray, Smart, and Thomson.

429 STEWART, Keith. "The Ballad and the *Genres* in the Eighteenth Century." *ELH* 24 (1957), 120–37.

430 SUTHERLAND, James. *A Preface to Eighteenth Century Poetry.* Oxford, 1948. Rpt. with additional notes, 1962.*†

431 THOMPSON, Elbert N. S. "The Octosyllabic Couplet." *PQ,* 18 (1939), 257–68.

432 THORPE, Peter. "Some Fallacies in the Study of Augustan Poetry." *Criticism,* 9 (1967), 326–36.

433 THORPE, Peter. "The Nonstructure of Augustan Verse." *PLL,* 5 (1969), 235–51.

434 THORPE, Peter. " 'No Metaphor Swell'd High': The Relative Unimportance of Imagery or Figurative Language in Augustan Poetry." *TSLL,* 13 (1972), 593–612.

435 TILLOTSON, Geoffrey. "Augustan Poetic Diction: Nature, Art and Man's 'Imperium.' " *TLS,* Jan. 4, 1936, pp. 1–2. Rpt. in his *Essays in Criticism and Research* (Cambridge, Eng., 1942), pp. 53–62.

436 TILLOTSON, Geoffrey. "Eighteenth-Century Poetic Diction." *E&S,* 25 (1940), 59–80. Rpt. in his *Essays in Criticism and Research,* (Cambridge, 1942), pp. 63–85, and rev. in his *Augustan Studies* (1961). Rpt. in 29.

437 TILLOTSON, Geoffrey. "Matthew Arnold and Eighteenth-Century Poetry." In 31, pp. 252–73.

438 TILLOTSON, Geoffrey. "The Manner of Proceeding in Certain Eighteenth- and Early Nineteenth-Century Poems." *PBA,* 34 (1948). Rpt. as Chap. 5 in his *Augustan Studies* (1961).

439 TILLOTSON, Geoffrey. *Augustan Poetic Diction.* Oxford, 1964. Chaps. 1–4 from *Augustan Studies* (1961) revised.

440 TRICKETT, Rachel. *The Honest Muse: A Study in Augustan Verse.* Oxford, 1967.

441 WASSERMAN, Earl R. "The Return of the Enjambed Couplet." *ELH,* 7 (1940), 239–52.

442 WASSERMAN, Earl R. *Elizabethan Poetry in the Eighteenth Century.* Urbana, 1947.

443 WASSERMAN, Earl R. "The Inherent Values of Eighteenth-Century Personification." *PMLA,* 65 (1950), 435–63.

444 WASSERMAN, Earl R. "Nature Moralized: The Divine Analogy in the Eighteenth Century." *ELH,* 20 (1953), 39–76.

445 WILLIAMS, Iolo A. *Points in Eighteenth Century Verse.* London, 1934.

446 WIMSATT, W. K., Jr. "Rhetoric and Poems: The Example of Pope." *English Institute Essays 1948* (New York, 1949), pp. 179–207. Rpt. in his *The Verbal Icon* (Lexington, Ky., 1954).

447 WIMSATT, W. K., Jr. "The Augustan Mode in English Poetry." *ELH,* 20 (1953), 1–14. Rpt. in his *Hateful Contraries* (Lexington, Ky., 1965).

448 WIMSATT, W. K., Jr. "Imitation as Freedom: 1717–1798." *New Literary History,* 1 (1970), 215–36.

449 YOHANNAN, John D. "The Persian Poetry Fad in England, 1770–1825." *CL,* 4 (1952), 136–60.

The Treatment of External Nature

450 ARTHOS, John. *The Language of Natural Description in Eighteenth-Century Poetry.* Ann Arbor, Mich., 1949. Rpt. 1966.

451 AUBIN, Robert A. *Topographical Poetry in XVIII-Century England.* New York, 1936.

452 BRAGG, Marion K. *The Formal Eclogue in Eighteenth-Century England.* Orono, Maine, 1926.

453 CHALKER, John. *The English Georgic: A Study in the Development of a Form.* Baltimore, 1969.

454 DEANE, Cecil V. *Aspects of Eighteenth Century Nature Poetry.* Oxford, 1935.

455 DURLING, Dwight L. *Georgic Tradition in English Poetry.* New York, 1935.

456 FOSTER, John W. "A Redefinition of Topographical Poetry." *JEGP,* 69 (1970), 394–406.

457/458 HAAS, C. E. de. *Nature and the Country in English Poetry of the First Half of the Eighteenth Century.* Amsterdam, 1928.

459 JONES, Richard F. "Eclogue Types in English Poetry of the Eighteenth Century." *JEGP,* 24 (1925), 33–60.

460 LITZ, Francis E. "Richard Bentley on Beauty, Irregularity, and Mountains." *ELH,* 12 (1945), 327–32.

461 MANWARING, Elizabeth W. *Italian Landscape in Eighteenth Century England: A Study Chiefly of the Influence of Claude Lorrain and Salvator Rosa on English Taste, 1700–1800.* New York, 1925. Rpt. 1965.

462 MOORE, Cecil A. "The Return to Nature in English Poetry of the Eighteenth Century." *SP,* 14 (1917), 243–91. Rpt. in his *Backgrounds of English Literature, 1700–1760* (Minneapolis, 1953).

463 NICOLSON, Marjorie H. *Newton Demands the Muse: Newton's "Opticks" and the Eighteenth-Century Poets.* Princeton, N. J., 1946.

464 OGDEN, H. V. S. "Thomas Burnet's *Telluris Theoria Sacra* and Mountain Scenery." *ELH,* 14 (1947), 139–50.

465 PRIESTLEY, F. E. L. "Newton and the Romantic Concept of Nature." *UTQ,* 17 (1948), 323–36.

466 REYNOLDS, Myra. *The Treatment of Nature in English Poetry Between Pope and Wordsworth.* Chicago, 1896. 2d ed., 1909. Rpt. New York, 1966, 1971.

467 SAMBROOK, A. J. "An Essay on Eighteenth-Century Pastoral, Pope to Wordsworth." *Trivium,* 5 (1970), 21–35; 6 (1971), 103–15.

468 SPENCER, Jeffrey B. *Heroic Nature: Ideal Landscape in English Poetry from Marvell to Thomson.* Evanston, Ill., 1973.

469 STUART, Dorothy M. "Landscape in Augustan Verse." *E&S,* 26 (1940), 73–87.

470 TILLOTSON, Geoffrey. "The Methods of Description in Eighteenth- and Nineteenth-Century Poetry." In 27, pp. 235–38.

471 WILLIAMS, George G. "The Beginnings of Nature Poetry in the Eighteenth Century." *SP,* 27 (1930), 583–608.

472 WILLIAMS, Raymond. " 'Nature's Threads.' " *ECS,* 2 (1968), 45–57.

Drama

Anthologies

In addition to the numerous anthologies of Restoration and eighteenth-century plays, the following on special types should be noted.

473 *Burlesque Plays of the Eighteenth Century.* Ed. Simon Trussler. Oxford, 1969.†

474 *Eighteenth-Century Drama: Afterpieces.* Ed. Richard W. Bevis. Oxford, 1970.†

475 *Ten English Farces.* Eds. Leo Hughes and A. H. Scouten. Austin, Tex., 1948.

Bibliography

476 ARNOTT, James F., and John W. ROBINSON. *English Theatrical Literature, 1559–1900: A Bibliography, Incorporating Robert W. Lowe's "A Bibliographical Account of English Theatrical Literature."* London, 1970.

477 STRATMAN, Carl J., David G. SPENCER, and Mary Elizabeth DEVINE. *Restoration and Eighteenth-Century Theatre Research: A Bibliographical Guide, 1900–1968.* Carbondale, Ill., 1971.

General Studies

478 APPLETON, William W. "The Double Gallant in Eighteenth-Century Comedy." In 43, pp. 145–57.

479 AVERY, Emmett L. "Dancing and Pantomime on the English Stage, 1700–1737." *SP,* 31 (1934), 417–52.

DRAMA

480 AVERY, Emmett L. "The Defence and Criticism of Pantomimic Entertainments in the Early Eighteenth Century." *ELH,* 5 (1938), 127–45.

481 AVERY, Emmett L. "Some New Prologues and Epilogues, 1704–1708." *SEL,* 5 (1965), 455–67.

482 BAKER, Herschel. *John Philip Kemble: The Actor in His Theatre.* Cambridge, Mass., 1942.

483 BASKERVILL, Charles Read. "Play-Lists and Afterpieces of the Mid-Eighteenth Century." *MP,* 23 (1926), 445–64.

484 BATESON, F. W. *English Comic Drama, 1700–1750.* Oxford, 1929, 1963.

485 BOAS, Frederick S. *An Introduction to Eighteenth-Century Drama, 1700–1780.* Oxford, 1953.

486 CLARK, William S. *The Irish Stage in the Country Towns, 1720–1800.* Oxford, 1965.

487 *A Comparison Between the Two Stages.* . . . Ed. Staring B. Wells. Princeton, N.J., 1942.

488 CONNOLLY, Leonard W. "The Censor's Wife at the Theatre: The Diary of Anna Margaretta Larpent, 1790–1800." *HLQ,* 35 (1971), 49–64.

489 DIRCKS, Richard J. *"Les Fêtes Champêtres* 1774: Literary and Theatrical Perspectives." *PQ,* 50 (1971), 647–56.

490 DONALDSON, Ian. *The World Upside Down: Comedy from Jonson to Fielding.* Oxford, 1970.

491 DOWNER, Alan S. "Nature to Advantage Dressed: Eighteenth-Century Acting." *PMLA,* 58 (1943), 1002–37.

492 DUNBAR, Janet. *Peg Woffington and Her World.* London, 1968.

493 EVANS, Bertrand. *Gothic Drama from Walpole to Shelley.* Berkeley, Cal., 1947.

494 FFRENCH, Yvonne. *Mrs. Siddons, Tragic Actress.* Rev. ed., London, 1954.

495 FOTHERGILL, Brian. *Mrs. Jordan: Portrait of an Actress.* 1965.

496 GORE-BROWN, Robert. *Gay Was the Pit: The Life and Times of Anne Oldfield, Actress (1688–1720).* London, 1957.

497 HIGHFILL, Philip H., Jr., Kalman A. BURNIM, and Edward A. LANGHANS. *A Biographical Dictionary of Actors, Actresses, Musicians, Dancers, Managers, and Other Stage Personnel in London, 1660–1800.* Carbondale, Ill., 1973– . In progress.*

498 HNATKO, Eugene. "The Failure of Eighteenth-Century Tragedy." *SEL,* 11 (1971), 459–68.

499 HUGHES, Leo. *A Century of English Farce.* Princeton, N.J., 1956.

500 HUGHES, Leo. *The Drama's Patrons: A Study of the Eighteenth-Century London Audience.* Austin, Tex., 1971.

501 KAUFMAN, Paul. "The Reading of Plays in the Eighteenth Century." *BNYPL,* 73 (1969), 562–80.

502 KELLY, John A. *German Visitors to English Theaters in the Eighteenth Century.* Princeton, N.J., 1936.

503 KENNY, Shirley S. "Theatrical Warfare, 1695–1710." *TN,* 27 (1972), 130–45.

504 KINNE, Willard A. *Revivals and Importations of French Comedies in England, 1749–1800.* New York, 1939.

505 KNAPP, Mary E. *Prologues and Epilogues of the Eighteenth Century.* New Haven, Conn., 1961.

506 KRONENBERGER, Louis. *The Thread of Laughter: Chapters on English Stage Comedy from Jonson to Maugham.* New York, 1953.

507 LANGHANS, Edward A. "Three Early Eighteenth-Century Promptbooks." *TN,* 20 (1966), 142–50. See also *MP,* 65 (1967), 114–29.

508 LOFTIS, John. *Comedy and Society from Congreve to Fielding.* Stanford, Cal., 1959.

509 LOFTIS, John. *The Politics of Drama in Augustan England.* Oxford, 1963.*

510 LOFTIS, John. "The Limits of Historical Veracity in Neoclassical Drama." In 51, pp. 27–50.

511 LOFTIS, John, ed. *Essays on the Theatre from Eighteenth-Century Periodicals.* (*ARS*) Los Angeles, 1960.

512 LOFTIS, John. *The Spanish Plays of Neoclassical England.* New Haven, Conn., 1973.

513 *The London Stage, 1660–1800. A Calendar of Plays, Entertainments and Afterpieces Together with Casts, Box-Receipts and Contemporary Comment, Compiled from the Playbills, Newspapers and Theatrical Diaries of the Period.* Carbondale, Ill., 1960–68.* 11 vols.
   Part 1, 1660–1700. Ed. William Van Lennep. 1965.†
   Part 2, 1700–1729. Ed. Emmett L. Avery. 2 vols. 1960.†
   Part 3, 1729–1747. Ed. A. H. Scouten. 2 vols. 1961.†
   Part 4, 1747–1776. Ed. George W. Stone, Jr. 3 vols. 1962.†
   Part 5, 1776–1800. Ed. Charles B. Hogan. 3 vols. 1968.†

514 LYNCH, James J. *Box, Pit, and Gallery: Stage and Society in Johnson's London.* Berkeley, Cal., 1953.

515 MACEY, Samuel. "Theatrical Satire: A Protest from the Stage Against Poor Taste in Theatrical Entertainment." In 36, pp. 121–29.

516 MacMILLAN, Dougald. *Drury Lane Calendar, 1747–1776.* Oxford, 1938.

517 MacMILLAN, Dougald. *Catalogue of the Larpent Plays in the Huntington Library.* San Marino, Cal., 1939. See also Ethel Pearce in *MLQ,* 6 (1943), 491–94.

518 MacMILLAN, Dougald. "The Rise of Social Comedy in the Eighteenth Century." *PQ,* 41 (1962), 330–38.

519 NICOLL, Allardyce. *A History of English Drama, 1660–1800.* Cambridge, 1952–59. 6 vols. Vols. 2–3 deal with the eighteenth century.*

520 PEDICORD, Harry W. *The Theatrical Public in the Time of Garrick.* New York, 1954.†

521 PEDICORD, Harry W. "Course of Plays, 1740–2: An Early Diary of Richard Cross, Prompter to the Theatre." *BJRL,* 40, no. 2 (1958), 1–46.

522 PEDICORD, Harry W. "White Gloves at Five: Fraternal Patronage of London Theatres in the Eighteenth Century." *PQ,* 45 (1966), 270–88.

523 PRICE, Cecil. *Theatre in the Age of Garrick.* Oxford, 1973.

524 RICHARDS, Kenneth, and Peter THOMSON, eds. *The Eighteenth-Century English Stage.* London, 1972.

525 ROSENFELD, Sybil. *The Theatres of the London Fairs in the Eighteenth Century.* Cambridge, 1960.

526 RUTHERFORD, Marie-Rose. "The Abbé Prévost and the English Theatre, 1730–1740." *TN,* 9 (1955), 111–18.

527 SANDS, Mollie. "Mrs. Tofts, 1685?–1756." *TN,* 20 (1966), 100–12.

528 SAWYER, Paul. "The Popularity of Various Types of Entertainment at Lincoln's Inn Fields and Covent Garden Theatres, 1720–1733." *TN,* 24 (1970), 154–63.

529 TAYLOR, Aline M. "The Patrimony of James Quin: The Legend and the Facts." *Tulane Studies in English,* 8 (1958), 55–106.

530 THOMAS, Russell. "Contemporary Taste in the Stage Directions of London Theaters, 1770–1800." *MP,* 42 (1944), 65–78.

531 THORP, Willard. "The Stage Adventures of Some Gothic Novels." *PMLA,* 43 (1928), 476–86.

532 TOBIN, Terence. "A List of Plays and Entertainments by Scottish Dramatists, 1660–1800." *SB,* 23 (1970), 103–17.

533 TOBIN, Terence. "A List of Anonymous Pieces Presented at the Theatre Royal, Edinburgh, 1767–1800." *SSL,* 7 (1970), 29–34.

534 TUCKER, Joseph. "The Eighteenth-Century English Translations of Molière." *MLQ,* 3 (1942), 83–104.

535 VINCENT, Howard P. "Rich and the First Covent Garden Theatre." *ELH,* 17 (1950), 296–306.

536 WASSERMAN, Earl R. "The Pleasures of Tragedy." *ELH,* 14 (1947), 283–307.

537 WASSERMAN, Earl R. "The Sympathetic Imagination in Eighteenth-Century Theories of Acting." *JEGP,* 46 (1947), 264–72.

538 WIMSATT, W. K., Jr., ed. *English Stage Comedy.* (English Institute Essays, 1954.) New York, 1955.

539 WIMSATT, W. K., Jr., ed. *The Idea of Comedy: Essays in Prose and Verse, Ben Jonson to George Meredith.* Englewood Cliffs, N.J., 1969.

540 WRAY, Edith. "English Adaptations of French Drama Between 1780 and 1815." *MLN,* 43 (1928), 87–90.

541 YEARLING, Elizabeth M. "The Good-Natured Heroes of Cumberland, Goldsmith, and Sheridan." *MLR,* 67 (1972), 490–500.

Sentimental Drama

542 BERNBAUM, Ernest. *The Drama of Sensibility: A Sketch of the History of English Sentimental Comedy and Domestic Tragedy, 1696–1780.* Boston, 1915. Rpt. 1958.

543 CASKEY, J. Homer. "Arthur Murphy and the War on Sentimental Comedy." *JEGP,* 30 (1931), 563–77.

544 CROISSANT, De W. C. "Early Sentimental Comedy." *Parrott Presentation Volume* (Princeton, N. J., 1935), pp. 47–71.

545 KRUTCH, Joseph W. *Comedy and Conscience After the Restoration.* New York, 1924.

546 LYNCH, Kathleen M. "Thomas D'Urfey's Contribution to Sentimental Comedy." *PQ,* 9 (1930), 249–59.

547 MAGILL, Lewis M. "Poetic Justice: The Dilemma of the Early Creators of Sentimental Tragedy." *RS,* 25 (1957), 24–32.

548 NOLTE, Fred O. *The Early Middle Class Drama, 1696–1774.* Lancaster, Pa., 1935.

549 PARNELL, Paul E. "The Sentimental Mask." *PMLA,* 78 (1963), 529–35.

550 SHERBO, Arthur. *English Sentimental Drama.* East Lansing, Mich., 1957.*

551 SMITH, John Harrington. "Shadwell, the Ladies, and the Change in Comedy." *MP,* 46 (1948), 22–33.

552 TYRE, Richard H. "Versions of Poetic Justice in the Early Eighteenth Century." *SP,* 54 (1957), 29–44.

553 WILLIAMS, S. T. "The English Sentimental Drama from Steele to Cumberland." *SR,* 33 (1925), 405–26.

554 WOOD, Frederick T. "Sentimental Comedy in the Eighteenth Century." *Neophilologus,* 18 (1932–33), 37–44, 281–89.

Opera

555 DORRIS, George E. *Paolo Rolli and the Italian Circle in London, 1715–1744.* The Hague, 1967.†

556 GAGEY, Edmond M. *Ballad Opera.* New York, 1937.

557 LOEWENBERG, Alfred. *Annals of Opera, 1597–1940. Compiled from the Original Sources.* 2d ed., rev. 2 vols. Geneva, 1955.*

558 LOEWENS, Irving. *"The Touch-Stone* (1728): A Neglected View of London Opera." *Musical Quarterly,* 45 (1959), 325–42.

559 NALBACH, Daniel. *The King's Theatre, 1704–1867: London's First Italian Opera House.* London, 1972.

560 ROSENTHAL, Harold. *Two Centuries of Opera at Covent Garden.* London, 1958.

561 WALSH, T. J. *Opera in Dublin, 1705–1797: The Social Scene.* Dublin, 1973.

Shakespeare

562 BRANAM, George C. *Eighteenth-Century Adaptations of Shakespearean Tragedy.* Berkeley, Cal., 1956.

563 COLEMAN, William S. E. "Post-Restoration Shylocks Prior to Macklin." *Theatre Survey,* 8 (1967), 17–36.

564 DONOHUE, Joseph W., Jr. "Kemble and Mrs. Siddons in *Macbeth:* The Romantic Approach to Tragic Character." *TN,* 22 (1967–68), 65–86.

565 HOBSBAUM, Philip. " 'King Lear' in the Eighteenth Century." *MLR,* 68 (1973), 494–506.

566 HOGAN, Charles B. *Shakespeare in the Theatre, 1701–1800: A Record of Performances in London.* 2 vols. Oxford, 1952–57.

567 SCOUTEN, Arthur H. "The Increase in Popularity of Shakespeare's Plays in the Eighteenth Century: A *Caveat* for Interpreters of Stage History." *SQ,* 7 (1956), 189–202.

568 SMITH, David Nichol. *Eighteenth Century Essays on Shakespeare.* 2d ed. Oxford, 1963. Reprints prefaces by Pope, Theobald, Hanmer, Warburton, and Johnson, and essays by Rowe, Dennis, Farmer, and Morgann.

569 STONE, George W., Jr. "The Poet and the Players." *Proc. Amer. Philos. Soc.,* 106 (1962), 412–21.

570 VELZ, John W. *Shakespeare and the Classical Tradition: A Critical Guide to Commentary, 1660–1960.* Minneapolis, 1968.

Literary Criticism

Collected Essays

571 DURHAM, W. H. *Critical Essays of the Eighteenth Century, 1700–25.* New Haven, Conn., 1915.

572 ELLEDGE, Scott. *Eighteenth-Century Critical Essays.* 2 vols. Ithaca, N.Y., 1961.

573 GILMORE, Thomas B. Jr. *Early Eighteenth-Century Essays on Taste.* (*SF&R.*) Gainesville, Fla., 1972.

574 HOOKER, Edward N. *Six Eighteenth-Century Essays on Wit.* (*ARS*) Los Angeles, 1946.

575 HYNES, Samuel. *English Literary Criticism, Restoration and Eighteenth Century.* New York, 1963.†

576 SIGWORTH, Oliver. *Criticism and Aesthetics, 1600–1800.* New York, 1971.†

577 SIMON, Irène. *Neo-Classical Criticism, 1660–1800.* Columbia, S.C., 1971.†

Individual Works

578 BAILLIE, John. *An Essay on the Sublime* (1747). Ed. Samuel H. Monk. (*ARS*) Los Angeles, 1953.

579 COHEN, Ralph, ed. *Essays on Taste by John Gilbert Cooper (1757) and John Armstrong (1770).* (*ARS*) Los Angeles, 1951.

580 COLLINS, Anthony. *A Discourse Concerning Ridicule and Irony in Writing* (1729). Eds. Edward A. Bloom and Lillian D. Bloom. (*ARS*) Los Angeles, 1970.

581 DACIER, André. *Preface to Aristotle's Art of Poetry* (1705). Ed. Samuel H. Monk. (*ARS*) Los Angeles, 1959.

582 DUFF, William. *An Essay on Original Genius. . . .* (1767). Ed. John L. Mahoney. (*SF&R*) Gainesville, Fla., 1964.

583 GERARD, Alexander. *Essay on Taste* (1759). Ed. Walter J. Hipple, Jr. (SF&R) Gainesville, Fla., 1963.

584 GERARD, Alexander, *Essay on Genius* (1774). Ed. Bernhard Fabian. (Facs. rpt.) Munich, 1966.

585 HAYLEY, William. *An Essay on Epic Poetry* (1789). Ed. Sister M. Celeste Williamson. (*SF&R*) Gainesville, Fla., 1968.

586 MORRIS, Corbyn. *An Essay Towards Fixing the True Standards of Wit, Humour, Raillery, Satire, and Ridicule* (1744). Ed. James L. Clifford. (*ARS*) Los Angeles, Cal., 1947.

587 OGILVIE, John. *An Essay on the Lyric Poetry of the Ancients* (1762). Ed. Wallace Jackson. (*ARS*) Los Angeles, Cal., 1970.

588 OLDMIXON, John. *An Essay on Criticism* (1728). Ed. R. J. Madden, C. S. B. (*ARS*) Los Angeles, Cal., 1964.

589 REYNOLDS, Frances. *An Enquiry Concerning . . . Taste* (1785). Ed. James L. Clifford. (*ARS*) Los Angeles, Cal., 1951.

590 SAY, Samuel. *An Essay on the Harmony, Variety, and Power of Numbers* (1745). Ed. Paul Fussell, Jr. (*ARS*) Los Angeles, Cal., 1956.

591 SCOTT, John Robert. *Dissertation on the Progress of the Fine Arts.* (1800). Ed. Roy Harvey Pearce. (*ARS*) Los Angeles, Cal., 1954.

592 WESLEY, Samuel. *Epistle to a Friend Concerning Poetry* (1700). *Essay on Heroic Poetry.* (2d ed., 1697). Ed. Edward N. Hooker. (*ARS*) Los Angeles, Cal., 1947.

Bibliography

593 DRAPER, John W. *Eighteenth Century English Aesthetics: A Bibliography.* Heidelberg, 1931. General Works on Aesthetics; Architecture and Gardening; Pictoral and Plastic Arts; Literature and Drama; Music, including Opera. Appendix: Some Modern Studies. Additions by R. D. Havens in *MLN,* 47 (1932), 118–20, and William D. Templeman in *MP,* 30 (1933), 309–16.

General Studies

594 ALKON, Paul K. "Critical and Logical Concepts of Method from Addison to Coleridge." *ECS,* 5 (1971), 97–121.

595 ATKINS, J. W. H. *English Literary Criticism: 17th and 18th Centuries.* London, 1951.†

596 BABCOCK, R. W. "The Idea of Taste in the Eighteenth Century." *PMLA,* 50 (1935), 922–26.

597 BAINE, Rodney M. "The First Anthologies of English Literary Criticism, Warton to Haslewood." *SB,* 3 (1951), 262–65.

598 BARBIER, Carl Paul. *William Gilpin: His Drawings, Teaching, and Theory of the Picturesque.* Oxford, 1963.

599 BATE, Walter J. *From Classic to Romantic: Premises of Taste in Eighteenth-Century England.* Cambridge, Mass., 1946.*†

600 BEVILACQUA, Vincent M. "Two Newtonian Arguments Concerning 'Taste.' " *PQ,* 47 (1968), 585–90.

601 BOND, Donald F. "The Neo-Classical Psychology of the Imagination." *ELH,* 4 (1937), 245–64.

602 BOSKER, A. *Literary Criticism in the Age of Johnson.* 2d ed., rev. Groningen and New York, 1953.

603 BOYD, John D., S. J. *The Function of Mimesis and Its Decline.* Cambridge, Mass., 1968. Rev. by G. S. Rousseau in *PQ,* 49 (1970), 134–37.

604 BRETT, R. L. "The Aesthetic Sense and Taste in the Literary Criticism of the Early Eighteenth Century." *RES,* 20 (1944), 199–213.

605 BULLITT, John M., and W. J. BATE. "Distinctions Between Fancy and Imagination in Eighteenth-Century English Criticism." *MLN,* 60 (1945), 8–15. See also Earl R. Wasserman, *ibid.,* 64 (1949), 23–25.

606 CARRITT, E. F. *A Calendar of British Taste from 1600–1800, Being a Museum of Specimens and Landmarks.* London, 1949.

607 CHAPMAN, Gerald W., ed. *Literary Criticism in England,, 1660–1800.* New York, 1966.

608 CLOUGH, Wilson O. "Reason and Genius: An Eighteenth-Century Dilemma (Hogarth, Hume, Burke, Reynolds)." *PQ,* 23 (1944), 33–54.

609 COHEN, Ralph. "Association of Ideas and Poetic Unity." *PQ,* 36 (1957), 465–74.

610 CONGLETON, James E. *Theories of Pastoral Poetry in England, 1684–1798.* Gainesville, Fla., 1952.

611 CRANE, R. S. "Imitation of Spenser and Milton in the Early Eighteenth Century: A New Document." *SP,* 15 (1918), 195–206. Henry Felton.

612 CRANE, R. S. *The Language of Criticism and the Structure of Poetry.* Toronto, 1953.

613 CRANE, R. S. *The Idea of the Humanities and Other Essays Critical and Historical.* 2 vols. Chicago, 1967.*

614 DAVIE, Donald. *The Language of Science and the Language of Literature, 1700–1740.* London, 1963.

615 DAVIES, Cicely. "Ut pictura poesis." *MLR,* 30 (1935), 159–69.

616 DRAPER, John W. "Poetry and Music in Eighteenth Century Aesthetics." *Englische Studien,* 67 (1932), 70–85.

617 ELLEDGE, Scott. "The Background and Development in English Criticism of the Theories of Generality and Particularity." *PMLA,* 62 (1947), 147–82. See also Jeffrey Hart in 38, pp. 71–82.

618 FOERSTER, Donald M. *Homer in English Criticism: The Historical Approach in the Eighteenth Century.* New Haven, Conn., 1947. Rpt. Hamden, Conn., 1969.

619 FOERSTER, Donald M. *The Fortunes of Epic Poetry: A Study in English and American Criticism, 1750–1950.* Washington, D.C., 1962.

620 FRYE, Northrop. *Anatomy of Criticism: Four Essays.* Princeton, N.J., 1957.†

621 GRAY, Charles H. *Theatrical Criticism in London to 1795.* New York, 1931.

622 GREEN, Clarence C. *The Neo-Classic Theory of Tragedy in England during the Eighteenth Century.* Cambridge, Mass., 1934.

623 GRENE, Marjorie. "Gerard's *Essay on Taste.*" *MP,* 41 (1943), 45–58.

624 HAGSTRUM, Jean H. *The Sister Arts: The Tradition of Literary Pictorialism and English Poetry from Dryden to Gray.* Chicago, 1958.*

625 HALEWOOD, William H. " 'The Reach of Art' in Augustan Poetic Theory." In 21, pp. 193–212.

626 HAVENS, Raymond D. "Changing Taste in the Eighteenth Century: A Study of Dryden's and Dodsley's Miscellanies." *PMLA,* 44 (1929), 501–36.

627 HAVENS, Raymond D. "Simplicity: A Changing Concept." *JHI,* 14 (1953), 3–32.

628 HIPPLE, Walter J., Jr. *The Beautiful, the Sublime, and the Picturesque in Eighteenth-Century British Aesthetic Theory.* Carbondale, Ill., 1957.*

629 HIPPLE, Walter J., Jr. "Philosophical Language and the Theory of Beauty in the Eighteenth Century." In 21, pp. 213–31.

630 HOOKER, Edward N. "The Discussion of Taste, from 1750 to 1770, and the New Trends in Literary Criticism." *PMLA,* 49 (1934), 577–92.

631 HOOKER, Edward N. "The Reviewers and the New Criticism, 1754–70." *PQ,* 13 (1934), 189–202.

632 HOOKER, Edward N. "The Reviewers and the New Trends in Poetry, 1754–1770." *MLN,* 51 (1936), 207–14.

633 HUSSEY, Christopher. *The Picturesque: Studies in a Point of View.* London, 1927.

634 JACKSON, Wallace. *Immediacy: The Development of a Critical Concept from Addison to Coleridge.* Amsterdam, 1973.

635 JONES, Claude E. "Poetry and the *Critical Review,* 1756–1785." *MLQ,* 9 (1948), 17–36.

636 JONES, Claude E. "Dramatic Criticism in the *Critical Review,* 1756–1785." *MLQ,* 20 (1959), 18–26, 133–44.

637 JONES, Richard Foster. "Science and Criticism in the Neo-Classical Age of English Literature." *JHI,* 1 (1940), 381–412.

638 KALLICH, Martin. *The Association of Ideas and Critical Theory in Eighteenth-Century England. . . .* The Hague, 1970.

639 KAUFMAN, Paul. "Heralds of Original Genius." *Essays in Memory of Barrett Wendell* (Cambridge, Mass., 1926), pp. 191–217.

640 KENNEDY, Wilma L. *The English Heritage of Coleridge of Bristol, 1798: The Basis in Eighteenth-Century English Thought for His Distinction Between Imagination and Fancy.* New Haven, Conn., 1947.

641 KINGHORN, A. M. "Literary Aesthetics and the Sympathetic Emotions—A Main Trend in Eighteenth-Century Scottish Criticism." *SSL,* 1 (1963), 35–47.

642 KNOX, Norman. *The Word "Irony" and its Context, 1500–1755.* Durham, N.C., 1961.

643 KNOX, Norman. "On the Classification of Ironies." *MP,* 70 (1972), 53–62.

644 LARRABEE, Stephen A. "*Il poco Più* and the School of Taste." *ELH,* 8 (1941), 47–50.

645/6 LOVEJOY, Arthur O. " 'Nature' as Aesthetic Norm." *MLN,* 42 (1927), 444–50. Rept. in his *Essays in the History of Ideas* (Baltimore, 1948).

647 LOVEJOY, Arthur O. "The Parallel of Deism and Classicism." *MP,* 29 (1932), 281–99. Rept. in his *Essays in the History of Ideas* (Baltimore, 1948). See also Roland N. Stromberg in *ECS,* 1 (1968), 381–95.

648 MACE, Dean T. "The Doctrine of Sound and Sense in Augustan Poetic Theory." *RES,* N.S. 2 (1951), 129–39.

649 McKENZIE, Gordon. *Critical Responsiveness: A Study of the Psychological Current in Later Eighteenth-Century Criticism.* Berkeley, Cal., 1949.

650 MACLEAN, Norman. "From Action to Image: Theories of the Lyric in the Eighteenth Century." *Critics and Criticism, Ancient and Modern,* ed. R. S. Crane (Chicago, 1952), pp. 408–60.

651 MALEK, James S. "The Influence of Empirical Psychology on Aesthetic Discourse: Two Eighteenth-Century Theories of Art." *Enlightenment Essays,* 1 (1970), 1–16. James Beattie and Sir William Jones.

652 MALEK, James S. "Art as Mind Shaped by Medium: The Significance of James Harris' 'A Discourse on Music, Painting and Poetry' in Eighteenth-Century Aesthetics." *TSLL,* 12 (1970), 221–39.

653 MALEK, James S. "Thomas Twining's Analysis of Poetry and Music as Imitative Arts." *MP,* 68 (1971), 260–68.

654 MANN, Elizabeth L. "The Problem of Originality in English Literary Criticism, 1750–1800." *PQ,* 18 (1939), 97–118.

655 MARESCA, Thomas E. "Language and Body in Augustan Poetic." *ELH,* 37 (1970), 374–88.

656 MARKS, Emerson R. *The Poetics of Reason: English Neoclassical Criticism.* New York, 1968.

657 MARSH, Robert. *Four Dialectical Theories of Poetry: An Aspect of English Neoclassical Criticism.* Chicago, 1965.* Shaftesbury, Akenside, David Hartley, and James Harris.

658 MONK, Samuel H. *The Sublime: A Study of Critical Theories in XVIIIth-Century England.* New York, 1935. Rpt. Ann Arbor, Mich., 1960.*

659 MYERS, R. M. "Neo-classical Criticism of the Ode for Music." *PMLA,* 62 (1947), 399–421.

660 NEIMAN, Fraser. "The Letters of William Gilpin to Samuel Healey." *HLQ,* 35 (1972), 159–69.

661 NETHERCOT, A. H. "The Reputation of the 'Metaphysical Poets' During the Age of Pope." *PQ,* 4 (1925), 161–79. Other articles by Nethercot in *SP,* 22 (1925), 81–132, and *MLR,* 25 (1930), 152–64.

662 NICOLSON, Marjorie. *Mountain Gloom and Mountain Glory: The Development of the Aesthetics of the Infinite.* Ithaca, N.Y., 1959.†

663 NITCHIE, Elizabeth. "Longinus and the Theory of Poetic Imitation in Seventeenth and Eighteenth Century England." *SP,* 32 (1935), 580–97.

664 ONG, Walter J. "Psyche and the Geometers: Aspects of the Associationist Critical Theory." *MP,* 48 (1951), 16–27.

665 PAGE, Alex. "Faculty Psychology and Metaphor in Eighteenth-Century Criticism." *MP,* 66 (1969), 237–47.

666 PAGE, Alex. "The Origin of Language and Eighteenth-Century English Criticism." *JEGP,* 71 (1972), 12–21.

667 PRICE, Martin. "The Picturesque Moment." In 35, pp. 259–92.

668 RAYSOR, Thomas M. "The Downfall of the Three Unities." *MLN,* 42 (1927), 1–9.

669 ROGERSON, Brewster. "The Art of Painting the Passions." *JHI,* 14 (1953), 68–94.

670/1 SANDERS, Charles. " 'First Follow Nature': An Annotation." *ES,* 49 (1968), 289–302.

672 SCHEFFER, John D. "The Idea of Decline in Literature and the Fine Arts in Eighteenth-Century England." *MP,* 34 (1936), 155–78.

673 SCHILLER, Jerome. "An Alternative to 'Aesthetic Disinterestedness.' " *JAAC,* 22 (1964), 295–302.

674 SCHUELLER, Herbert M. "Literature and Music as Sister Arts: An Aspect of Aesthetic Theory in Eighteenth-Century Britain." *PQ,* 26 (1947), 193–205. Other Articles by Schueller in *JAAC,* 8 (1950), 155–71; in *JHI,* 13 (1952), 73–93; in *JAAC,* 11 (1953), 334–59.

675 SCHWEIGER, Niklaus R. *The Ut pictura poesis Controversy in Eighteenth Century England and Germany.* Bern, 1972.

676 STOLNITZ, Jerome. " 'Beauty': Some Stages in the History of an Idea." *JHI,* 22 (1961), 185–204.

677 STOLNITZ, Jerome. "On the Origins of 'Aesthetic Disinterestedness.' " *JAAC,* 20 (1961), 131–43. See also Marcia Allentuck and Rémy G. Saisselin, *ibid.,* 21 (1962), 89–90, 209–10; and Stolnitz, *ibid.,* 22 (1963), 69–70.

678 STOLNITZ, Jerome. "Locke and the Categories of Value in Eighteenth-Century British Aesthetic Theory." *Philosophy,* 38 (1963), 40–51.

679 STONE, P. W. K. *The Art of Poetry, 1750–1820: Theories of Poetic Composition and Style. . . .* London, 1967.

680 SWEDENBERG, H. T., Jr. *The Theory of the Epic in England, 1650–1800.* Berkeley, Cal. 1944.

681 THORPE, Clarence D. "Two Augustans Cross the Alps: Dennis and Addison on Mountain Scenery." *SP,* 32 (1935), 463–82.

682/3 TUVESON, Ernest Lee. *The Imagination as a Means of Grace: Locke and the Aesthetics of Romanticism.* Berkeley, Cal. 1960.*

684 WATSON, George. "Contributions to a Dictionary of Critical Terms: *Imagination* and *Fancy.*" *EIC,* 3 (1953), 201–14.

685 WATSON, George. *The Literary Critics: A Study of English Descriptive Criticism.* (Penguin) London, 1962.†

686 WELLEK, René. *A History of Modern Criticism, 1750–1950.* Vol. 1: *The Later Eighteenth Century.* New Haven, Conn., 1955.*

687 WILEY, Margaret Lee. "Genius: A Problem in Definition." *Texas Studies in English,* 16 (1936), 77–83.

688 WIMSATT, W. K., Jr. "The Structure of the 'Concrete Universal' in Literature." *PMLA,* 62 (1947), 262–80. Rpt. in his *The Verbal Icon: Studies in the Meaning of Poetry* (Lexington, Ky., 1954).

689 WIMSATT, W. K., Jr. and Cleanth BROOKS. *Literary Criticism: A Short History.* New York, 1957. Rev. by Robert Marsh in *MP,* 55 (1958), 263–75.

690 WITTKOWER, R. "Imitation, Eclecticism, and Genius." In 52, pp. 143–61.

691 WOOD, Theodore E. B. *The Word "Sublime" and its Context, 1650–1760.* The Hague, 1972.

692 YOST, Calvin D., Jr. *The Poetry of the Gentleman's Magazine: A Study in Eighteenth-Century Literary Taste.* Philadelphia, 1936.

Periodicals

Bibliography

693 CRANE, R. S. and F. B. KAYE. *A Census of British Newspapers and Periodicals, 1620–1800.* Chapel Hill, N.C., 1927.

694 GABLER, Anthony J. "Check List of English Newspapers and Periodicals Before 1801 in the Huntington Library." *Huntington Lib. Bull.,* No. 2 (1931), 1–66.

695 MILFORD, R. T., and D. M. SUTHERLAND. *A Catalogue of English Newspapers and Periodicals in the Bodleian Library, 1622–1800.* Oxford, 1936.

696 MUDDIMAN, J. G. *et al.* "The History and Bibliography of English Newspapers." *N&Q,* 160–61 (1931), *passim.*

697 RIFFE, Nancy L. "Contributions to a Finding List of Eighteenth-Century Periodicals." *BNYPL,* 67 (1963), 431–34.

698 STEWART, Powell. *British Newspapers and Periodicals, 1632–1800.* Austin, Tex., 1950.

699 WEED, Katherine K., and Richmond P. BOND. *Studies of British Newspapers and Periodicals from their Beginning to 1800: a Bibliography.* Chapel Hill, N.C., 1946. Additions and corrections in *MP,* 45 (1947), 65–66.

General Studies

700 BLOOM, Edward A. "Labors of the Learned: Neoclassic Book Reviewing Aims and Techniques." *SP,* 54 (1957), 537–63.

701 BLOOM, Edward A. "Neoclassic 'Paper Wars' for a Free Press." *MLR,* 56 (1961), 481–96.

702 BOND, Richmond P., ed. *Studies in the Early English Periodical.* Chapel Hill, N.C., 1957. Introduction, pp. 3–48.

703 CRAIG, Mary E. *The Scottish Periodical Press, 1750–1789.* Edinburgh, 1931.

704 CRANFIELD, G. A. *The Development of the Provincial Newspaper, 1700–1760.* Oxford, 1962.

705 GRAHAM, Walter. *The Beginnings of English Literary Periodicals: A Study of Periodical Literature, 1665–1715.* New York, 1926. Rev. by R. S. Crane in *MP,* 24 (1926), 245–47.

706 GRAHAM, Walter. *English Literary Periodicals.* New York, 1930.

707 HANSON, Laurence. *Government and the Press, 1695–1765.* London, 1936.

708 MORISON, Stanley. *The English Newspaper: Some Account of the Physical Development of Journals Printed in London Between 1622 and the Present Day.* Cambridge, Eng., 1932.

709 MUNTER, Robert L. *The History of the Irish Newspaper, 1685–1760.* Cambridge, Eng., 1967.

710 REA, Robert R. *The English Press in Politics, 1760–1774.* Lincoln, Neb., 1963.

711 SIEBERT, Frederick S. *Freedom of the Press in England, 1476–1776: The Rise and Decline of Government Controls.* Urbana, Ill., 1952.

712 SNYDER, Henry L. "The Circulation of Newspapers in the Reign of Queen Anne." *The Library,* 5th ser., 23 (1968), 206–35.

713 SPECTOR, Robert D. *English Literary Periodicals and the Climate of Opinion During the Seven Years' War.* The Hague, 1966.

714 STEARNS, Bertha Monica. "Early English Periodicals for Ladies (1700–1760)." *PMLA,* 48 (1933), 38–60.

715 SUTHERLAND, James R. "The Circulation of Newspapers and Literary Periodicals, 1700–30." *The Library,* 4th ser., 15 (1934), 110–24.

716 THOMAS, Peter D. G. "The Beginning of Parliamentary Reporting in Newspapers, 1768–1774." *EHR,* 74 (1959), 623–36.

717 WATSON, Melvin R. *Magazine Serials and the Essay Tradition, 1746–1820.* Baton Rouge, La., 1956.

718 WERKMEISTER, Lucyle, *The London Daily Press, 1772–1792.* Lincoln, Neb., 1963.

719 WHITE, Cynthia L. *Women's Magazines, 1693–1968.* London, 1970.

720 WILES, Roy M. "Early Georgian Provincial Magazines." *The Library,* 5th ser., 19 (1964), 187–95.

721 WILES, Roy M. *Freshest Advices: Early Provincial Newspapers in England.* Columbus, Ohio, 1965.

722 WILES, Roy M. "The Periodical Essay: Lures to Readership." *Eng. Symposium Papers,* 2 (1972), 3–40.

Individual Periodicals and Journalists

The Annual Register

723 COPELAND, Thomas W. "Burke and Dodsley's *Annual Register.*" *PMLA,* 54 (1939), 223–45.

724 COPELAND, Thomas W. "Edmund Burke and the Book Reviews in Dodsley's *Annual Register.*" *PMLA,* 57 (1942), 446–68.

725 SARASON, Bertram D. "Editorial Mannerisms in the Early 'Annual Register.' " *PBSA,* 52 (1958), 131–37.

726 TODD, William B. "A Bibliographical Account of the *Annual Register,* 1758–1825." *The Library,* 5th ser., 16 (1961), 104–20.

The Critical Review

727 JONES, Claude E. *Smollett Studies.* Berkeley, Cal., 1942. Pp. 77–102: "Smollett and the 'Critical Review.' "

728 JONES, Claude E. "Contributors to *The Critical Review,* 1756–1785." *MLN,* 61 (1946), 433–41.

729 ROPER, Derek. "Smollett's 'Four Gentlemen': The First Contributors to the *Critical Review,*" *RES,* N.S. 10 (1959), 38–44.

730 ROPER, Derek. "The Politics of the *Critical Review,* 1756–1817." *DUJ,* 53 (1961), 117–22.

Ichabod Dawks

731 MORISON, Stanley. *Ichabod Dawks and His News-Letter, with an Account of the Dawks Family of Booksellers and Stationers, 1635–1731.* Cambridge, Eng., 1931.

Pierre Desmaizeaux

732 BROOME, J. H. "Pierre Desmaizeaux, journaliste: Les Nouvelles littéraires de Londres entre 1700 et 1740." *RLC,* 29 (1955), 184–204.

John Dunton

733 HATFIELD, Theodore M. "John Dunton's Periodicals." *Journalism Quarterly,* 10 (1933), 209–25.

734 McCUTCHEON, Roger P. "John Dunton's Connection with Book-Reviewing." *SP,* 25 (1928), 346–61.

735 McEWEN, Gilbert D. *The Oracle of the Coffee-House: John Dunton's "Athenian Mercury."* San Marino, Cal., 1972.

736 MOORE, C. A. "John Dunton, Pietist and Impostor." *SP,* 22 (1925), 467–99. Rpt. in his *Backgrounds of English Literature, 1700–1760* (Minneapolis, 1953).

737 PARKS, Stephen. "John Dunton and *The Works of the Learned.*" *The Library,* 5th ser., 23 (1968), 13–24.

The Examiner

738 ALLEN, Robert J. "William Oldisworth: 'The Author of *The Examiner.*' " *PQ,* 26 (1947), 159–80.

739 ANDERSON, Paul B. "Mistress Delarivière's Biography." *MP,* 33 (1936), 261–78.

740 COOK, Richard I. " 'Mr. *Examiner*' and 'Mr. *Review*': The Tory Apologetics of Swift and Defoe." *HLQ,* 29 (1966), 127–46.

741 NEEDHAM, Gwendolyn B. "Mary de la Rivière Manley: Tory Defender." *HLQ,* 12 (1949), 253–88.

742 TODD, William B. "The Printing of Eighteenth-Century Periodicals: With Notes on the *Examiner* and the *World.*" *The Library,* 5th ser., 10 (1955), 49–54.

The Female Spectator

743 HODGES, James. "The *Female Spectator,* a Courtesy Periodical." In 702, pp. 151–82.

The Female Tatler

744 ANDERSON, Paul B. "The History and Authorship of Mrs. Crackenthorpe's *Female Tatler.*" *MP,* 28 (1931), 354–60. See also R. T. Milford, *ibid.,* 29 (1932), 350–51. Other articles by Anderson on this periodical in *PQ,* 15 (1936), 286–300; in *PMLA,* 52 (1937), 100–103; in *PQ,* 16 (1937), 358–75.

745 GRAHAM, Walter. "Thomas Baker, Mrs. Manley, and the *Female Tatler.*" *MP,* 34 (1937), 267–72.

746 SMITH, John Harrington. "Thomas Baker and the *Female Tatler.*" *MP,* 49 (1952), 182–88.

The Free-Thinker

747 JOOST, Nicholas. "The Authorship of the *Free-Thinker.*" In 702, pp. 103–34.

The Gazetteer

748 HAIG, Robert L. *"The Gazetteer," 1735–1797: A Study in the Eighteenth-Century English Newspaper.* Carbondale, Ill., 1960.

The General Magazine of Arts and Sciences

749 MILLBURN, John R. *"Martin's Magazine: The General Magazine of Arts and Sciences,* 1755–65." *The Library,* 5th ser., 28 (1973), 221–39.

The Gentleman's Magazine

750 CARLSON, C. Lennart. *The First Magazine: A History of The Gentleman's Magazine. . . .* Providence, R.I., 1938. Rev. by Donald F. Bond in *MP,* 38 (1940), 85–100.

751 TODD, William B. "A Bibliographical Account of the *Gentleman's Magazine,* 1731–1754." *SB,* 18 (1965), 81–109.

The Grub-Street Journal

752 HILLHOUSE, James T. *The Grub-Street Journal.* Durham, N.C., 1928. Rev. by George Sherburn in *MP,* 26 (1929), 361–67.

753 WILLIAMSON, Raymond. "John Martyn and *The Grub-Street Journal.*" *Medical History,* 5 (1961), 361–74.

John Hawkesworth

754 EDDY, Donald D. "John Hawkesworth, Book Reviewer in the *Gentleman's Magazine.*" *PQ,* 43 (1964), 223–38.

755 GRIFFITH, Philip M. "The Authorship of the Papers Signed 'A' in Hawkesworth's *Adventurer:* A Strong Case for Dr. Richard Bathurst." *Tulane Studies in Eng.,* 12 (1962), 63–70.

756 LAMS, Victor J., Jr. "The 'A' Papers in the *Adventurer:* Bonnell Thornton, not Dr. Bathurst, Their Author." *SP,* 64 (1967), 83–96.

The London Evening Post

757 CRANFIELD, G. A. "The *London Evening Post,* 1727–1744: A Study in the Development of the Political Press." *Historical Journal,* 6 (1963), 20–37.

The London Gazette

758 HANDOVER, P. M. *A History of the London Gazette, 1665–1965.* London, 1965.

The London Journal

759 HEALEY, Charles B. *The London Journal and its Authors, 1720–1723.* Lawrence, Kans., 1935.

The Medley

760 POSTON, H. L. "The *Medleys* of 1712." *The Library,* 5th ser., 13 (1958), 205–7.

The Monthly Mercury

761 BLAGDEN, Cyprian. "Henry Rhodes and the *Monthly Mercury,* 1702 to 1720." *BC,* 5 (1956), 343–53.

The Monthly Review

762 KNAPP, Lewis M. "Ralph Griffiths, Author and Publisher, 1746–1750." *The Library,* 4th ser., 20 (1939), 197–213.

763 LONSDALE, Roger. "Dr. Burney and the *Monthly Review."* *RES,* N.S., 14 (1963), 346–58; 15 (1964), 27–37.

764 NANGLE, Benjamin C. *The Monthly Review, First Series, 1749–1789, Indexes of Contributors and Articles.* Oxford, 1934. See also Roger Lonsdale in *PBSA,* 55 (1961), 309–18 (on William Bewley's articles).

765 NANGLE, Benjamin C. *The Monthly Review, Second Series, 1790–1815. . . .* Oxford, 1955.

766 SPECTOR, Robert D. "The *Monthly* and Its Rival." *BNYPL,* 64 (1960): 159–61.

The Morning Post

767 HINDLE, Wilfrid. *The Morning Post, 1772–1937: Portrait of a Newspaper.* London, 1937.

The Museum

768 RYSKAMP, Charles. "John Gilbert Cooper and Dodsley's 'Museum.' " *N&Q,* 203 (1958), 210–11.

769 TIERNEY, James E. "*The Museum,* the 'Super-Excellent Magazine.' " *SEL,* 13 (1973), 503–15.

770 TIERNEY, James E. "*Museum* Attributions in John [Gilbert] Cooper's Unpublished Letters." *SB,* 27 (1974), 232–35.

William Pittis

771 NEWTON, Theodore F. M. "William Pittis and Queen Anne Journalism." *MP,* 33 (1935–36), 169–86, 279–302.

The Universal Chronicle

772 KOLB, Gwin J. "John Newbery, Projector of the *Universal Chronicle:* A Study of the Advertisements." *SB,* 11 (1958), 249–51.

The World

773 CASKEY, J. Homer. "The Two Issues of *The World." MLN,* 45 (1930), 29–31.

774 TODD, William B. "The First Edition of *The World." The Library,* 5th ser., 11 (1956), 283–84.

775 WINSHIP, George P., Jr. "The Printing History of the *World."* In 702, pp. 183–95.

The Writing of History

776 BLACK, J. B. *The Art of History: A Study of Four Great Historians of the Eighteenth Century.* London, 1926. Voltaire, Hume, Robertson, Gibbon.

777 BRAUDY, Leo. *Narrative Form in History and Fiction: Hume, Fielding and Gibbon.* Princeton, N.J., 1970.

778 DAVIS, Herbert. "The Augustan Concept of History." In 42, pp. 213–29.

779 HALE, John R., ed. *The Evolution of British Historiography: From Bacon to Namier.* London, 1967.

780 PEARDON, Thomas P. *The Transition in English Historical Writing, 1760–1830.* New York, 1933.

781 PRESTON, Thomas R. "Historiography as Art in Eighteenth-Century England." *TSLL,* 11 (1969), 1209–21.

782 THOMSON, M[ark] A. *Some Developments in English Historiography During the Eighteenth Century.* London, 1957. Inaugural lecture, University College, London.

783 WARD, Addison. "The Tory View of Roman History." *SEL,* 4 (1964), 413–56.

784 WELLEK, René. *The Rise of English Literary History: The Origin and Development of Literary Historiography from Bacon to the Wartons.* Chapel Hill, N.C., 1941. Rpt. New York, 1966.

785 WHALLEY, P. *An Essay on the Manner of Writing History* (1746). Ed. Keith Stewart. (*ARS*) Los Angeles, 1960.

Biography and Autobiography

786 BUTT, John. *Biography in the Hands of Walton, Johnson, and Boswell.* Ewing Lectures. Los Angeles, 1966.

787 CLIFFORD, James L., ed. *Biography as an Art. Selected Criticism, 1560–1960.* New York, 1962.

788 CLIFFORD, James L. *From Puzzles to Portraits: Problems of a Literary Biographer.* Chapel Hill, N.C., 1970.

789 DAGHLIAN, Philip B., ed. *Essays in Eighteenth-Century Biography.* Bloomington, Ind., 1968. Ralph W. Rader, "Literary Form in Factual Narrative: The Example of Boswell's *Johnson*"; Donald Greene, "The Uses of Autobiography in the Eighteenth Century"; James L. Clifford, "How Much Should a Biographer Tell? Some Eighteenth-Century Views"; Robert Kelley, "A Selected Bibliography"; Donald Greene, "A Reading Course in Autobiography."

790 LONGAKER, Mark. *English Biography in the Eighteenth Century.* Philadelphia, 1931.

791 MATTHEWS, William. *British Diaries: An Annotated Bibliography of British Diaries Written Between 1442 and 1942.* Berkeley, Cal., 1950.

792 MATTHEWS, William. *British Autobiographies: An Annotated Bibliography of British Autobiographies Published or Written Before 1951.* Berkeley, Cal., 1955.

793 MORRIS, John N. *Versions of the Self: Studies in English Autobiography from John Bunyan to John Stuart Mill.* New York, 1966.

794 SHUMAKER, Wayne. *English Autobiography: Its Emergence, Materials, and Form.* Berkeley, Cal., 1954.

795 STAUFFER, Donald A. *The Art of Biography in Eighteenth-Century England.* 2 vols. Princeton, N.J., 1941.*

Satire

796/7 BISHOP, Carter R. " 'Peace is my Dear Delight.' " *West Va. Univ. Bull.: Philological Studies,* 4 (1943), 64–76.

798 BLOOM, Edward A. and Lillian D. BLOOM. "The Satiric Mode of Feeling: A Theory of Intention." *Criticism,* 11 (1969), 115–39.

799 BOYCE, Benjamin. "News from Hell: Satiric Communications with the Nether World in English Writing of the Seventeenth and Eighteenth Centuries." *PMLA,* 58 (1943), 402–37.

800 BREDVOLD, Louis I. "A Note in Defence of Satire." *ELH,* 7 (1940), 253–64. Rpt. in 23.

801 BREDVOLD, Louis I. "The Gloom of the Tory Satirists." In 28, pp. 3–19. Rpt. in 29.

802 BROOKS, Harold F. "The 'Imitation' in English Poetry, especially in Formal Satire, before the Age of Pope." *RES,* 25 (1949), 124–40.

803 CARNOCHAN, W. B. "Satire, Sublimity, and Sentiment: Theory and Practice in Post-Augustan Satire." *PMLA,* 85 (1970), 260–67. Discussion by Thomas B. Gilmore and Carnochan, *Ibid.,* 86 (1971), 277–80; by William Kupersmith and Carnochan, *Ibid.,* 87 (1972), 508–11, 1125–26, and 88 (1973), 144.

804 CLARK, Arthur M. *Studies in Literary Modes.* Edinburgh, 1946.

805 COLLINS, Anthony. *A Discourse Concerning Ridicule and Irony in Writing* (1729). Eds. Edward A. Bloom and Lillian D. Bloom. (ARS) Los Angeles, 1970.

806 DALNEKOFF, Donna I. "A Familiar Stranger: The Outsider of Eighteenth-Century Satire." *Neophilologus,* 57 (1973), 121–34.

807 ELKIN, P. K. *The Augustan Defence of Satire.* Oxford, 1973.

808 ELLIOTT, Robert C. *The Power of Satire: Magic, Ritual, Art.* Princeton, N.J., 1960.[†]

809 FEINBERG, Leonard. *An Introduction to Satire.* Ames, Iowa, 1967.[†]

810 FEINBERG, Leonard. "Satire: The Inadequacy of Recent Definitions." *Genre,* 1 (1968), 31–37.

811 GILMORE, Thomas B., Jr. *The Eighteenth-Century Controversy over Ridicule as a Test of Truth: A Reconsideration.* Atlanta, Ga., 1970.

812 GOLDGAR, Bertrand A. "Satires on Man and 'The Dignity of Human Nature.'" *PMLA,* 80 (1965), 535–41.

813 GUITE, Harold. "An 18th-Century View of Roman Satire." In 36, pp. 113–20.

814 HARTE, Walter. *An Essay on Satire, Particularly on the Dunciad.* (1730). Ed. Thomas B. Gilmore, Jr. (ARS) Los Angeles, 1968.

815 HEATH-STUBBS, John. *The Verse-Satire.* London, 1969.[†]

816 HIGHET, Gilbert. *The Anatomy of Satire.* Princeton, N.J., 1962.[†]

817 HODGART, Matthew. *Satire.* London, 1969.[†]

818 HOPKINS, Kenneth. *Portraits in Satire.* London, 1958. Churchill and poets of the late eighteenth-century.

819 JACK, Ian. *Augustan Satire: Intention and Idiom in English Poetry, 1660–1750.* Oxford, 1952.[*†]

820 JACKSON, Wallace. "Satire: An Augustan Idea of Disorder." In 38, pp. 13–26.

821 JENSEN, H. James, and Malvin R. ZIRKER, eds. *The Satirist's Art.* Bloomington, Ind., 1972. Includes: "Pope's Illusive Temple of Infamy," by Michael Rosenblum, and "Swift: The View from Within the Satire," by Ernest Tuveson.

822 KEENER, Frederick M. *English Dialogues of the Dead: A Critical History, an Anthology, and a Check-List.* New York, 1973.

823 KERNAN, Alvin B. *The Plot of Satire.* New Haven, Conn. 1965.

824 KINSLEY, William. " 'The Malicious World' and the Meaning of Satire." *Genre,* 3 (1970), 137–55.

825 KITCHIN, George. *A Survey of Burlesque and Parody in English.* Edinburgh, 1931.

826 LEYBURN, Ellen D. *Satiric Allegory: Mirror of Man.* New Haven, Conn., 1956.

827 LOCKWOOD, Thomas. "The Augustan Author-Audience Relationship: Satiric vs. Comic Forms." *ELH,* 36 (1969), 648–58.

828 MILLER, Henry K. "The Paradoxical Encomium with Special Reference to Its Vogue in England, 1600–1800." *MP,* 53 (1956), 145–78.

829 PAULSON, Ronald. *The Fictions of Satire.* Baltimore, 1967.

830 PAULSON, Ronald, ed. *Satire: Modern Essays in Criticism.* Englewood Cliffs, N.J., 1971.†

831 PINKUS, Philip. "Satire and St. George." *Queen's Quarterly,* 70 (1963), 30–49.

832 PINKUS, Philip. "The New Satire of Augustan England." *UTQ,* 38 (1969), 136–58.

833 RANDOLPH, Mary C. "The Structural Design of the Formal Verse Satire." *PQ,* 21 (1942), 368–84.

834 RANDOLPH, Mary C. " 'Candour' in XVIIIth-Century Satire." *RES,* 20 (1944), 45–62.

835 SPACKS, Patricia M. "Some Reflections on Satire." *Genre,* 1 (1968), 13–30.

836 SUTHERLAND, James. *English Satire.* Cambridge, Eng., 1958.*†

837 SUTHERLAND, W. O. S., Jr. *The Art of the Satirist: Essays on the Satire of Augustan England.* Austin, Tex., 1965.

838 THORPE, Peter. "The Economics of Satire: Towards a New Definition." *Western Humanities Rev.,* 23 (1969), 187–96.

839 THORPE, Peter "Satire as Pre-Comedy." *Genre,* 4 (1971), 125–34.

840 VINER, Jacob. "Satire and Economics in the Augustan Age of Satire." In 45, pp. 77–101.

841 WALKER, Hugh. *English Satire and Satirists.* London, 1925.

842 WEINBROT, Howard D. *The Formal Strain: Studies in Augustan Imitation and Satire.* Chicago, 1969.

843 WEINBROT, Howard D. "On the Discrimination of Augustan Satires." in 38, pp. 5–12.

844 WILKINSON, Andrew M. "The Decline of English Verse Satire in the Middle Years of the Eighteenth Century." *RES,* N.S. 3 (1952), 222–33.

845 WILKINSON, Andrew M. "The Rise of English Verse Satire in the Eighteenth Century." *ES,* 34 (1953), 97–108.

846 WORCESTER, David. *The Art of Satire.* Cambridge, Mass., 1940. Rpt. New York, 1968.

847 YOUNGREN, William H. "Generality in Augustan Satire." *In Defense of Reading,* eds. R. A. Brower and R. Poirier, (New York, 1962), pp. 206–34.

Humor

848 CAZAMIAN, Louis. *The Development of English Humor, Parts I and II.* Durham, N.C., 1952. Rev. by Stuart M. Tave in *MP,* 50 (1953), 206–8.

849 DRAPER, John W. "The Theory of the Comic in Eighteenth-Century England." *JEGP,* 37 (1938), 207–23.

850 ESAR, Evan. "The Legend of Joe Miller." *American Book Collector,* 13 (1962), 11–26.

851 HELTZEL, Virgil B. "Chesterfield and the Anti-Laughter Tradition." *MP,* 26 (1928), 73–90.

852 HOOKER, Edward N. "Humor in the Age of Pope." *HLQ,* 11 (1948), 361–85.

853 NEVO, Ruth. "Toward a Theory of Comedy." *JAAC,* 21 (1963), 327–32.

854 RAMONDT, Marie. "Between Laughter and Humour in the Eighteenth Century." *Neophilologus,* 40 (1956), 128–38.

855 SNUGGS, Henry L. "The Comic Humours: A New Interpretation." *PMLA,* 62 (1947), 114–22.

856 TAVE, Stuart M. *The Amiable Humorist: A Study in the Comic Theory and Criticism of the Eighteenth and Early Nineteenth Centuries.* Chicago, 1960.*

Rhetoric and Oratory

857 BEVILACQUA, Vincent M. "Alexander Gerard's Lectures on Rhetoric: Edinburgh University Library MS Dc 5.61." *SM,* 34 (1967), 384–88.

858 BRYANT, Donald C., ed. "After Goodrich: New Resources in British Public Address—A Symposium," *QJS,* 48 (1962), 1–14.

859 BURWICK, Frederick. "Associational Rhetoric and Scottish Prose Style." *SM,* 34 (1967), 21–34.

860 EHNINGER, Douglas. "Dominant Trends in British Rhetorical Thought, 1750–1800." *Southern Speech Journal,* 18 (1952), 3–12.

861 HARDING, Harold F. "The Listener on Eloquence, 1750–1800." *Studies in Speech and Drama in Honor of Alexander M. Drummond* (Ithaca, N.Y., 1944), pp. 341–53.

862 HOWELL, Wilbur S. *Eighteenth-Century British Logic and Rhetoric.* Princeton, N.J., 1971.*

863 HOWES, Raymond F., ed. *Historical Studies of Rhetoric and Rhetoricians.* Ithaca, N.Y., 1961.

864 RAGSDALE, J. Donald. "Invention in English 'Stylistic' Rhetoric, 1600–1800." *QJS,* 51 (1965), 164–67.

865 SANDFORD, William P. *English Theories of Public Address, 1530–1828.* Columbus, Ohio, 1931.

Letter Writing

866 ANDERSON, Howard, Philip B. DAGHLIAN, and Irvin EHRENPREIS, eds. *The Familiar Letter in the Eighteenth-Century.* Lawrence, Kans., 1966.† Includes essays on Boswell (by Rufus Reiberg), Burke (by James T. Boulton), Chesterfield (by Cecil Price), Cowper (by William R. Cagle), Gibbon (by Patricia Craddock), Gray (by R. W. Ketton-Cremer), Johnson (by Philip B. Daghlian), Lady Mary Wortley Montagu (by Robert Halsband), Pope (by Rosemary Cowler), Swift (by Oliver W. Ferguson), and Walpole (by William N. Free).

867 DAVIS, Herbert. "The Correspondence of the Augustans." In 41, pp. 195–212.

868 HORNBEAK, Katherine Gee. *The Complete Letter-Writer in English, 1568–1800.* Northampton, Mass., 1934.

869 HUMILIATA, Sister Mary. "Standards of Taste Advocated for Feminine Letter Writing, 1640–1797." *HLQ,* 13 (1950), 261–77.

870 IRVING, William H. *The Providence of Wit in the English Letter Writers.* Durham, N.C., 1955.

871 ROBERTSON, Jean. *The Art of Letter Writing: An Essay on the Hand-Books Published in England During the Sixteenth and Seventeenth Centuries.* Liverpool and London, 1942. Pp. 67–80. "A Bibliography of Complete Letter-Writers, 1568–1700."

Language and Prose Style

872 AARSLEFF, Hans. *The Study of Language in England, 1780–1860.* Princeton, N.J., 1967.

873 ADOLPH, Robert. *The Rise of Modern Prose Style.* Cambridge, Mass., 1968.

874 BAILEY, Richard W., and Dolores M. BURTON. *English Stylistics: A Bibliography.* Cambridge, Mass., 1968.

875 ELLEDGE, Scott. "The Naked Science of Language, 1747–1786." In 21, pp. 266–95.

876 EMSLEY, Bert. "James Buchanan and the Eighteenth-Century Regulation of English Usage." *PMLA,* 48 (1933), 1154–66.

876A *English Linguistics.* Microfiche ed. 365 vols. Ilkley, Yorks, 1974.

877 FREIMARCK, Vincent. "The Bible and Neo-Classical Views of Style." *JEGP,* 51 (1952), 507–26.

878 FRIES, Charles C. "The Rules of Common School Grammars." *PMLA,* 42 (1927), 221–37.

879 GREENE, Donald J. "Is There a 'Tory' Prose Style?" *BNYPL,* 66 (1962), 449–54. See also Frank Brady, "Prose Style and the 'Whig' Tradition." *Ibid.,* pp. 455–63.

880 KENNEY, William. "Addison, Johnson, and the 'Energetick' Style." *SN,* 33 (1961), 103–14.

881 LEONARD, S. A. *The Doctrine of Correctness in English Usage, 1700–1800.* Madison, Wis., 1929.

882 MICHAEL, Ian. *English Grammatical Categories and the Tradition to 1800.* Cambridge, Eng., 1970.

883 NEUMANN, J. H. "Jonathan Swift and English Pronunciation." *QJS,* 28 (1942), 198–201. Other articles by Neumann on Swift and language in *MLQ,* 4 (1943), 191–204; in *SP,* 41 (1944), 79–85; in *American Speech,* 21 (1946), 253–63.

884 NEUMANN, J. H. "Chesterfield and the Standard of Usage in English." *MLQ,* 7 (1946), 465–75.

885 OSSELTON, N. E. "Formal and Informal Spelling in the 18th Century." *ES,* 44 (1963), 267–75.

886 PLATT, Joan. "The Development of English Colloquial Idiom during the Eighteenth Century." *RES,* 2 (1926), 70–81, 189–96.

887 SEARS, Donald A. "Eighteenth-Century Work on Language." *Bull. of Bibliography,* 28 (1971), 120–23.

888 STARNES, De Witt T., and Gertrude E. NOYES. *The English Dictionary from Cawdrey to Johnson, 1604–1755.* Chapel Hill, N.C., 1946.

889 SUTHERLAND, James. "Some Aspects of Eighteenth-Century Prose." In 31, pp. 94–110.

890 SUTHERLAND, James. *On English Prose.* Toronto, 1957.

891 TUCKER, Susie I. *Protean Shape: A Study in Eighteenth-Century Vocabulary and Usage.* London, 1967.

Part Two
Individual Authors

Joseph Addison (1672–1719)

Works

892 *Miscellaneous Works.* Ed. A. C. Guthkelch. 2 vols. London, 1914.

893 *The Spectator.* Ed. Donald F. Bond. 5 vols. Oxford, 1965.

894 *Critical Essays from the Spectator, by Joseph Addison, with Four Essays by Richard Steele.* Ed. Donald F. Bond. Oxford, 1970.†

895 *Letters.* Ed. Walter Graham. Oxford, 1941. See also Pat Rogers, "Addison's Official Correspondence: A Supplement to Graham." *MP,* 69 (1972), 328–29.

Studies

896 AULT, Norman. "Pope and Addison." *RES,* 17 (1943), 428–51. Rpt. in his *New Light on Pope* (1949), chap. 6, and in 2012.

897 BAKER, Donald C. "Witchcraft, Addison, and *The Drummer.*" *SN,* 31 (1959), 174–81.

898 BATTERSBY, James L. "Johnson and Shiels: Biographers of Addison." *SEL,* 9 (1969), 521–37.

899 BATTERSBY, James L. "The Serino Biography of Joseph Addison." *PBSA,* 65 (1971), 67–69.

900 BLOOM, Edward A., and Lillian D. BLOOM. *Joseph Addison's Sociable Animal: In the Market-Place, On the Hustings, In the Pulpit.* Providence, R.I., 1971.*

901 BLOOM, Lillian D. "Addison as Translator: A Problem in Neo-Classical Scholarship." *SP,* 46 (1949), 31–53.

902 BRADNER, Leicester. "The Composition and Publication of Addison's Latin Poems." *MP,* 35 (1938), 359–67.

903 CAMPBELL, Hilbert H. "The Sale Catalogue of Addison's Library." *ELN,* 4 (1967), 269–73.

904 CHAMBERS, Robert D. "Addison at Work on the *Spectator."* *MP,* 56 (1959), 145–53.

905 COOKE, Arthur L. "Addison vs. Steele, 1708." *PMLA,* 68 (1953), 313–20.

906 COOKE, Arthur L. "Addison's Aristocratic Wife." *PMLA,* 72 (1957), 373–89.

907 CRUM, M. C. "A Manuscript of Essays by Joseph Addison." *Bodl. Lib. Record,* 5 (1954), 98–103.

908 DOBRÉE, Bonamy. "The First Victorian." In his *Essays in Biography* (1925), pp. 197–345.

909 ELIOSEFF, Lee A. *The Cultural Milieu of Addison's Literary Criticism.* Austin, Tex., 1963.

910 FRIEDMAN, Albert B. "Addison's 'Chevy Chase' Papers." In his *The Ballad Revival* (Chicago, 1961), chap. 4.

911 GAY, Peter. "The Spectator as Actor: Addison in Perspective." *Encounter,* 29, vi (1967), 27–32. Rpt. in 53.

912 GREENOUGH, Chester N. "Did Joseph Addison Write 'The Play-House'?" In his *Collected Studies* (Cambridge, Mass., 1940), pp. 181–94.

913 HANSEN, David A. "Addison on Ornament and Poetic Style." In 21, pp. 94–127.

914 HORN, Robert D. "Addison's *Campaign* and Macaulay." *PMLA,* 63 (1948), 886–902.

915 HORN, Robert D. "The Early Editions of Addison's *Campaign."* *SB,* 3 (1950–51), 256–61.

916 HUBBELL, Jay B. "Some Uncollected Poems by Joseph Addison." *MP,* 36 (1939), 277–81.

917 HUMPHREYS, A. R. *Steele, Addison and Their Periodical Essays.* (*WTW*) London, 1959.†

918 KELSALL, M. M. "The Meaning of Addison's *Cato."* *RES,* N.S., 17 (1966), 149–62.

919 KINSLEY, William. "Meaning and Format: Mr. Spectator and His Folio Half-Sheets." *ELH,* 34 (1967), 482–94.

920 LANNERING, Jan. *Studies in the Prose Style of Joseph Addison.* Upsala, 1951.†

921 LEWIS, C. S. "Addison." In 31, pp. 1–14. Rpt. in 29.

922 McDONALD, Daniel. "The 'Logic' of Addison's *Freeholder.*" *PLL,* 4 (1968), 20–34.

923 RAU, Fritz. "Zum Gehalt des *Tatler* und *Spectator:* Forschungsbericht." *Anglia,* 88 (1970), 42–93.*

924 SALTER, C. H. "Dryden and Addison." *MLR,* 69 (1974), 29–39.

925 SMITHERS, Peter. *The Life of Joseph Addison.* 2d ed., rev. Oxford, 1968.*

926 SUTHERLAND, James. "The Last Years of Joseph Addison." In his *Background for Queen Anne* (London, 1939), pp. 127–44.

927 THORPE, Clarence D. "Addison and Hutcheson on the Imagination." *ELH,* 2 (1935), 215–34.

928 THORPE, Clarence D. "Addison's Theory of the Imagination as 'Perceptive Response.' " *PMASAL,* 21 (1935), 509–30.

929 THORPE, Clarence D. "Addison and Some of his Predecessors on 'Novelty.' " *PMLA,* 52 (1937), 1114–29.

930 THORPE, Clarence D. "Addison's Contribution to Criticism." In 37, pp. 318–29.*

931 TURNER, Margaret. "The Influence of La Bruyère on the 'Tatler' and the 'Spectator.' " *MLR,* 48 (1953), 10–16.

932 WILKINSON, Jean. "Some Aspects of Addison's Philosophy of Art." *HLQ,* 28 (1964), 31–44.*

Mark Akenside (1721–1770)

Bibliography

933 WILLIAMS, Iolo A. *Seven XVIIIth Century Bibliographies* (1924), pp. 75–97.

Studies

934 ALDRIDGE, Alfred O. *"The Eclecticism of Mark Akenside's 'The Pleasures of Imagination.' "* *JHI,* 5 (1944), 292–314.

935 ALDRIDGE, Alfred O. "Akenside and Imagination." *SP,* 42 (1945), 769–92.

936 HART, Jeffrey. "Akenside's Revision of *The Pleasures of Imagination.*" *PMLA,* 74 (1959), 67–74.

937 HOUPT, Charles T. *Mark Akenside: A Biographical and Critical Study.* Philadelphia, 1944.

938 MAHONEY, John L. "Akenside and Shaftesbury: The Influence of Philosophy on English Romantic Theory." *Discourse,* 4 (1961), 241–47.

939 MAHONEY, John L. "Addison and Akenside: The Impact of Psychological Criticism on Early English Romantic Poetry." *BJA,* 6 (1966), 365–74.

940/1 MARSH, Robert. "Akenside and Addison: The Problem of Ideational Debt." *MP,* 59 (1961), 36–48.

942 NORTON, John. "Akenside's *The Pleasures of Imagination:* An Exercise in Poetics." *ECS,* 3 (1970), 366–83.

943 POTTER, George R. "Mark Akenside, Prophet of Evolution." *MP,* 24 (1926), 55–64.

944 SILBER, C. Anderson. "The Evolution of Akenside's *The Pleasures of the Imagination:* The Missing Link Established." *PBSA,* 65 (1971), 357–63. Akenside's revisions.

945 WILLIAMS, Ralph M. "Two Unpublished Poems by Mark Akenside." *MLN,* 57 1942), 626–31.

For Dodsley's *Museum,* which Akenside edited, see "Periodicals."

John Arbuthnot (1667–1735)

Works

946 *Life and Works.* Ed. George A. Aitken. Oxford, 1892.

947 *The History of John Bull.* Ed. H. Teerink. Amsterdam, 1925.

948 *Memoirs of the Extraordinary Life, Works, and Discoveries of Martinus Scriblerus.* Ed. Charles Kerby-Miller. New Haven, 1950. Rpt. New York, 1966.

Studies

949 BEATTIE, Lester M. *John Arbuthnot, Mathematician and Satirist.* Cambridge, Mass., 1935. Rpt. New York, 1967.*

950 ERICKSON, Robert A. "Situations of Identity in the *Memoirs of Martinus Scriblerus.*" *MLQ,* 26 (1965), 388–400.

951 FREEHAFER, John. "Arbuthnot and the Dublin Pirates." *Scriblerian,* 2 (1970), 65–67.

952 KÖSTER, P. J. "Arbuthnot's Use of Quotation and Parody in the Account of the Sacheverell Affair." *PQ,* 48 (1969), 201–11.

953 KÖSTER, P. J., ed. *Arbuthnotiana: The Story of the St. Alb-ns Ghost (1712). A Catalogue of Dr. Arbuthnot's Library (1779).* (ARS) Los Angeles, 1972.

954 MAYO, Thomas F. "The Authorship of *The History of John Bull.*" *PMLA,* 45 (1930), 274–82.

James Beattie (1735–1803)

Works

955 *London Diary, 1773.* Ed. Ralph S. Walker. Aberdeen, 1946.

956 *Day-Book, 1773–1798.* Ed. Ralph S. Walker. Aberdeen, 1948.

Bibliography

957 KLOTH, Karen, and Bernhard FABIAN. "James Beattie: Contributions Towards a Bibliography." *Bibliotheck,* 5 (1970), 232–45.

Studies

958 BEVILACQUA, Vincent M. "The Authorship of 'Alexander Gerard's' Lectures on Logic and Rhetoric . . . " *ELN,* 5 (1967), 101–5.

959 BEVILACQUA, Vincent M. "James Beattie's Theory of Rhetoric." *SM,* 34 (1967), 109–24.

960 EBERWEIN, Robert T. "James Beattie and David Hume on the Imagination and Truth." *TSLL,* 12 (1971), 595–603.

961 LAND, Stephen K. "James Beattie on Language." *PQ,* 51 (1972), 887–904.

962 MOSSNER, Ernest C. "Beattie's 'The Castle of Scepticism': An Unpublished Allegory Against Hume, Voltaire, and Hobbes." Texas *Studies in English,* 27 (1948), 108–45.

963 MOSSNER, Ernest C. "Beattie on Voltaire: An Unpublished Parody." *Romanic Review,* 41 (1950), 26–32.

964 TAVE, Stuart M. "Some Essays by James Beattie in the 'London Magazine.' " *N&Q,* 197 (1952), 534–37.

George Berkeley (1685–1723)

965 *Works.* Ed. A. A. Luce and T. E. Jessop. 9 vols. London, 1948–57.

966 *Philosophical Writings.* Ed. David M. Armstrong. New York, 1965.†

967 *Principles, Dialogues, and Philosophical Correspondence.* Ed. Colin M. Turbayne. Indianapolis, 1965.†

968 *Three Dialogues between Hylas and Philonous.* Ed. Colin M. Turbayne. Indianapolis, 1954.†

969 *A Treatise Concerning the Principles of Human Knowledge.* Ed. Colin M. Turbayne. Indianapolis, 1957.†

970 *Works on Vision.* Ed. Colin M. Turbayne. Indianapolis, 1963.†

Bibliography

971 JESSOP, T. E. *A Bibliography of George Berkeley: With an Inventory of Berkeley's Literary Remains by A. A. Luce.* London, 1934. Rpt. New York, 1968.

972 TURBAYNE, C. M., and R. WARE. "A Bibliography of George Berkeley, 1933–1962." *Journal of Philosophy,* 60 (1963), 93–112.

Studies

973 AARON, R. I. "A Catalogue of Berkeley's Library." *Mind,* 41 (1932), 465–75.

974 ATTFIELD, R. "Berkeley and Imagination." *Philosophy,* 45 (1970), 237–39.

975 BENNETT, Jonathan. *Locke, Berkeley, Hume: Central Themes.* Oxford, 1971. †

976 BRACKEN, Harry M. *The Early Reception of Berkeley's Immaterialism, 1710–1733.* The Hague, 1959. Rev. ed., 1965.

977 HERSCHBELL, Jackson P. "Berkeley and the Problem of Evil." *JHI,* 31 (1970), 543–54.

978 JESSOP, T. E. *George Berkeley.* (WTW) London, 1959.[†]

979 JOHNSTON, Joseph. *Berkeley's "Querist" in Historical Perspective.* Dundalk, 1970.

980 LUCE, A. A. *Berkeley and Malebranche: A Study in the Origins of Berkeley's Thought.* London, 1934.

981 LUCE, A. A. *The Life of George Berkeley, Bishop of Cloyne.* London, Eng., 1949.[*]

982 MARTIN, C. B., and D. M. ARMSTRONG, eds. *Locke and Berkeley: A Collection of Critical Essays.* 1968.

983 NICOLSON, Marjorie, and George S. ROUSSEAU. "Bishop Berkeley and Tar-Water." In 45, pp. 102-37.

984 RITCHIE, A. D. *George Berkeley: A Re-appraisal.* Ed. G. E. Davie. Manchester, 1967.

985 STEINKRAUS, Warren E., ed. *New Studies in Berkeley's Philosophy.* New York, 1966.

986 TIPTON, Ian. "Two Questions on Bishop Berkeley's Panacea." *JHI,* 30 (1969), 203–24.

987 WARNOCK, G. J. *Berkeley.* (Penguin) London, 1953.[†]

988 WILD, John. *George Berkeley: A Study of his Life and Philosophy.* Cambridge, Mass., 1936. Rpt. New York, 1962.[*]

Sir Richard Blackmore (1654–1729)

Works

989 *Essay upon Wit (1716).* Ed. Richard C. Boys. (ARS) Los Angeles, 1946.

990 *Prince Arthur* (1695). Facsimile. Menston, Yorkshire, 1971.

Studies

991 BOYS, Richard C. *Sir Richard Blackmore and the Wits: A Study of "Commendatory Verses on the Author of the Two Arthurs and the Satyr Against Wit" (1700).* Ann Arbor, Mich., 1949.

992 BOYS, Richard C. "The Authorship of Poems in *Commendatory Verses* (1700)." *PQ,* 30 (1951), 261–62. See also W. J. Cameron in *N&Q,* 208 (1963), 63–66.

993 NEWTON, Theodore F. M. "Blackmore's *Eliza.*" *HSNPL,* 18 (1935), 113–23.

994 ROSENBERG, Albert. *Sir Richard Blackmore.* Lincoln, Neb., 1953.[*]

Hugh Blair (1718–1800)

Works

995 *Lectures on Rhetoric and Belles-Lettres.* Ed. Harold Harding. 2 vols. Carbondale, Ill., 1965.

996 *The Rhetoric of Blair, Campbell and Whately.* Ed. James L. Golden and Edward P. J. Corbett. [Selections.] New York, 1968.

Studies

997 BEVILACQUA, Vincent M. "Philosophical Assumptions Underlying Hugh Blair's *Lectures . . .*" *Western Speech,* 31 (1967), 150–64.

998 BOWERS, John W. "A Comparative Criticism of Hugh Blair's Essay on Taste." *QJS,* 47 (1961), 384–89.

999 COHEN, Herman. "Hugh Blair's Theory of Taste." *QJS,* 44 (1958), 265–74.

1000 CORBETT, Edward P. J. "Hugh Blair as an Analyzer of English Prose Style." *CCC,* 4 (1958), 98–103.

1001 MAYS, Morley J. "Johnson and Blair on Addison's Prose Style." *SP,* 39 (1942), 638–49.

1002 SCHMITZ, Robert M. *Hugh Blair.* New York, 1948.*

Henry St. John, Viscount Bolingbroke (1678–1751)

Works

1003 *Historical Writings.* Ed. Isaac Kramnick. Chicago, 1972.

1004 *The Idea of a Patriot King.* Ed. Sydney W. Jackman. Indianapolis, 1965. †

Studies

1005 ALDRIDGE, Alfred O. "Shaftesbury and Bolingbroke." *PQ,* 31 (1952), 1–16.

1006 BARBER, Giles. "Bolingbroke, Pope, and the *Patriot King.*" *The Library,* 5 ser., 19 (1964), 67–89.

1007 BARBER, Giles. "Some Uncollected Authors: XLI. Henry Saint John, Viscount Bolingbroke, 1678–1751." *BC,* 14 (1965), 528–37.

1008 CABLE, Mabel Hessler. "*The Idea of a Patriot King* in the Propaganda of the Opposition to Walpole, 1735–39." *PQ,* 18 (1939), 119–30.

1009 DICKINSON, H. T. *Bolingbroke.* London, 1970.

1010 HART, Jeffrey. *Viscount Bolingbroke, Tory Humanist.* Toronto, 1965.

1011 JACKMAN, Sydney W. *Man of Mercury: An Appreciation of the Mind of Henry St. John, Viscount Bolingbroke.* London, 1966.

1012 JAMES, D. G. *The Life of Reason: Hobbes, Locke, Bolingbroke.* London, Eng., 1949.

1013/14 KRAMNICK, Isaac. *Bolingbroke and His Circle: The Politics of Nostalgia in the Age of Walpole.* Cambridge, Mass., 1968.*

1015 ROGERS, Pat. "Swift and Bolingbroke on Faction." *JBS,* 9 (1970), 71–101.

1016 SMALLWOOD, Frank T. "Bolingbroke *vs.* Alexander Pope: The Publication of the *Patriot King.*" *PBSA,* 65 (1971), 225–41.

James Boswell (1740–1795)

Works

1017 *Private Papers of James Boswell from Malahide Castle in the Collection of Lieut.- Col. Ralph Heyward Isham.* Eds. Geoffrey Scott and F. A. Pottle. 19 vols. New York, 1928–37.

1018 Yale Edition of the Private Papers. Ed. F. W. Hilles *et al.* New York and London, 1950– . In progress. *The London Journal, 1762–63* (1950); *Boswell in Holland, 1763–64* (1952); *Portraits by Sir Joshua Reynolds* (1952); *Boswell on the Grand Tour: Germany and Switzerland, 1764* (1953); *Boswell on the Grand Tour: Italy, Corsica, and France, 1763–66* (1955); *Boswell in Search of a Wife, 1766–69* (1956); *Boswell for the Defence, 1769–74* (1959); *Journal of a Tour to the Hebrides with Samuel Johnson, 1773* (1961); *Boswell: The Ominous Years, 1774–76* (1963); *Boswell in Extremes, 1776–78* (1971).

1019 "Research Edition" of the Private Papers. New York and London, 1966– . In progress. *Correspondence of James Boswell and John Johnston of Grange.* Ed. Ralph S. Walker. (1966); *Correspondence and Other Papers of James Boswell Relating to the Making of the "Life of Johnson."* Ed. Marshall Waingrow (1969).

1020 *The Hypochondriack.* Ed. Margery Bailey. 2 vols. Stanford, Cal., 1928. [Essays in the *London Magazine,* 1777–83.] Rpt. London, 1951, under the title *Boswell's Column.*

1021 *Journal of a Tour to Corsica; and Memoirs of Pascal Paoli.* Ed. S. C. Roberts. Cambridge, Eng., 1923.

1022 *Journal of a Tour to the Hebrides* (with Johnson's *Journey to the Western Islands of Scotland*). Ed. R. W. Chapmen. London, 1924. Rpt. (without notes and appendixes), 1930.†

1023 *Boswell's Life of Johnson. Together with Boswell's Journal of a Tour to the Hebrides and Johnson's Diary of a Journey into North Wales.* Ed. G. B. Hill. Revised and enlarged edition by L. F. Powell. Vols. 1–4, Oxford, 1934: Vols. 5–6, 1950; Vols. 5–6, 2d ed. 1964.*†

1024 *Letters.* Ed. Chauncey B. Tinker. 2 vols. Oxford, 1924.

Bibliography

1025 ABBOTT, Claude C. *A Catalogue of Papers relating to Boswell, Johnson, and Sir William Forbes, Found at Fettercairn House.* Oxford, 1936.

1026 BROWN, Anthony E. *Boswellian Studies: A Bibliography.* 2d ed., rev. Hamden, Conn., 1972.

1027 POTTLE, Frederick A., and Marion S. POTTLE. *The Private Papers of James Boswell from Malahide Castle . . . : A Catalogue.* London, 1931.

Studies

1028 ALKON, Paul K. "Boswell's Control of Aesthetic Distance." *UTQ,* 38 (1969), 174–91.

1029 BRADY, Frank. *Boswell's Political Career.* New Haven, Conn., 1965.

1030 BRADY, Frank. "Boswell's Self-Presentation and His Critics." *SEL,* 12 (1972), 545–55.

1031 BROOKS, A. Russell. *James Boswell.* (*TEAS*) New York, 1971.

1032 CLIFFORD, James L., ed. *Twentieth-Century Interpretations of Boswell's Life of Johnson.* Englewood Cliffs, N.J., 1970.†

1033 COLLINS, P. A. W. *James Boswell.* (*WTW*) London, 1956.†

1034 DAMROSCH, Leopold, Jr. "*The Life of Johnson*: An Anti-Theory." *ECS,* 6 (1973), 486–505.

1035 DOWLING, William C. "The Boswellian Hero." *SSL,* 10 (1972), 79–93.

1036 FUSSELL, Paul, Jr. "The Force of Literary Memory in Boswell's *London Journal.*" *SEL,* 2 (1962), 351–57.

1037 GOLDEN, James L. "James Boswell on Rhetoric and Belles-Lettres." *QJS,* 50 (1964), 266–76.

1038 HART, Edward. "The Contributions of John Nichols to Boswell's *Life of Johnson.*" *PMLA,* 67 (1952), 391–410.

1039 LUSTIG, Irma S. "Boswell on Politics in the *Life of Johnson.*" *PMLA,* 80 (1965), 387–93.

1040 LUSTIG, Irma S. "Boswell's Literary Criticism in the *Life of Johnson.*" *SEL,* 6 (1966), 529–41.

1041 LUSTIG, Irma S. "Boswell at Work: The 'Animadversions' on Mrs. Piozzi." *MLR,* 67 (1972), 11–30.

1042 MOLIN, Sven Eric. "Boswell's Account of the Johnson-Wilkes Meeting." *SEL,* 3 (1963), 307–22.

1043 OSBORN, James M. "Edmond Malone and Dr. Johnson." In 27, pp. 1–20. [Malone and the *Life of Johnson.*]

1044 PASSLER, David L. *Time, Form, and Style in Boswell's "Life of Johnson."* New Haven, Conn., 1971.

1045 POTTLE, Frederick A. *The Literary Career of James Boswell, Esq., Being the Bibliographical Materials for a Life of Boswell.* Oxford, 1929. Reissued with New Introduction, 1966.

1046 POTTLE, Frederick A. "Boswell Revalued." In *Literary Views: Critical and Historical Essays,* ed. Carroll Camden (Chicago, 1964), pp. 79–91.

1047 POTTLE, Frederick A. *James Boswell: The Earlier Years, 1740–1769.* London, 1966.*

1048 SIEBENSCHUH, William R. *Form and Purpose in Boswell's Biographical Works.* Berkeley, Cal., 1973.

1049 STEWART, Mary M. "Boswell's Denominational Dilemma." *PMLA*, 76 (1961), 503–11.

1050 STEWART, Mary M. "Boswell and the Infidels." *SEL*, 4 (1964), 475–83.

1051 STEWART, Mary M. "James Boswell and the National Church of Scotland." *MLQ*, 30 (1967), 369–87.

1052 TRACY, Clarence. "Boswell: The Cautious Empiricist." In 32, pp. 225–43.

1053 WOOLLEY, James D. "Johnson as Despot: Anna Seward's Rejected Contribution to Boswell's *Life*." *MP*, 70 (1972), 140–45.

John Brown (1715–1766)

Works

1054 *Essays on the Characteristicks of the Earl of Shaftesbury (1751)*. Ed. Donald D. Eddy. New York, 1969.

Studies

1055 EDDY, Donald D. *A Bibliography of John Brown*. New York, 1971.

1056 FLASDIECK, Hermann M. *John Brown (1715–1766) und seine Dissertation on Poetry and Music*. Halle, Germany, 1924.

1057 TEMPLEMAN, William D. "Warburton and Brown Continue the Battle over Ridicule." *HLQ*, 17 (1953), 17–36.

Edmund Burke (1729–1797)

Works

1058 *A Note-Book of Edmund Burke: Poems, Characters, Essays and Other Sketches*. Ed. H. V. F. Somerset. Cambridge, Eng., 1957.

1059 *A Philosophical Inquiry into the Origin of Our Ideas of the Sublime and Beautiful*. Ed. J. T. Boulton. London, Eng., 1958.[†]

1060 *The Philosophy of Edmund Burke: A Selection from His Speeches and Writings*. Eds. Louis I. Bredvold and Ralph G. Ross. Ann Arbor, Mich., 1960, 1967.[†]

1061 *Reflections on the Revolution in France*. Ed. William B. Todd. New York, 1959.[†]

1062 *Selected Writings and Speeches on America*. Ed. Thomas Mahoney. Indianapolis, 1964.[†]

1063 *Correspondence*. Eds. Thomas W. Copeland *et al.* 9 vols. Cambridge, Eng., and Chicago, 1958–70.

Bibliography

1064 BRYANT, Donald C. "Edmund Burke: A Generation of Scholarship and Discovery." *JBS,* 2 (1962), 91–114; "Edmund Burke: The New Images 1966." *QJS,* 52 (1966), 329–36.

1065 "Doctoral Dissertations in Literature on Burke 1916–1963." *SBHT,* 10 (1969), 1250–51.

1066 STANLIS, Peter J. *A Bibliography of Edmund Burke 1748–1968.* London, 1972.

1067 TODD, William B. *A Bibliography of Edmund Burke.* London, 1964.

Studies

1068 BOULTON, James T. *The Language of Politics in the Age of Wilkes and Burke.* Toronto, 1963.

1069 BRYANT, Donald C. *Edmund Burke and his Literary Friends.* St. Louis, 1939.

1070 CAMPBELL, John A. "Edmund Burke's Argument from Circumstance in *Reflections on the Revolution in France.*" *SBHT,* 12 (1970–71), 1764–83.

1071 CHAPMAN, Gerald W. *Edmund Burke: The Practical Imagination.* Cambridge, Mass., 1967.

1072 COBBAN, Alfred. *Edmund Burke and the Revolt Against the Eighteenth Century* ... 1929. 2d ed., London, 1960.

1073 CONE, Carl B. "Edmund Burke's Library." *PBSA,* 44 (1950), 153–72.

1074 CONE, Carl B. *Burke and the Nature of Politics.* 2 vols. Lexington, Ky., 1957–64.*

1075 COPELAND, Thomas W. *Our Eminent Friend Edmund Burke: Six Essays.* New Haven, Conn., 1949; London, 1950.

1076 DREYER, Frederick. "Edmund Burke: The Philosopher in Action." *SBHT,* 15 (1973–74), 121–42.

1077 FAULKNER, John E. "Edmund Burke's Early Conception of Poetry and Rhetoric." *SBHT,* 12 (1970–71), 1747–63.

1078 GOODWIN, A. "The Political Genesis of Edmund Burke's *Reflections on the Revolution in France.*" *BJRL,* 50 (1968), 336–64.

1079 HARRIS, Eileen. "Burke and Chambers on the Sublime and Beautiful." *Essays on the History of Architecture Presented to Rudolph Wittkower* (London, 1967), pp. 207–13.

1080 JOY, Neill R. "Burke's Speech on Conciliation with the Colonies: Epic Prophecy and Satire." *SBHT,* 9 (1967), 753–72.

1081 KAUFMAN, Pamela. "Burke, Freud, and the Gothic." *SBHT,* 13 (1972). 2178–92.

1082 LOVE, Walter D. "Edmund Burke's Idea of the Body Corporate: A Study in Imagery." *Rev. of Politics,* 27 (1965), 184–97.

1083 MAHONEY, Thomas H. D. *Edmund Burke and Ireland.* Cambridge, Mass., 1960.

1084 MANSFIELD, Harvey C., Jr. *Statesmanship and Party Government: A Study of Burke and Bolingbroke.* Chicago, 1965.*

1085 MURRAY, Robert H. *Edmund Burke, A Biography.* London, 1931.

1086 O'GORMAN, Frank. *Edmund Burke: His Political Philosophy.* Bloomington, Ind., 1973.

1087 OLIVER, Barbara C. "Edmund Burke's Enquiry and the Baroque Theory of Passions." *SBHT,* 12 (1970), 1661–76.

1088 PARKIN, Charles. *The Moral Basis of Burke's Political Thought.* Cambridge, Eng., 1956.

1089 SPEER, Richard. "The Rhetoric of Burke's Select Committee Reports." *QJS,* 57 (1971), 306–15.

1090 STANLIS, Peter J. *Edmund Burke and the Natural Law.* Ann Arbor, Mich., 1958.

1091 STANLIS, Peter J., ed. *Edmund Burke: The Enlightenment and the Modern World.* Detroit, 1967.

1092 UTLEY, Thomas E. *Edmund Burke. (WTW)* London, 1957.†

1093 WAAGE, Frederick O., Jr. "Burke's *Short Account* and Its 'Answer.' " *HLQ,* 36 (1973), 255–66.

1094 WECTER, Dixon. "Burke's Theory of Words, Images, and Emotion." *PMLA,* 55 (1940), 167–81.

1095 WESTON, John C., Jr. "Edmund Burke's View of History." *Rev. of Politics,* 23 (1961), 203–29.

1096 WICHELNS, Herbert A. "Burke's Essay on the Sublime and Its Reviewers." *JEGP,* 21 (1922), 645–61.

1097 WILKINS, Burleigh T. *The Problem of Burke's Political Philosophy.* Oxford, 1967.

Robert Burns (1759–1796)

Works

1098 *Poems and Songs.* Ed. James Kinsley. 3 vols. Oxford, 1968. Also published in one volume, texts alone, 1969.†

1099 *Letters.* Ed. J. DeLancey Ferguson. 2 vols. Oxford, 1931.

1100 *Selected Letters.* Ed. DeLancey Ferguson. (*WC*) London, 1953.

Bibliography

1101 EGERER, Joel W. *A Bibliography of Robert Burns.* Edinburgh, 1964; Carbondale, Ill., 1965.

Studies

1102 BEATY, Frederick L. "Burns's Comedy of Romantic Love." *PMLA,* 83 (1968), 429–38.

1103 BENTMAN, Raymond. "Robert Burns's Declining Fame." *Studies in Romanticism,* (1972), 207–24.

1104 CRAWFORD, Thomas. *Burns: A Study of the Poems and Songs.* Stanford, Cal., 1960.*†

1105 DAICHES, David. *Robert Burns.* New York, 1950; London, 1952, 1966.†

1106 DAICHES, David. *Robert Burns.* (*WTW*) London, 1957.†

1107 DAICHES, David. *Robert Burns and His World.* New York, 1972.

1108 FERGUSON, J. DeLancey. *Pride and Passion: Robert Burns, 1759–1796.* New York, 1959, 1964.

1109 FITZHUGH, Robert T. *Robert Burns, the Man and the Poet: A Round, Unvarnished Account.* Boston, 1970.

1110 LINDSAY, John Maurice. *Robert Burns: The Man, his Work, the Legend.* London, 1954. Rev. ed., 1968.

1111 LINDSAY, John Maurice. *The Burns Encyclopaedia.* London, 1959. Rev. ed., 1970.

1112 LOW, Donald A. *Burns: The Critical Heritage.* London, 1974.

1113 ROBOTHEN, John S. "The Reading of Robert Burns." *BNYPL,* 74 (1970), 561–76.

1114 SNYDER, Franklyn B. *The Life of Robert Burns.* New York, 1932. Rpt. Hamden, Conn., 1968.

1115 SNYDER, Franklyn B. *Robert Burns: His Personality, His Reputation, and His Art.* Toronto, 1936. Rpt. 1970.

1116 THORNTON, Robert D. "Twentieth-Century Scholarship on the Songs of Robert Burns." *University of Colorado Studies* (Series in Language and Literature), No. 4 (1953), 75–92.

1117 THORNTON, Robert D. *James Currie, the Entire Stranger, and Robert Burns.* Edinburgh, 1963.

1118 THORNTON, Robert D. "Robert Burns and the Scottish Enlightenment." *SVEC,* 58 (1967), 1533–49.

1119 WESTON, John C. "The Narrator of *Tam o'Shanter.*" *SEL,* 8 (1968), 537–50.

1120 WESTON, John C. "The Text of Burns' 'The Jolly Beggars.'" *SB,* 13 (1960), 239–47.

1121 WESTON, John C. "Robert Burns' Use of the Scots Verse–Epistle Form." *PQ,* 49 (1970), 188–210.

Joseph Butler (1692–1752)

Works

1122 *The Analogy of Religion.* Ed. Ernest C. Mossner. New York, 1961.†

1123 *Five Sermons.* Ed. Stuart M. Brown. Indianapolis, 1950.†

1124 *Butler's Fifteen Sermons Preached at the Rolls Chapel.* Ed. T. A. Roberts. London, 1970.

Studies

1125 DUNCAN-JONES, Austin. *Butler's Moral Philosophy.* London, 1952.

1126 MOSSNER, Ernest C. *Bishop Butler and the Age of Reason: A Study in the History of Thought.* New York, 1936.*

1127 NORTON, William J., Jr. *Bishop Butler, Moralist and Divine.* New Brunswick, N. J., 1940.

1128 SYKES, Norman. "Bishop Butler and the Church of His Age." *DUJ,* 43 (1950), 1–14.

1129 WINDSOR, A. C. "Bishop Butler and Contemporary Ethics." *Church Quarterly Review,* 168 (1967), 181–90.

Susanna Centlivre (c. 1670–1723)

Works

1130 *A Bold Stroke for a Wife.* Ed. Thalia Stathas. Lincoln, Neb., 1968.†

1131 *The Busie Body (1709).* Ed. Jess Byrd. (*ARS*) Los Angeles, 1949.

Studies

1132 ANDERSON, Paul B. "Innocence and Artifice; or, Mrs. Centilivre and *The Female Tatler.*" *PQ,* 16 (1937), 358–75.

1133 BOWYER, John W. *The Celebrated Mrs. Centilivre.* Durham, N.C., 1952.*

1134 STROZIER, Robert. "A Short View of Some of Mrs. Centilivre's Celebrated Plays ... " *Discourse,* 7 (1964), 62–80.

1135 SUTHERLAND, James R. "The Progress of Error: Mrs. Centlivre and the Biographers." *RES,* 18 (1942), 167–82.

Thomas Chatterton (1752–1770)

Works

1136 *Complete Works.* Ed. Donald S. Taylor, with Benjamin B. Hoover. 2 vols. Oxford, 1971.

Studies

1137 BRONSON, Bertrand H. "Thomas Chatterton." In 40, pp. 239–55.

1138 BRONSON, Bertrand H. "Chattertoniana." *MLQ,* 11 (1950), 417–24.

1139 KELLY, Linda. *The Marvellous Boy: The Life and Myth of Thomas Chatterton.* London, 1971.

1140 KROESE, Irvin B. "Chatterton's *Aella* and Chatterton." *SEL,* 12 (1972), 557–66.

1141 MALONE, Edmond. *Cursory Observations on the Poems Attributed to Thomas Rowley (1782)*. Ed. James M. Kuist. (*ARS*) Los Angeles, 1966.

1142 POWELL, L. F. "Thomas Tyrwhitt and the Rowley Poems." *RES*, 7 (1931), 314–28.

Philip Dormer Stanhope, 4th Earl of Chesterfield (1694–1773)

Works

1143 *Letters*. Ed. Bonamy Dobrée. 6 vols. London and New York, 1932.

1144 *Some Unpublished Letters*. Ed. Sidney L. Gulick, Jr. Berkeley, Cal. 1957.

Bibliography

1145 GULICK, Sidney L. *A Chesterfield Bibliography to 1800*. Chicago, 1935.

1146 TODD, William B. "The Number, Order, and Authorship of the Hanover Pamphlets Attributed to Chesterfield." *PBSA*, 44 (1950), 224–38.

Studies

1147 BARRELL, Rex A. *Chesterfield et la France*. Paris, 1968.

1148 GULICK, Sidney L., Jr. "The Publication of Chesterfield's *Letters to His Son*." *PMLA*, 51 (1936), 165–77.

1149 LEED, Jacob. "Johnson and Chesterfield, 1746–47." *SBHT*, 12 (1970), 1676–90. Comment by Paul J. Korshin, pp. 1804–11; reply by Leed, *ibid.*, 13 (1971), 2011–15.

1150 NELICK, Frank C. "Lord Chesterfield's Adoption of Philip Stanhope." *PQ*, 38 (1959), 370–78.

1151 PRICE, Cecil. "Some New Light on Chesterfield." *NM*, 54 (1953), 272–84.

1152 PRICE, Cecil. "Further Chesterfield Gleanings." *NM*, 56 (1955), 112–21.

1153 PULLEN, Charles. "The Chesterfield Myth and Eighteenth-Century Ethics." *Dalhousie Review*, 47 (1967), 369–79.

1154 PULLEN, Charles. "Lord Chesterfield and Eighteenth-Century Appearance and Reality." *SEL*, 8 (1968), 501–15.

1155 SHELLABARGER, Samuel. *Lord Chesterfield and His World*. Boston, 1951.

1156 WEINBROT, Howard D. "Johnson's *Dictionary* and *The World*: The Papers of Lord Chesterfield and Richard Owen Cambridge." *PQ*, 50 (1971), 663–69.

Charles Churchill (1731–1764)

Works

1157 *Poetical Works.* Ed. Douglas Grant. Oxford, 1956.

1158 *Correspondence of John Wilkes and Charles Churchill.* Ed. Edward H. Weatherly. New York, 1954.

Bibliography

1159 WILLIAMS, Iolo A. *Seven XVIIIth Century Bibliographies* (1924), pp. 181–205.

Studies

1160 BEATTY, Joseph M., Jr. "An Essay in Critical Biography—Charles Churchill." *PMLA,* 35 (1920), 226–46.

1161 BEATTY, Joseph M., Jr. "Churchill's Influence on Minor Eighteenth-Century Satirists." *PMLA,* 42 (1927), 162–76. See also Robert C. Whitford, *MLN,* 43 (1928), 30–34.

1162 BROWN, Wallace Cable. *Charles Churchill: Poet, Rake, and Rebel.* Lawrence, Kans., 1953.

1163 FISHER, Alan S. "The Stretching of Augustan Satire: Charles Churchill's 'Dedication' to Warburton." *JEGP,* 72 (1973), 360–77.

1164 GOLDEN, Morris. "Churchill's Literary Influence on Cowper." *JEGP,* 58 (1959), 655–65.

1165 GOLDEN, Morris. "Sterility and Eminence in the Poetry of Charles Churchill." *JEGP,* 66 (1967), 333–46.

1166 McADAMS, William L. "Monstrous Birth: Charles Churchill's Image Cluster." *Satire Newsletter,* 8 (1971), 101–04.

1167 WINTERS, Yvor. "The Poetry of Charles Churchill." *Poetry,* 98 (1961), 44–53, 104–17. Rpt. in his *Forms of Discovery* (Denver, 1967), pp. 121–45.

Colley Cibber (1671–1757)

Works

1168 *An Apology for the Life of Mr. Colley Cibber, Comedian.* Ed. B. R. S. Fone. Ann Arbor, Mich., 1968.

1169 *The Careless Husband.* Ed. William W. Appleton. Lincoln, Neb., 1966.†

1170 *The Rival Queens, with the Humours of Alexander the Great.* Ed. William M. Peterson. Painesville, Ohio, 1965.

1171 *Three Sentimental Comedies.* Ed. Maureen Sullivan. New Haven, Conn., 1973. *Love's Last Shift, The Careless Husband, The Lady's Last Stake.*

1172 *The Provoked Husband,* by Vanbrugh and Cibber. Ed. Peter Dixon. Lincoln, Neb., 1973.†

Bibliography

1173 ASHLEY, L. R. N. "Colley Cibber: A Bibliography." *RECTR*, 6, No. 1 (1967), 14–27; 6, No. 2 (1967) , 51–57; 7, No. 1 (1968), 17.

Studies

1174 ASHLEY, Leonard R. N. *Colley Cibber.* New York, 1965.

1175 BARKER, Richard H. *Mr. Cibber of Drury Lane.* New York, 1939.*

1176 FONE, B. R. S. "Colley Cibber's *Love's Last Shift* and Sentimental Comedy." *RECTR*, 7, No. 1 (1968), 33–43.

1177 GILMORE, Thomas B., Jr. "Colley Cibber's Good Nature and his Reaction to Pope's Satire." *PLL*, 2 (1966), 361–71.

1178 HAYLEY, R. L. "The Scriblerians and the South Sea Bubble: A Hit by Cibber." *RES*, N. S. 24 (1973), 452–58. [*The Refusal.*]

1179 KALSON, Albert E. "The Chronicles in Cibber's *Richard III.*" *SEL*, 3 (1963), 253–67.

1180 KALSON, Albert E. "Eighteenth-Century Editions of Colley Cibber's *Richard III.*" *RECTR*, 7, No. 1 (1968), 7–17.

1181 PARNELL, Paul E. "Equivocation in Cibber's *Love's Last Shift.*" *SP*, 57 (1960), 519–34.

1182 PEAVY, Charles D. "The Pope-Cibber Controversy: A Bibliography." *RECTR*, 3 (1964), 51–55.

William Collins (1721–1759)

Works

1183 *Minor Poets of the Eighteenth Century.* Ed. Hugh I'Anson Fausset. (*EL*) London, 1930.

1184 *Poems of Thomas Gray, William Collins, and Oliver Goldsmith.* Ed. Roger Lonsdale. London, 1969.

1185 *Drafts and Fragments of Verse.* Ed. J. S. Cunningham. Oxford, 1956.

Bibliography and Concordance

1186 WILLIAMS, Iolo A. *Seven XVIIIth Century Bibliographies.* (1924), pp. 101–14.

1187 BOOTH, Bradford A., and Claude E. Jones. *A Concordance to the Poetical Works of William Collins.* Berkeley, Cal., 1939.

Studies

1188 AINSWORTH, Edward G., Jr. *Poor Collins: His Life, His Art, and His Influence.* Ithaca, N.Y., 1937.

1189 BROWN, Merle E. "On William Collins' 'Ode to Evening.'" *EIC,* 11 (1961), 136–53.

1190 CARVER, P. L. *The Life of a Poet: A Biographical Sketch of William Collins.* London, 1967.*

1191 CRIDER, John R. "Structure and Effect in Collins' Progress Poems." *SP,* 60 (1963), 57–72.

1192 DOUGHTY, Oswald. *William Collins.* (*WTW*) London, 1964.†

1193 GARROD, H. W. *Collins.* Oxford, 1928.

1194 LAMONT, Claire. "William Collins's 'Ode on the Popular Superstitions of the Highlands of Scotland'—A Newly Discovered Manuscript." *RES,* N. S., 19 (1968), 137–47.

1195 McKILLOP, Alan D. "The Romanticism of William Collins." *SP,* 20 (1923), 1–16.

1196 McKILLOP, Alan D. "Collin's *Ode to Evening*—Background and Structure." *TSL,* 5 (1960), 73–83.

1197 PETTIT, Henry. "Collins's 'Ode to Evening' and the Critics." *SEL,* 4 (1964), 361–69.

1198 QUINTANA, Ricardo. "The Scheme of Collins's *Odes on Several . . . Subjects.*" In 27, pp. 371–80.

1199 SIGWORTH, Oliver F. *William Collins.* (*TEAS*) New York, 1965.

1200 STEWART, Mary M. "William Collins and Thomas Barrow." *PQ,* 48 (1969), 212–19.

1201 STEWART, Mary M. "Further Notes on William Collins." *SEL,* 10 (1970), 569–78.

1202 TOMPKINS, J. M. S. "'In Yonder Grave a Druid Lies.'" *RES,* 22 (1946), 1–16.

1203 WASSERMAN, Earl R. "Collins' 'Ode on the Poetical Character.'" *ELH,* 34 (1967), 92–115.

1204 WHITE, H. O. "The Letters of William Collins." *RES,* 3 (1927), 12–21.

1205 WOODHOUSE, A. S. P. "Collins and the Creative Imagination: A Study in the Critical Background of His Odes (1746)." *Studies in English by Members of University College, Toronto* (Toronto, 1931), pp. 59–130.

1206 WOODHOUSE, A. S. P. "The Poetry of Collins Reconsidered." In 35, pp. 93–137.

George Colman the Elder (1732–1794)

Studies

1207 BERGMANN, Frederick L. "David Garrick and *The Clandestine Marriage.*" *PMLA,* 67 (1952), 148–62.

1208 GERBER, Helmut E. "*The Clandestine Marriage* and its Hogarthian Associations." *MLN,* 72 (1957), 267–71.

1209 PAGE, Eugene R. *George Colman the Elder, Essayist, Dramatist, and Theatrical Manager. 1732–1794.* New York, 1935.*

1210 SPECTOR, Robert D. "*The Connoisseur*: A Study of the Functions of a Persona." In 43, pp. 109–21.

1211/12 VINCENT, Howard P. "Christopher George Colman, 'Lunatick.'" *RES,* 18 (1942), 38–48.

William Cowper (1731–1800)

Works

1213 *Poetical Works.* Ed. H. Milford. 4th ed., rev. by Norma Russell. London, 1967.

1214 *Correspondence.* Ed. Thomas Wright. 1904. 4 vols. *Unpublished and Uncollected Letters.* Ed. Thomas Wright. London, Eng., 1925.

1215 "Memoir of William Cowper: An Autobiography." Ed. Maurice J. Quinlan. *Proc. Amer. Philos. Soc.,* 97 (1953), 359–82.

1216 *The Cast-Away: The Test of the Original Manuscript and the First Printing of Cowper's Latin Translation.* Ed. Charles Ryskamp. Princeton, N.J., 1963.

Bibliographies and Concordance

1217 RUSSELL, Norma. *A Bibliography of William Cowper to 1837.* Oxford, 1963.

1218 HARTLEY, Lodwick. *William Cowper: The Continuing Revaluation: An Essay and A Bibliography of Cowperian Studies from 1895 to 1960.* Chapel Hill, N.C., 1960.

1219 POVEY, K. "Handlist of Manuscripts in the Cowper and Newton Museum, Olney, Bucks." *TCBL,* 4 (1965), 107–27.

1220 RYSKAMP, Charles. "William Cowper and His Circle: A Study of the Hannay Collection." *Princeton Univ. Lib. Chronicle,* 24 (1962), 3–26.

1221 NEVE, John. *A Concordance to the Poetical Works of Cowper.* London, 1887. Rpt. New York, 1969.

Studies

1222 CECIL, David. *The Stricken Deer, or, The Life of Cowper.* London, 1929.

1223 DANCHIN, Pierre. "William Cowper's Poetic Purpose as Seen in His Letters." *ES,* 46 (1965), 235–44.

1224 DAVIE, Donald A. "The Critical Principles of William Cowper." *Camb. J.,* 7 (1953), 182–88.

1225 DESAI, R. W. "William Cowper and the Visual Arts." *BNYPL,* 72 (1968), 359–72.

1226 FÖRSTER, M. "Cowpers Ballade 'John Gilpin': Textgestalt, Verbreitung und Fortsetzungen." *Englische Studien,* 64 (1929), 380–416; 65 (1930), 26–48.

1227 FREE, William N. *William Cowper.* (*TEAS*) New York, 1970.

1228 GOLDEN, Morris. *In Search of Stability: The Poetry of William Cowper.* New York, 1960.

1229 HARTLEY, Lodwick C. *William Cowper, Humanitarian.* Chapel Hill, N.C., 1938.*

1230 HARTLEY, Lodwick C. " 'The Stricken Deer' and his Contemporary Reputation." *SP,* 36 (1939), 637–50.

1231 HARTLEY, Lodwick C. "Cowper and the Evangelicals: Notes on Early Biographical Interpretations." *PMLA,* 65 (1950), 719–31.

1232 HUANG, Roderick. *William Cowper: Nature Poet.* London, 1957.

1233 KEYNES, Geoffrey. "The Library of William Cowper." *TCBL,* 3 (1959–60), 47–69, 167. See also Norma Russell, *Ibid.,* 3 (1961), 225–31.

1234 KROITOR, Harry P. "Cowper, Deism, and the Divinization of Nature." *JHI,* 21 (1960), 511–26.

1235 KROITOR, Harry P. "The Influence of Popular Science on William Cowper." *MP,* 61 (1964), 281–87.

1236 LINK, Frederick M. "Two Cowper Letters." *MP,* 62 (1964), 137–38.

1237 MANDEL, Barrett J. "Artistry and Psychology in William Cowper's *Memoir.*" *TSLL,* 12 (1970), 431–42.

1238 NICHOLSON, Norman. *William Cowper.* London, 1951.

1239 NICHOLSON, Norman, *William Cowper.* (*WTW*) London, 1960.†

1240 PALEY, Morton D. "Cowper as Blake's Spectre." *ECS,* 1 (1968), 236–52.

1241 POVEY, Kenneth. "The Text of Cowper's Letters." *MLR,* 22 (1927), 22–27.

1242 POVEY, Kenneth. "Notes for a Bibliography of Cowper's Letters." *RES,* 7 (1931), 182–87; 8 (1932), 316–19; 10 (1934), 76–78; 12 (1936), 333–35.

1243 POVEY, Kenneth. "Cowper and Lady Austen." *RES,* 10 (1934), 417–27.

1244 QUINLAN, Maurice J. *William Cowper: A Critical Life.* Minneapolis, 1953.*

1245 RYSKAMP, Charles. *William Cowper of the Inner Temple, Esq.: A Study of His Life and Works to the Year 1768.* Cambridge, Eng., 1959.*

1246 SHERBO, Arthur. "Cowper's Connoisseur Essays." *MLN,* 70 (1955), 340–42.

1247 THOMAS, Gilbert. *William Cowper and the Eighteenth Century.* London, 1935. Rev. ed., 1948; New York, 1949.

1248 WEISS, Harry B. "William Cowper's Frolic in Rhyme: *The Diverting History of John Gilpin.*" *BNYPL,* 41 (1937), 675–80.

George Crabbe (1754–1832)

Works

1249 *Poetical Works,* Ed. A. J. and R. M. Carlyle. Oxford, 1908, 1914.

1250 *New Poems.* Ed. Arthur Pollard. Liverpool, 1960.

Studies

1251 BRETT, R. L. *Crabbe.* (*WTW*) London, 1956.†

1252 BROMAN, Walter E. "Factors in Crabbe's Eminence in the Early Nineteenth Century." *MP,* 51 (1953), 42–49.

1253 CHAMBERLAIN, Robert L. *George Crabbe.* (*TEAS*) New York, 1965.

1254 CRUTTWELL, Patrick. "The Last Augustan." *Hudson Review,* 7 (1955), 533–54.

1255 GALLON, D. N. " 'Silford Hall or the Happy Day.' " *MLR,* 61 (1966), 384–94.

1256 HADDAKIN, Lilian. *The Poetry of Crabbe.* London, 1955.

1257 HATCH, R. B. "George Crabbe, the Duke of Rutland, and the Tories." *RES,* N. S., 24 (1973), 429–43.

1258 HIBBARD, G. R. "Crabbe and Shakespeare." In 34, pp. 83–93.

1258A HUCHON, René. *Un Poète réaliste anglais, George Crabbe, 1754–1832.* Paris, 1906. Eng. trans. by Frederick Clarke, 1907, rpt. 1968.

1259 LANG, Varley. "Crabbe and the Eighteenth Century." *ELH,* 5 (1938), 305–33.

1260 *The Life of George Crabbe by His Son* [1834]. Ed. E. M. Forster. (*WC*) London, 1932.

1261 POLLARD, Arthur. *Crabbe: The Critical Heritage.* London, 1972.

1262 POLLARD, Graham. "The Early Poems of George Crabbe and *The Lady's Magazine.*" *Bodl. Lib. Record,* 5 (1955), 149–56.

1263 SALE, Arthur. "The Development of Crabbe's Narrative Art." *Camb. J.,* 5 (1952), 480–98.

1264 SIGWORTH, Oliver F. *Nature's Sternest Painter: Five Essays on the Poetry of George Crabbe.* Tucson, Ariz., 1965. See also W. K. Thomas, "George Crabbe: Not Quite the Sternest." *Studies in Romanticism,* 7 (1968), 166–75.

1265 SPEIRS, John. "Crabbe as Master of the Verse Tale." *Oxford Rev.* 1 (1966), 3–40.

1266 THALE, Rose M. "Crabbe's *Village* and Topographical Poetry." *JEGP,* 55 (1956), 618–23.

1267 THOMAS, W. K. "Crabbe's Borough: The Process of Montage." *UTQ,* 36 (1967), 181–92.

1268 THOMAS, W. K. "Crabbe's *Workhouse.*" *HLQ,* 32 (1969), 149–61.

Richard Cumberland (1732–1811)

Studies

1269 CASKEY, J. Homer. "Richard Cumberland's Mission in Spain." *PQ,* 9 (1930), 82–86.

1270 DETISCH, Robert J. "The Synthesis of Laughing and Sentimental Comedy in *The West Indian.*" *ETJ,* 22 (1970), 291–300.

1271 DIRCKS, Richard J. "Richard Cumberland's Political Associations." *SBHT,* 11 (1970), 1555–70.

1272 FLETCHER, Ifan Kyrle. "Cumberland's *The Princess of Parma.*" *TLS,* March 15, 1934, p. 187. See also William Van Lennep, *Ibid.,* Oct. 24, 1936, p. 863, and Sybil Rosenfeld, Apr. 16, 1938, p. 264.

1273 WILLIAMS, S. T. *Cumberland: His Life and Dramatic Works.* New Haven, Conn., 1917.*

John Dennis (1657–1734)

Works

1274 *Critical Works.* Ed. Edward N. Hooker. 2 vols. Baltimore, 1939–43. Rpt. Baltimore, 1965.

Studies

1275 HEFFERNAN, James A. W. "Wordsworth and Dennis: The Discrimination of Feelings." *PMLA,* 82 (1967), 430–36.

1276 HOOKER, Edward N. "Pope and Dennis." *ELH,* 7 (1940), 188–98.

1277 KRAMER, Dale. "Passion in Poetic Theory: John Dennis and Wordsworth." *NM,* 69 (1968), 421–27.

1278 LOGAN, Terence P. "John Dennis's *Select Works,* 1718, 1721." *PBSA,* 65 (1971), 155–56.

1279 SAXENA, M. N. "John Dennis and the Unities." *IJES,* 10 (1969), 26–39.

1280 SINGH, Amri. "The Argument on Poetic Justice (Addison *Versus* Dennis)." *IJES,* 3 (1962), 61–77.

1281 TUPPER, Fred S. "Notes on the Life of John Dennis." *ELH,* 5 (1938), 211–17.

1282 WILKINS, Arthur N. "John Dennis and Poetic Justice." *N&Q,* 202 (1957), 421–24.

1283 WILKINS, Arthur N. "John Dennis on Love as a 'Tragical Passion.' " *N&Q,* 203 (1958), 396–98, 417–19.

John Dyer (1699–1757)

Works

1284 *Minor Poets of the Eighteenth Century.* Ed. Hugh I'Anson Fausset. (EL) London, 1930.

1285 *Grongar Hill.* Ed. Richard C. Boys. Baltimore, 1941.

Studies

1286 HUGHES, Helen S. "John Dyer and the Countess of Hertford." *MP,* 27 (1930), 311–20.

1287 REICHERT, John F. " 'Grongar Hill': Its Origin and Development." *PLL,* 5 (1969), 123–29.

1288 SPATE, O. H. K. "The Muse of Mercantilism: Jago, Grainger, and Dyer." In 25, pp. 119–31.

1289 TILLOTSON, Geoffrey. " 'Grongar Hill': An Introduction and Texts." In his *Augustan Studies* (London, 1961), pp. 184–203.

1290 WILLIAMS, Ralph M. *Poet, Painter, and Parson: The Life of John Dyer.* New York, 1956.

Adam Ferguson (1723–1816)

Works

1291 *An Essay on the History of Civil Society, 1767.* Ed. Duncan Forbes. Edinburgh, 1966.

1292 " 'Of the Principle of Moral Estimation: A Discourse between David Hume, Robert Clark, and Adam Smith': An Unpublished MS. by Adam Ferguson." Ed. Ernest C. Mossner. *JHI,* 21 (1960), 222–32.

Studies

1293 KETTLER, David. *The Social and Political Thought of Adam Ferguson.* Columbus, Ohio, 1965.

1294 KETTLER, David. "The Political Vision of Adam Ferguson." *SBHT,* 9 (1967), 773–78.

1295 LEHMANN, William C. *Adam Ferguson and the Beginnings of Modern Sociology* . . . New York, 1930.

1296 MOSSNER, Ernest C. "Adam Ferguson's 'Dialogue on a Highland Jaunt' with Robert Adam, William Cleghorn, David Hume, and William Wilkie." In 27, pp. 297–308.

Robert Fergusson (1750–1774)

Works

1297 *Poems.* Ed. Matthew P. McDiarmid. 2 vols. Edinburgh, 1955–57.

1298 *The Unpublished Poems.* Ed. William E. Gillis. Edinburgh, 1955.

Bibliography

1299 FAIRLEY, John A. *Bibliography of Robert Fergusson.* Glasgow, 1915. See also Gordon Lindstrand in *SSL,* 7 (1970), 159–68.

Studies

1300 BUTT, John. "The Revival of Vernacular Scottish Poetry in the Eighteenth Century." In 35, pp. 219–37.

1301 DAICHES, David. *The Paradox of Scottish Culture: The Eighteenth Century Experience.* London, 1964.

1302 MacLAINE, Allan H. *Robert Fergusson.* (*TEAS*) New York, 1965.

1303 ROY, James A. "Robert Fergusson and Eighteenth-Century Scotland." *UTQ,* 17 (1948), 179–89.

1304 SMITH, Sydney Goodsir, ed. *Robert Fergusson, 1750–1774: Essays by Various Hands To Commemorate the Bicentenary of His Birth.* Edinburgh, 1952.

Samuel Foote (1720–1777)

1305 BELDEN, Mary M. *The Dramatic Work of Samuel Foote.* New Haven, Conn., 1929.

1306 TREFMAN, Simon. *Sam. Foote, Comedian, 1720–1777.* New York, 1971.

1307 WEATHERLY, Edward H. "Foote's Revenge on Churchill and Lloyd." *HLQ,* 9 (1945), 49–60.

1308 WHARTON, Robert. "The Divided Sensibility of Samuel Foote." *ETJ,* 17 (1965), 31–37.

1309 WIMSATT, W. K., Jr. "Foote and a Friend of Boswell's: A Note on *The Nabob.*" *MLN,* 57 (1942), 325–35.

David Garrick (1717–1779)

Works

1310 *The Diary of David Garrick, Being a Record of His Memorable Trip to Paris in 1751.* Ed. Ryllis C. Alexander. New York, 1928.

1311 *The Journal of David Garrick Describing his Visit to France and Italy in 1763.* Ed. George W. Stone, Jr. New York, 1939.

1312 *Three Farces.* Ed. Louise B. Osborn. New Haven, Conn., 1925. *The Lying Valet. A Peep Behind the Curtain. Bon Ton.*

1313 *Three Plays.* Ed. Elizabeth P. Stein. New York, 1926. *Harlequin's Invasion. The Jubilee. The Meeting of the Company, or Bayes's Art of Acting.*

1314 *Letters.* Ed. David M. Little and George M. Kahrl. 3 vols. Cambridge, Mass., 1963.

Bibliography

1315 BERKOWITZ, Gerald M. "David Garrick: An Annotated Bibliography." *RECTR,* 11, i (1972), 1–18.

1316 KNAPP, Mary E. *A Checklist of Verse by David Garrick.* Charlottesville, Va., 1955.

Studies

1317 ANGUS, William. "An Appraisal of David Garrick; Based Mainly upon Contemporary Sources." *QJS,* 25 (1939), 30–42.

1318 BARTON, Margaret. *Garrick.* London, 1948.

DAVID GARRICK

1319 BERGMANN, Frederick L. "David Garrick and *The Clandestine Marriage*." *PMLA,* 67 (1952), 148–62.

1320 BERGMANN, Frederick L. "Garrick's *Zara*." *PMLA,* 74 (1959), 225–32.

1321 BURNIM, Kalman A. *David Garrick, Director.* Pittsburgh, 1961.†

1322 ENGLAND, Martha W. *Garrick's Jubilee.* Columbus, Ohio, 1964.

1323 MacMILLAN, Dougald. "David Garrick as Critic." *SP,* 31 (1934), 69–83.

1324 MacMILLAN, Dougald. "David Garrick, Manager . . . " *SP,* 45 (1948), 630–46.

1325 MARTZ, Louis L., and Edwine M. MARTZ. "Notes on Some Manuscripts Relating to David Garrick." *RES,* 19 (1943), 186–200.

1326 MOTTER, T. H. Vail. "Garrick and the Private Theatres, with a List of Amateur Performances in the Eighteenth Century." *ELH,* 11 (1944), 63–75.

1327 STEIN, Elizabeth P. *David Garrick, Dramatist.* New York, 1938.*

1328 STOCHHOLM, Johanne M. *Garrick's Folly: The Shakespeare Jubilee of 1769 at Stratford and Drury Lane.* London, 1964.

1329 STONE, George Winchester, Jr. "Garrick's Long Lost Alteration of *Hamlet.*" *PMLA,* 49 (1934), 890–921.

1330 STONE, George Winchester, Jr. "Garrick's Presentation of *Antony and Cleopatra.*" *RES,* 13 (1937), 20–38.

1331 STONE, George Winchester, Jr. "Garrick, and an Unknown Operatic Version of *Love's Labour's Lost.*" *RES,* 15 (1939), 323–28.

1332 STONE, George Winchester, Jr. "*A Midsummer Night's Dream* in the Hands of Garrick and Colman." *PMLA,* 54 (1939), 467–82.

1333 STONE, George Winchester, Jr. "Garrick's Handling of Macbeth." *SP,* 38 (1941), 609–28.

1334 STONE, George Winchester, Jr. "Garrick's Production of *King Lear. . . .*" *SP,* 45 (1948), 89–103.

1335 STONE, George Winchester, Jr. "The God of his Idolatry: Garrick's Theory of Acting and Dramatic Composition with Special Reference to Shakespeare." *Joseph Quincy Adams Memorial Studies* (Washington, 1948), pp. 115–28.

1336 STONE, George Winchester, Jr. "David Garrick's Significance in the History of Shakespearean Criticism. . . ." *PMLA,* 65 (1950), 183–97.

1337 STONE, George Winchester, Jr. "*Romeo and Juliet:* The Source of Its Modern Stage Career." *SQ,* 15 (1964), 191–206.

1338 STONE, George Winchester, Jr. "Garrick and Othello." *PQ,* 45 (1966), 304–20.

1339 STONE, George Winchester, Jr. "Bloody, Cold, and Complex Richard: David Garrick's Interpretation." In *On Stage and Off: Eight Essays in English Literature,* ed. John W. Ehrstine et al (Pullman, Wash., 1968), pp. 14–26.

1340 TASCH, Peter A. "Garrick's Revisions of Bickerstaff's *The Sultan.*" *PQ,* 50 (1971), 141–49.

1341 WALCH, Peter. "David Garrick in Italy." *ECS,* 3 (1970), 523–31.

1342 WOODS, Charles B. "The 'Miss Lucy' Plays of Fielding and Garrick." *PQ,* 41 (1962), 294–310.

John Gay (1685–1732)

Works

1343   *Poetical Works, Including "Polly," "The Beggar's Opera," and Selections from the Other Dramatic Works.* Ed. G. C. Faber. London, 1926. Rpt. New York, 1969.

1344   *The Beggar's Opera.* Ed. Edgar V. Roberts and Edward Smith. Lincoln, Neb., 1969.[†]

1345   *The Beggar's Opera and Companion Pieces.* Ed. C. F. Burgess. New York, 1966.[†]

1346   *Fables (1727, 1738).* Ed. Vinton A. Dearing. (ARS) Los Angeles, 1967.

1347   *The Present State of Wit (1711).* Ed. Donald F. Bond. (ARS) Ann Arbor, Mich., 1947.[†]

1348   *Three Hours After Marriage* [by Gay, Pope, and Arbuthnot]. Ed. John Harrington Smith. (*ARS*) Los Angeles, 1961.[†]

1349   *Three Hours After Marriage* [by Gay, Pope, and Arbuthnot.] Ed. Richard Morton and William M. Peterson. Painesville, Ohio, 1961.[†]

1350   *Letters.* Ed. C. F. Burgess. Oxford, 1966.

Studies

1351   ARMENS, Sven M. *John Gay, Social Critic.* New York, 1954.

1352   BATTESTIN, Martin C. "Menalcas' Song: The Meaning of Art and Artifice in Gay's Poetry." *JEGP,* 65 (1966), 662–79.

1353   BRONSON, Bertrand H. "The Beggar's Opera." *Studies in the Comic* (Univ. of California Publications in English, 7, ii. 1941), pp. 197–231. Rpt. in 23.

1354   BRONSON, Bertrand H. "The True Proportions of Gay's *Acis and Galatea.*" *PMLA,* 80 (1965), 325–31.

1355   ELLIS, William D., Jr. "Thomas D'Urfey, the Pope-Philips Quarrel, and *The Shepherd's Week.*" *PMLA,* 74 (1959), 203–12.

1356   FORSGREN, Adina. *John Gay: Poet "of a Lower Order."* 2 vols. Stockholm, 1964–71.*

1357   FULLER, John. "Cibber, *The Rehearsal at Gotham,* and the Suppression of *Polly.*" *RES,* N.S. 13 (1962), 125–34.

1358   GRAHAM, Edwin. "John Gay's Second Series, the *Craftsman* in Fable." *PLL,* 5 (1969), 17–25.

1359   HEUSTON, Edward. "Gay's *Trivia* and the *What D'Ye Call It.*" *Scriblerian,* 5 (1972), 39–42.

1360   IRVING, William H. *John Gay, Favorite of the Wits.* Durham, N.C., 1940.*

1361   LEWIS, Peter E. "Gay's Burlesque Method in *The What D'Ye Call It.*" *DUJ,* 59 (1967), 13–25.

1362   LEWIS, Peter E. "Another Look at John Gay's *The Mohocks.*" *MLR,* 63 (1968), 790–93.

1363 LEWIS, Peter E. "Dramatic Burlesque in *Three Hours After Marriage.*" *DUJ,* 33 (1972), 232–39.

1364 MACK, Maynard. "Gay Augustan." *Yale Univ. Lib. Gazette,* 21 (1946), 6–10. The Tinker collection at Yale.

1365 SCHULTZ, William Eben. *Gay's "Beggar's Opera": Its Content, History, and Influence.* New Haven, Conn., 1923.*

1366 SHERBO, Arthur. "Virgil, Dryden, Gay, and Matters Trivial." *PMLA,* 85 (1970), 1063–71.

1367 SHERBURN, George. "The Fortunes and Misfortunes of *Three Hours After Marriage.*" *MP,* 24 (1926), 91–109.

1368 SPACKS, Patricia M. *John Gay.* (TEAS) New York, 1965.

1369 STROUP, T. B. "Gay's *Mohocks* and Milton." *JEGP,* 46 (1947), 164–67.

1370 SUTHERLAND, James. "John Gay." In 28, pp. 201–14. Rpt. in 29.

1371 SUTHERLAND, James. "*Polly* Among the Pirates." *MLR,* 37 (1942), 291–303.

1372 SWAEN, A. E. H. "The Airs and Tunes of John Gay's *Beggar's Opera.*" *Anglia,* 43 (1919), 152–90.

1373 SWAEN, A. E. H. "The Airs and Tunes of John Gay's *Polly.*" *Anglia,* 60 (1936), 403–22.

1374 TROWBRIDGE, Hoyt. "Pope, Gay, and *The Shepherd's Week.*" *MLQ,* 5 (1944), 79–88.

1375 WARNER, Oliver. *John Gay.* (WTW) London, 1964.†

Edward Gibbon (1737–1794)

Works

1376 *Autobiographies.* Ed. Dero A. Saunders. Cleveland, 1961.†

1377 *The Decline and Fall of the Roman Empire.* 6 vols. (*EL*) London 1954.†

1378 *The Decline and Fall of the Roman Empire and Other Selected Writings.* Abr. and ed. H. R. Trevor-Roper. New York, 1963.†

1379 *Gibbon's Journal to January 28th, 1763.* With Journals I-III and Ephemerides. Ed. D. M. Low. London, 1929.

1380 *Le Journal de Gibbon à Lausanne, 17 août 1763–19 avril 1764.* Ed. Georges A. Bonnard. Lausanne, 1945.

1381 *Gibbon's Journey from Geneva to Rome: His Journal from 20 April to 2 October 1764.* Ed. Georges A. Bonnard. London, 1961.

1382 *Memoirs of My Life.* Ed. Georges A. Bonnard. London, 1966; New York, 1969.

1383 *Miscellanea Gibboniana.* Ed. G. R. de Beer et al. Lausanne, 1952.

1384 *English Essays.* Ed. Patricia B. Craddock. Oxford, 1972.

1385 *Letters.* Ed. J. E. Norton. 3 vols. London, 1956.

Bibliography

1386 NORTON, J. E. *A Bibliography of the Works of Edward Gibbon.* London, 1940. Rpt. 1970.

1387 BARKER, Nicolas. "A Note on the Bibliography of Gibbon, 1776–1802." *The Library,* 5th ser., 18 (1963), 40–50.

Studies

1388 BOND, Harold L. *The Literary Art of Edward Gibbon.* Oxford, 1960.*

1389 CRADDOCK, Patricia B. "Gibbon's Revision of the *Decline and Fall." SB,* 21 (1968), 191–204.

1390 JORDAN, David P. *Gibbon and His Roman Empire.* Urbana, Ill., 1971.

1391 JOYCE, Michael. *Edward Gibbon.* London, 1953.

1392 KEAST, William R. "The Element of Art in Gibbon's *History." ELH,* 23 (1956), 153–62.

1393 *The Library of Edward Gibbon: A Catalogue of His Books.* With an Introduction by Geoffrey Keynes. London, 1940.

1394 LOW, D. M. *Edward Gibbon, 1737–1794.* London, 1937.

1395 McCLOY, Shelby T. *Gibbon's Antagonism to Christianity.* Chapel Hill, N.C., 1933.*

1396 MANDEL, Barrett J. "The Problem of Narration in Edward Gibbon's *Autobiography." SP,* 67 (1970), 550–64.

1397 MASON, H. A. "Gibbon's Irony." *Camb. Quarterly,* 3 (1968), 309–17.

1398 MOWAT, R. B. *Gibbon.* London, 1936.

1399 OLIVER, Dennis M. "The Character of an Historian: Edward Gibbon." *ELH,* 38 (1971), 254–73.

1400 OLIVER, Dennis M. "Gibbons Use of Architecture as Symbol." *TSLL,* 14 (1972), 77–92.

1401 SARTON, George. "The Missing Factor in Gibbon's Concept of History." *HLB,* 11 (1957), 271–95.

1402 SAUNDERS, J. J. "The Debate on the Fall of Rome." *History,* 48 (1963), 1–17.

1403 SWAIN, Joseph Ward. *Edward Gibbon the Historian.* London, 1966.

1404 TREVOR-ROPER, Hugh. "Gibbon: Greatest of Historians." *J. Historical Studies,* 1 (1968), 109–16.

1405 TROWBRIDGE, Hoyt. "Edward Gibbon, Literary Critic." *ECS,* 4 (1971), 403–19.

1406 WEDGWOOD, C. V. *Edward Gibbon.* (*WTW*) London, 1955.†

1407 WHITE, Ian. "The Subject of Gibbon's History." *Camb. Quarterly,* 3 (1968), 299–309.

1408 WHITE, Lynn, Jr., ed. *The Transformation of the Roman World; Gibbon's Problem After Two Centuries.* Berkeley, Cal., 1966.†

Charles Gildon (1685–1724)

Studies

1409 ANDERSON, G. L. "Lord Halifax in Gildon's *New Rehearsal.*" *PQ,* 33 (1954), 423–26.

1410 ANDERSON, G. L. "Charles Gildon's Total Academy." *JHI,* 16 (1955), 247–51.

1411 ANDERSON, G. L. "The Authorship of *Cato Examin'd* (1713)." *PBSA,* 51 (1957), 84–90.

1412 LITZ, Francis E. "The Sources of Charles Gildon's *Complete Art of Poetry.*" *ELH,* 9 (1942), 118–35.

1413 MAXWELL, J. C. "Charles Gildon and the Quarrel of the Ancients and Moderns." *RES,* N.S. 1 (1950), 55–57.

1414 MOORE, John Robert. "*The Groans of Great Britain:* An Unassigned Tract by Charles Gildon." *PBSA,* 40 (1946), 22–31.

1415 MOORE, John Robert. "Gildon's Attack on Steele and Defoe in *The Battle of the Authors.*" *PMLA,* 66 (1951), 534–38.

1416 WELLS, Staring B. "An Eighteenth-Century Attribution." *JEGP,* 38 (1939), 233–46. [Against Gildon's authorship of *A Comparison Between the Two Stages.*]

William Godwin (1756–1836)

Works

1417 *Enquiry Concerning Political Justice and Its Influence on Morals and Happiness.* Ed. F. E. L. Priestley. 3 vols. Toronto, 1946.

1418 *Enquiry Concerning Political Justice. With Selections from Godwin's Other Writings.* Abr. and ed. by K. Codell Carter. Oxford, 1971.†

1419 *Four Early Pamphlets.* Ed. Burton R. Pollin. Gainesville, Fla. 1965.

1420 *Godwin and Mary: Letters of William Godwin and Mary Wollstonecraft.* Ed. Ralph M. Wardle. Lawrence, Kans., 1966.

1421 *Uncollected Writings, 1785–1822.* Ed. Jack W. Marken and Burton R. Pollin. Gainesville, Fla., 1968.

Bibliography

1422 POLLIN, Burton R. *Godwin Criticism: A Synoptic Bibliography.* Toronto, 1967.

Studies

1423 ALLEN, B. Sprague. "William Godwin as a Sentimentalist." *PMLA,* 33 (1918), 1–29.

1424 ALLEN, B. Sprague. "The Reaction against William Godwin." *MP,* 16 (1918), 225–43.

1425 ALLEN, B. Sprague. "William Godwin and the Stage." *PMLA,* 35 (1920), 358–74.

1426 BROWN, Ford K. *The Life of William Godwin.* London, 1926.

1427 FLEISHER, David. *William Godwin: A Study in Liberalism.* London, 1951.

1428 McCRACKEN, David. "Godwin's Reading in Burke." *ELN,* 7 (1970), 264–70.

1429 McCRACKEN, David. "Godwin's Literary Theory. . . ." *PQ,* 49 (1970), 113–33.

1430 MARKEN, Jack W. "The Canon and Chronology of William Godwin's Early Works." *MLN,* 69 (1954), 176–80.

1431 MONRO, D. H. *Godwin's Moral Philosophy: An Interpretation.* . . . Oxford, 1953.

1432 POLLIN, Burton R. *Education and Enlightenment in the Works of William Godwin.* New York, 1962.

1433 PREU, James A. *The Dean and the Anarchist.* Tallahassee, Fla., 1959. Swift's influence on Godwin.

1434 SMITH, Elton E., and Esther G. SMITH *William Godwin.* (TEAS) New York, 1966.

1435 STALLBAUMER, Virgil R. "Holcroft's Influence on *Political Justice.*" *MLQ,* 14 (1953), 21–30.

Oliver Goldsmith (1730?–1774)

Works

1436 *Collected Works.* Ed. Arthur Friedman. 5 vols. Oxford, 1966.

1437/8 *Collected Letters* Ed. Katharine C. Balderston. Cambridge, Eng., 1928. See also K. C. Balderston in *Yale Univ. Lib. Gazette,* 39 (1964), 67–72.

Bibliographies and Concordance

1439 SCOTT, Temple. *Oliver Goldsmith, Bibliographically and Biographically Considered.* . . . New York and London, 1928.

1440 WILLIAMS, Iolo A. *Seven XVIIIth Century Bibliographies* (1924), pp. 117–77.

1441 PADEN, William D., and Clyde K. HYDER. *A Concordance to the Poems of Oliver Goldsmith.* Lawrence, Kans., 1940.

General Studies

1442 ARTHOS, John. "The Prose of Goldsmith." *Michigan Quarterly Rev.,* 1 (1962), 51–55.

1443 COLE, Richard C. "Oliver Goldsmith's Reputation in Ireland, 1762–74." *MP,* 68 (1970), 65–70.

1444 DUSSINGER, John A. "Oliver Goldsmith, Citizen of the World." *SVEC,* 55 (1967), 445–61.

1445 FERGUSON, Oliver W. "The Materials of History: Goldsmith's *Life of Nash.*" *PMLA,* 80 (1965), 372–86.

1446 FERGUSON, Oliver W. "Goldsmith." *SAQ,* 66 (1967), 465–72.

1447 FRASER, G. S. "Johnson and Goldsmith: The Mid-Augustan Norm." *E&S,* 23 (1970), 51–70.

1448 GWYNN, Stephen. *Oliver Goldsmith.* London, 1935.

1449 HELGERSON, Richard. "The Two Worlds of Oliver Goldsmith." *SEL,* 13 (1973), 516–34.

1450 HOPKINS, Robert H. *The True Genius of Oliver Goldsmith.* Baltimore, 1969.*

1451 JEFFARES, A Norman. *Oliver Goldsmith.* (*WTW*) London, 1959.†

1452 KIRK, Clara M. *Oliver Goldsmith.* (*TEAS*) New York, 1967.

1453 LYNSKEY, Winifred. "Goldsmith and the Chain of Being." *JHI,* 6 (1945), 363–74. Comment by A. O. Lovejoy, *Ibid.,* 7 (1946), 91–98.

1454/5 PATRICK, Michael D. "Oliver Goldsmith's *Citizen of the World:* A Rational Accommodation of Human Existence." *Enlightenment Essays,* 2 (1971), 82–90.

1456 PITMAN, James Hall. *Goldsmith's Animated Nature* . . . New Haven, Conn., 1924.

1457 QUINTANA, Ricardo. *Oliver Goldsmith: A Georgian Study.* New York, 1967.

1458 REYNOLDS, W. Vaughan. "Goldsmith's Critical Outlook." *RES,* 14 (1938), 155–72.

1459 ROUSSEAU, G. S. *Goldsmith: The Critical Heritage.* London, 1974.

1460 SMITH, Hamilton J. *Oliver Goldsmith's The Citizen of the World: A Study,* New Haven, Conn., 1926.

1461 WARDLE, Ralph M. *Oliver Goldsmith.* Lawrence, Kans., 1957.

1462 WINCHCOMBE, George. *Oliver Goldsmith and the Moonrakers.* London, 1972.

1463 WINTER, David. "Girtin's Sketching Club." *HLQ,* 37 (1974), 123–49.

Plays

1464 GASSMAN, Byron. "French Sources of Goldsmith's *The Good Natur'd Man.*" *PQ,* 39 (1960), 56–65.

1465 HUME, Robert D. "Goldsmith and Sheridan and the Supposed Revolution of 'Laughing' Against 'Sentimental' Comedy." In 39, pp. 237–76.

1466 JEFFARES, A. Norman. *A Critical Commentary on Goldsmith's "She Stoops to Conquer."* London, 1966.

1467 McCARTHY, B. Eugene. "The Theme of Liberty in *She Stoops to Conquer.*" *Univ. of Windsor Rev.,* 7 (1971), 1–8.

1468 QUINTANA, Ricardo. "Oliver Goldsmith as a Critic of the Drama." *SEL,* 5 (1965), 435–54.

1469 QUINTANA, Ricardo. "Goldsmith's Achievement as Dramatist." *UTQ,* 34 (1965), 159–77.

1470 RODWAY, Allan. "Goldsmith and Sheridan: Satirists of Sentiment." In 34, pp. 65–72.

1471 SMITH, John Harrington. "Tony Lumpkin and the Country Booby Type in Antecedent English Comedy." *PMLA,* 58 (1943), 1038–49.

1472 TODD, William B. "The First Editions of *The Good Natur'd Man* and *She Stoops to Conquer.*" *SB,* 11 (1958), 133–42.

Poems

1473 BELL, Howard J., Jr. "*The Deserted Village* and Goldsmith's Social Doctrines." *PMLA,* 59 (1944), 747–72.

1474 DAVIE, Donald. "*The Deserted Village:* Poem as Virtual History." *Twentieth Century,* 156 (1954), 161–74.

1475 EVERSOLE, Richard. "The Oratorical Design of *The Deserted Village.*" *ELN,* 4 (1966), 99–104.

1476 FERGUSON, Oliver W. "Goldsmith's 'Retaliation.'" *SAQ,* 70 (1971), 149–60.

1477 JAARSMA, Richard J. "Ethics in the Wasteland: Image and Structure in Goldsmith's *The Deserted Village.*" *TSLL* 13 (1971), 447–59.

1478 JAARSMA, Richard J: "Satire, Theme, and Structure in *The Traveller.*" *TSL,* 16 (1971), 47–65.

1479 MINER, Earl. "The Making of *The Deserted Village.*" *HLQ,* 22 (1959), 125–41.

1480 STORM, Leo F. "Literary Convention in Goldsmith's *Deserted Village.*" *HLQ,* 33 (1970), 243–56.

"The Vicar of Wakefield"

1481 ADELSTEIN, Michael. "Duality of Theme in *The Vicar of Wakefield.*" *College English,* 22 (1961), 315–21.

1482 BÄCKMAN, Sven. *This Singular Tale: A Study of "The Vicar of Wakefield" and Its Literary Background.* Lund, 1971.

1483 DAHL, Curtis. "Patterns of Disguise in *The Vicar of Wakefield.*" *ELH,* 25 (1958), 90–104.

1484 EMSLIE, Macdonald. *Goldsmith: "The Vicar of Wakefield."* ("Studies in English Literature.") London, 1963.†

1485 GOLDEN, Morris. "The Time of Writing of the *Vicar of Wakefield.*" *BNYPL,* 65 (1961), 442–50.

1486 JAARSMA, Richard J. "Satiric Intent in *The Vicar of Wakefield.*" *Studies in Short Fiction,* 5 (1968), 331–41.

1487 McDONALD, Daniel. "*The Vicar of Wakefield:* A Paradox." *College Language Association Journal,* 10 (1966), 23–33.

Thomas Gray (1716–1771)

Works

1488 *Complete Poems: English, Latin and Greek.* Eds. H. W. Starr and J. R. Hendrickson. Oxford, 1966.

1489 *Correspondence.* Eds. Paget Toynbee and Leonard Whibley. With Corrections and Additions by H. W. Starr. 3 vols. Oxford, 1971.

Bibliographies and Concordance

1490 NORTHUP, Clark S. *A Bibliography of Thomas Gray*. New Haven, Conn., 1917.

1491 STARR, Herbert W. *A Bibliography of Thomas Gray, 1917–1951, With Material Supplementary to C. S. Northup's Bibliography* . . . Philadelphia, 1953. See also E. B. Basden in *N&Q,* 207 (1962), 249–61, 283–96, 336–49.

1492 COOK, Albert S. *A Concordance to the English Poems of Thomas Gray*. Boston, 1908.

Collected Studies

1493 DOWNEY, James, and Ben JONES, eds. *Fearful Joy: Papers from the Thomas Gray Bicentenary Conference at Carleton University*. Montreal, 1973.

General Studies

1494 CECIL, David. *Two Quiet Lives.* 1948.

1495 DOHERTY, F. "The Two Voices of Gray." *EIC,* 13 (1963), 222–30.

1496 EHRENPREIS, Irvin. "The Cistern and the Fountain: Art and Reality in Pope and Gray." In 21, pp. 156–75.

1497 ELLIS, Frank H. "Gray's Eton College Ode: The Problem of Tone." *PLL,* 5 (1969), 130–38.

1498 FOLADARE, Joseph. "Gray's 'Frail Memorial' to West." *PMLA,* 75 (1960), 61–65.

1499 GOLDEN, Morris. *Thomas Gray. (TEAS)* New York, 1964.

1500 GUILHEMET, Leon M. "Imitation and Originality in the Poems of Thomas Gray." In 38, pp. 33–52.

1501 JOHNSTON, Arthur. "Gray's 'The Triumphs of Owen.' " *RES,* N.S., 11 (1960), 275–85.

1502 JOHNSTON, Arthur. " 'The Purple Year' in Pope and Gray." *RES,* N.S. 14 (1963), 389–93.

1503 JOHNSTON, Arthur. *Thomas Gray and "The Bard."* Cardiff, Wales, 1966.

1504 JONES, William Powell. *Thomas Gray, Scholar.* . . . Cambridge, Mass., 1937.

1505 JONES, William Powell. "Thomas Gray's Library." *MP,* 35 (1938), 257–78.

1506 JONES, William Powell. "Johnson and Gray: A Study in Literary Antagonism." *MP,* 56 (1959), 243–53.

1507 KETTON-CREMER, Robert W. *Thomas Gray: A Biography.* Cambridge, Eng., 1955.†

1508 KEETON-CREMER, Robert W. *Thomas Gray.* (WTW) London, 1958.†

1509 MACDONALD, Alastair. "The Poet Gray in Scotland." *RES,* N.S. 13 (1962), 245–56.

1510 MACDONALD, Alastair. "Thomas Gray: An Uncommitted Life." *Humanities Assn. Bull.* (Canada), 13 (1962–63), 13–25.

1511 MARTIN, Roger. *Essai sur Thomas Gray.* Paris and London, 1934.*

1512 MELL, Donald C. "Form as Meaning in Augustan Elegy: A Reading of Thomas Gray's 'Sonnet on the Death of Richard West.'" *PLL*, 4 (1968), 131–43.

1513 SASLOW, E. L. "Richard West: A Correction." *PQ*, 47 (1968), 592–96.

1514 SPARROW, John. "Gray's 'Spring of Tears.'" *RES*, N.S., 14 (1963), 58–61.

1515 STARR, Herbert W. *Gray as a Literary Critic.* Philadelphia, 1941.

1516 STARR, Herbert W. "Gray's Craftsmanship." *JEGP*, 45 (1946), 415–29.

1517 SWEARINGEN, James E. "Johnson's 'Life of Gray.'" *TSLL*, 14 (1972), 283–302.

1518 TAYLER, Irene. *Blake's Illustrations to the Poems of Gray.* Princeton, N.J., 1971.

1519 TILLOTSON, Geoffrey. "On Gray's Letters"; "Gray the Scholar-Poet." In his *Essays in Criticism and Research* (Cambridge, 1942), pp. 117–23, 124–26.

1520 TILLOTSON, Geoffrey. "Gray's 'Ode on the Spring' "; "Gray's 'Ode on the Death of a Favourite Cat. . . .' " In his *Augustan Studies* (London, 1961), pp. 204–15, 216–23.

1521 TRACY, Clarence. " 'Melancholy Mark'd Him for Her Own'; Thomas Gray Two Hundred Years Afterwards." *Proc. & Trans. Royal Society of Canada*, 9 (1971), 313–25.

1522 VAN HOOK, La Rue. "New Light on the Classical Scholarship of Thomas Gray." *Amer. J. of Philology*, 57 (1936), 1–9.

1523 VERNON, P. F. "The Structure of Gray's Early Poems." *EIC*, 15 (1965), 381–93.

The "Elegy"

Texts

1524 *An Elegy Written in a Country Churchyard. The Text of the First Quarto with the Variants of the MSS and of the Early Editions (1757–71).* Ed. Francis Griffin Stokes. Oxford, 1929.

1525 *An Elegy Wrote in a Country Church Yard (1751) and the Eton College Manuscript.* Ed. George Sherburn. (*ARS*) Los Angeles, Cal., 1951.†

1526 *Elegy Written in a Country Churchyard.* (Merrill Literary Casebooks) Ed. Herbert W. Starr. Columbus, Ohio, 1968.†

Studies

1527 BERRY, Francis. "The Sound of Personification in Gray's 'Elegy.'" *EIC*, 12 (1962), 442–45.

1528 BRADY, Frank "Structure and Meaning in Gray's *Elegy.*" In 35, pp. 177–89.

1529 BRONSON, Bertrand H. "On a Special Decorum in Gray's *Elegy.*" In 35, pp. 171–76.

1530 BROOKS, Cleanth. "Gray's Storied Urn." In his *The Well Wrought Urn: Studies in the Structure of Poetry* (New York, 1947), pp. 96–113.

1531 DYSON, A. E. "The Ambivalence of Gray's 'Elegy.'" *EIC*, 7 (1957), 257–61.

1532 ELLIS, Frank H. "Gray's *Elegy:* The Biographical Problem in Literary Criticism." *PMLA*, 66 (1951), 971–1008.

1533 GARROD, H. W. "Note on the Composition of Gray's 'Elegy.'" In 31, pp. 111–16.

1534 GLAZIER, Lyle. "Gray's *Elegy:* 'The Skull beneath the Skin.'" *Univ. of Kansas City Rev.,* 19 (1953), 174–80.

1535 JACK, Ian. "Gray's *Elegy* Reconsidered." In 35, pp. 139–69.

1536 JONES, Myrddin. "Gray, Jacques, and the Man of Feeling." *RES,* N.S. 25 (1974), 39–48.

1536A KUIST, James M. "The Conclusion of Gray's *Elegy." SAQ,* 70 (1971), 203–14.

1537 NEWMAN, W. M. "When Curfew Tolled the Knell." *National Rev.,* 127 (1946), 244–48.

1538 PECKHAM, Morse. "Gray's 'Epitaph' Revisited." *MLN,* 71 (1956), 409–11.

1539 SHEPARD, Odell. "A Youth to Fortune and to Fame Unknown." *MP,* 20 (1923), 347–73.

1540 STARR, Herbert W. "'A Youth to Fortune and to Fame Unknown': A Reestimation." *JEGP,* 48 (1949), 97–107.

1541 STARR, Herbert W., ed. *Twentieth-Century Interpretations of Gray's "Elegy."* Englewood Cliffs, N.J., 1968.

1542 SUTHERLAND, John H. "The Stonecutter in Gray's 'Elegy.'" *MP,* 55 (1957), 11–13.

Aaron Hill (1685–1750)

Works

1543 *Preface to "The Creation"* (1720). Ed. Gretchen Graf Pahl. (ARS) Los Angeles, 1949.

1544 *The Prompter* (1734–36) [by Hill and William Popple]. Eds. William W. Appleton and K. A. Burnim. New York, 1966.

Studies

1545 BERGMANN, Fred L. "Garrick's *Zara." PMLA,* 74 (1959), 225–32. Garrick's production and adaptation of Hill's play.

1546 BREWSTER, Dorothy. *Aaron Hill, Poet, Dramatist, Projector.* New York, 1913.*

1547 DUNKIN, Paul S. "The Authorship of *The Fatal Extravagance." MLN,* 60 (1945), 328–30. See also Paul P. Kies in *RS,* 13 (1945), 155–58; 14 (1946), 88.

1548 McKILLOP, Alan D. "Letters from Aaron Hill to Richard Savage." *N&Q,* 199 (1954), 388–91.

1549 SCHIER, Donald. "Aaron Hill's Translation of Voltaire's *Alzire." SVEC,* 67 (1969), 45–57.

1550 SUTHERLAND, W. O. S., Jr. "Essay Forms in *The Prompter."* In 702, pp. 135–49.

William Hogarth (1697–1764)

Works

1551 *Graphic Works.* Ed. Ronald Paulson 2 vols. Enl. and rev. ed. New Haven, Conn., 1970.*

1552 *The Complete Engravings.* Eds. Joseph Burke and Colin Caldwell. London, 1968.

1553 *The Analysis of Beauty, with the Rejected Passages from the Manuscript Drafts and Autobiographical Notes.* Ed. Joseph Burke. Oxford, 1955.

1554 *Hogarth on High Life: The Marriage à la Mode Series from G. C. Lichtenberg's Commentaries.* Tr. and ed. by Arthur S. Wensinger with W. B. Coley. Middletown, Conn., 1970.

Bibliography

1555 REED, Stanley E. *Bibliography of Hogarth Books and Studies . . . 1764–1940.* Chicago, 1941.

Studies

1556 ANTAL, Frederick. *Hogarth and His Place in European Art.* London, 1962.*

1557 JACKSON, Wallace. "Hogarth's *Analysis:* The Fate of a Late Rococo Document." *SEL,* 6 (1966), 545–50.

1558 MOORE, Robert E. *Hogarth's Literary Relationships.* Minneapolis, 1948.

1559 PAULSON, Ronald. "The *Harlot's Progress* and the Tradition of History Painting." *ECS,* 1 (1967), 69–92.

1560 PAULSON, Ronald. *Hogarth: His Life, Art, and Times.* 2 vols. New Haven, Conn., 1971.*

1561 SHIPLEY, John B. "Ralph, Ellys, Hogarth, and Fielding: The Cabal Against Jacopo Amigoni." *ECS,* 1 (1968), 313–31. Comment by W. B. Coley, *Ibid.,* 2 (1969), 303–07; reply by Shipley, 307–11.

1562 WARK, Robert R. "Hogarth's Narrative Method in Practice and Theory." In 51, pp. 161–72.

David Hume (1711–1776)

Works

1563 *Dialogues Concerning Natural Religion.* Ed. Norman Kemp Smith. Oxford, 1935.

1564 *An Enquiry Concerning Human Understanding and Other Essays.* Ed. Ernest C. Mossner. New York, 1963.

1565 *An Inquiry Concerning the Principles of Morals, with a Supplement: A Dialogue.* Ed. Charles W. Hendel. New York, 1957.†

1566 *Of the Standard of Taste and Other Essays.* Ed. John W. Lenz. Indianapolis, 1965.

1567 *A Treatise of Human Nature.* Ed. E. C. Mossner. (Penguin) London, 1969.[†]

1568 *Letters.* Ed. J. Y. T. Greig. 2 vols. Oxford, 1932.

1569 *New Letters.* Eds. Raymond Klibansky and Ernest C. Mossner. Oxford, 1954. See also Geoffrey Hunter in *TSLL,* 2 (1960), 127–50; E. Mossner, *ibid.,* 4 (1962), 431–60; Ian Ross, *ibid.,* 10 (1969), 537–45; J. C. Hilson in *Forum for Modern Language Studies,* 6 (1970), 315–26.

Bibliography

1570 JESSOP, T. E. *A Bibliography of David Hume and of Scottish Philosophy from Francis Hutcheson to Lord Balfour.* London, 1938. Rev. ed., 1972.

1571 MATCZAK, S. A. "A Select and Classified Bibliography of David Hume." *Modern Schoolman,* 42 (1964), 70–81.

1572 HALL, Roland. *A Hume Bibliography from 1930.* Heslington, York, 1971.

Collected Studies

1573 CHAPPELL, V. C. ed. *Hume: A Collection of Critical Essays.* New York, 1966.

Other Studies

1574 ANDERSON, Robert F. *Hume's First Principles.* Lincoln, Neb., 1966.

1575 BASSON, A. H. *David Hume.* (Penguin) London, 1958.[†]

1576 BELGION, Montgomery. *David Hume.* (WTW) London, 1965.[†]

1577 BONGIE, Laurence. *David Hume: Prophet of the Counter-Revolution.* Oxford, 1965.

1578 CHURCH, Ralph W. *Hume's Theory of the Understanding.* London, 1935. Rpt. 1968.

1579 COHEN, Ralph. "David Hume's Experimental Method and the Theory of Taste." *ELH,* 25 (1958), 270–87.

1580 COHEN, Ralph. "The Transformation of Passion: A Study of Hume's Theories of Tragedy." *PQ,* 41 (1962), 450–64.

1581 FLEW, Antony. *Hume's Philosophy of Belief: A Study of His First "Inquiry."* London, 1961.

1582 FRAZER, Catherine S. "Hume on Imagination and Natural Relations." *SBHT,* 13 (1971–72), 2111–18.

1583 FURLONG, E. J. "Imagination in Hume's *Treatise* and *Enquiry Concerning the Human Understanding.*" *Philosophy,* 36 (1961), 62–70.

1584 GLATHE, Alfred B. *Hume's Theory of the Passions and of Morals: A Study of Books II and III of the "Treatise."* Berkeley, Cal., 1950.

1585 HALBERSTADT, William H. "A Problem in Hume's Aesthetics." *JAAC,* 30 (1971), 209–14.

1586 HENDEL, Charles W., Jr. *Studies in the Philosophy of David Hume.* Princeton, N.J., 1925.

DAVID HUME

1587 HIPPLE, Walter J., Jr. "The Logic of Hume's Essay 'Of Tragedy.'" *Philosophical Quarterly,* 6 (1956), 43–52.

1588 HURLBUTT, Robert H., III. *Hume, Newton, and the Design Argument.* Lincoln, Neb., 1965.

1589 KUHNS, Richard. "Hume's Republic and the Universe of Newton." In 33, pp. 75–95.

1590 LAIRD, John. *Hume's Philosophy of Human Nature.* London, 1932.

1591 McGUINESS, Arthur E. "Hume and Kames: The Burden of Friendship." *SSL,* 6 (1968–69), 3–19. See also Ian Ross, *ibid.,* 186–89.

1592 MALL, R. A. *Hume's Concept of Man.* New York, 1967.

1593 MERCER, Philip. *Sympathy and Ethics: A Study of the Relationship Between Sympathy and Morality with Special Reference to Hume's Treatise.* Oxford, 1972.

1594 MORRISROE, Michael, Jr. "Hume's Rhetorical Strategy: A Solution to the Riddle of the *Dialogues Concerning Natural Religion.*" *TSLL,* 11 (1969), 963–74.

1595 MORRISROE, Michael, Jr. "Did Hume Read Berkeley: A Conclusive Answer." *PQ,* 52 (1973), 310–15.

1596 MOSSNER, Ernest C. *The Forgotten Hume: Le bon David.* New York, 1943.

1597 MOSSNER, Ernest C. "An Apology for David Hume, Historian." *PMLA,* 56 (1941), 657–90.

1598 MOSSNER, Ernest C. "Was Hume a Tory Historian?" *JHI,* 2 (1941), 225–36.

1599 MOSSNER, Ernest C. "Hume's *Four Dissertations:* An Essay in Biography and Bibliography." *MP,* 48 (1950), 37–57.

1600 MOSSNER, Ernest C. *The Life of David Hume.* Austin, Tex., 1954. Rpt. 1970.*

1601 MOSSNER, Ernest C. "Hume's 'Of Criticism.'" In 21, pp. 232–48.

1602 NOXON, James. *Hume's Philosophical Development: A Study of his Methods.* Oxford, 1973.

1603 PRICE, John V. *The Ironic Hume.* Austin, Tex., 1965.

1604 PRICE, John V. *David Hume. (TEAS)* New York, 1969.

1605 STEWART, John B. *The Moral and Political Philosophy of David Hume.* New York, 1963.*

1606 STOCKTON, Constant N. "David Hume among the Historiographers." *Studies in History and Society,* 3, ii (1971), 14–29.

1607 STOCKTON, Constant N. "Hume — Historian of the English Constitution." *ECS,* 4 (1971), 277–93.

1608 STOVE, D. C. *Probability and Hume's Inductive Scepticism.* London, 1973.

1609 SUGG, Redding S., Jr. "Hume's Search for the Key with the Leathern Thong." *JAAC,* 16 (1957), 96–102.

1610 TAYLOR, Harold. "Hume's Theory of Imagination." *UTQ,* 12 (1943), 180–90.

1611 WERNER, John M. "David Hume and America." *JHI,* 33 (1972), 439–56.

1612 WILLIAMS, Raymond. "David Hume: Reasoning and Experience." In 30, pp. 123–45.

Richard Hurd (1720–1808)

Works

1613 *The Correspondence of Richard Hurd and William Mason and Letters of Richard Hurd to Thomas Gray, with Introduction and Notes by Ernest H. Pearce.* Ed. Leonard Whibley. Cambridge, Eng., 1932.

1614 *Letters on Chivalry and Romance (1762).* Ed. Hoyt TROWBRIDGE. (ARS) Los Angeles, 1963.

Studies

1615 CURRY, Stephen J. "The Use of History in Bishop Hurd's Literary Criticism." *TWA.,* 54 (1965), 79–91.

1616 CURRY, Stephen J. "Richard Hurd's Genre Criticism." *TSLL,* 8 (1966), 207–17.

1617 HAMM, Victor M. "A Seventeenth-Century Source for Hurd's *Letters on Chivalry and Romance.*" *PMLA,* 52 (1937), 820–28. [Chapelain's "De la lecture des vieux romans."]

1618 MONTAGUE, Edwine. "Bishop Hurd's Association with Thomas Warton." *Stanford Studies in Language and Literature 1941,* (Stanford, Cal., 1941), pp. 233–56.

1619 NANKIVELL, James. "Extracts from the Destroyed Letters of Richard Hurd to William Mason." *MLR,* 45 (1950), 153–63.

1620 SMITH, Audley L. "Richard Hurd's *Letters on Chivalry and Romance.*" *ELH,* 6 (1939), 58–81.

1621 TROWBRIDGE, Hoyt. "Bishop Hurd: A Reinterpretation." *PMLA,* 58 (1943), 450–65.

Francis Hutcheson (1694–1746)

Works

1622 *Collected Works.* Ed. Bernhard Fabian. 7 vols. Hildesheim, Ger., 1968.

1623 *Illustrations on the Moral Sense.* Ed. Bernard Peach. Cambridge, Mass., 1971.

Studies

1624 ALDRIDGE, Alfred Owen. "A Preview of Hutcheson's Ethics." *MLN,* 61 (1946), 153–61. [Hutcheson's article, signed "Philanthropos," in *London Journal,* Nov. 14 and 21, 1724.]

1625 ALDRIDGE, Alfred Owen. "A French Critic of Hutcheson's Aesthetics." *MP,* 45 (1948), 169–84. [Charles Louis de Villette.]

1626 BLACKSTONE, William T. *Francis Hutcheson and Contemporary Ethical Theory.* Athens, Ga., 1965.[†]

1627/8 FRANKENA, William. "Hutcheson's Moral Sense Theory." *JHI,* 16 (1955), 356–75.

Samuel Johnson (1709–1784)

Works

1629 *Works* ("Yale Edition"). General editors: Allen T. Hazen and John H. Middendorf. New Haven, Conn., 1958. In progress.
    1. *Diaries, Prayers, and Annals.* Ed. E. L. McAdam, Jr., with Donald and Mary Hyde. 1958.
    2. *"The Idler" and "The Adventurer."* Eds. W. J. Bate, John M. Bullitt, and L. F. Powell. 1963.†
  3–5. *The Rambler.* Eds. W. J. Bate and Albrecht B. Strauss. 3 vols. 1969.
    6. *Poems.* Ed. E. L. McAdam, Jr., with George Milne. 1964.
  7–8. *Johnson on Shakespeare.* Ed. Arthur Sherbo. 2 vols. 1968.
    9. *A Journey to the Western Islands of Scotland.* Ed. Mary Lascelles. 1971.

1630 *A Johnson Reader.* Eds. E. L. McAdam, Jr. and George Milne. New York, 1964.

1631 *Johnson as Critic.* Ed. John Wain. London, 1973.

1632 *Early Biographical Writings.* Ed. J. D. Fleeman. Farnborough, Hants, 1973.

1633 *Political Writings.* Ed. J. P. Hardy. London., 1968.

1634 *Prefaces and Dedications.* Ed. Allen T. Hazen. New Haven, Conn., 1937. Rpt. 1973.

1635 *Letters. With Mrs. Thrale's Genuine Letters [to Johnson].* Ed. R. W. Chapman. 3 vols. Oxford, 1952. For additions and comment see Mary Hyde in 1647, pp. 286–319; Duncan E. Isles in *TLS,* July 29 and Aug. 5, 1965, pp. 666, 685; Gwin J. Kolb in *PQ,* 38 (1959), 379–83; Frederick W. Hilles in *PQ,* 48 (1969), 226–33.

Bibliography

1636 COURTNEY, William P., and David Nichol SMITH. *A Bibliography of Samuel Johnson.* Oxford, 1915, 1925. Rpt. 1968. Supplement by R. W. Chapman and Allen T. Hazen, *Proc. and Papers Oxford Bibl. Soc.,* 5 (1938), 119–66.

1637 FLEEMAN, J. D. *A Preliminary Handlist of Documents and Manuscripts of Samuel Johnson.* Oxford, 1967.

1638 *The R. B. Adam Library Relating to Dr. Samuel Johnson and His Era.* 4 vols. London, 1929–30.

1639 HYDE, Mary C. "The History of the Johnson Papers." *PBSA,* 45 (1951), 103–24.

1640 CHAPMAN, R. W. *Two Centuries of Johnsonian Scholarship.* Glasgow, 1945.

1641 WINANS, Robert B. "Works by and About Samuel Johnson in Eighteenth-Century America." *PBSA,* 62 (1968), 537–46.

1642 CLIFFORD, James L. and Donald J. GREENE. *Samuel Johnson: A Survey and Bibliography of Critical Studies.* Minneapolis, 1970.

Collected Studies

1643 BOULTON, James T. *Johnson: The Critical Heritage.* London, 1971.

1644 CHAPMAN, R. W. *Johnsonian and Other Essays and Reviews.* Oxford, 1953.

1645 HILLES, Frederick W. ed. *New Light on Dr. Johnson: Essays on the Occasion of His 250th Birthday.* New Haven, Conn., 1959.

1646 WAHBA, Magdi, ed. *Johnsonian Studies.* . . . Cairo, 1962.

1647 *Johnson, Boswell and Their Circle: Essays Presented to Lawrence Fitzroy Powell in Honour of his Eighty-Fourth Birthday.* Oxford, 1965.

1648 GREENE, Donald J. ed. *Samuel Johnson: A Collection of Critical Essays.* Englewood Cliffs, N.J., 1965.

The Early Biographies

Texts

1649 TYERS, Thomas. *A Biographical Sketch of Dr. Samuel Johnson (1785).* Ed. Gerald D. Meyer. (ARS) Los Angeles, 1952.†

1650 PIOZZI, Hester Lynch (Mrs. Thrale). *Anecdotes of the Late Samuel Johnson (1786).* Ed. S. C. Roberts. Cambridge, Eng., 1925, 1932.

1651 HAWKINS, Sir John. *The Life of Samuel Johnson* (1787). Abr. and ed. Bertram H. Davis. New York, 1961. See also Davis' *Johnson Before Boswell: A Study of Sir John Hawkins' "Life of Samuel Johnson"* (New Haven, Conn., 1960).

1652 BOSWELL, James. *The Life of Samuel Johnson (1791).* See entry under Boswell.†

1652A *The Early Biographies of Samuel Johnson.* Ed. Robert E. KELLY and O. M. BRACK, Jr. Iowa City, Iowa, 1974.

Studies

1653 KELLEY, Robert E., and O. M. BRACK, Jr. *Samuel Johnson's Early Biographers.* Iowa City, 1971.

1654 KORSHIN, Paul J. "Robert Anderson's *Life of Johnson* and Early Interpretative Biography." *HLQ,* 36 (1973), 239–53.

General Studies

1655 ALKON, Paul K. *Samuel Johnson and Moral Discipline.* Evanston, Ill., 1967.

1655A AUSTIN, M. N. "The Classical Learning of Samuel Johnson." In 25, pp. 285–306.

1656 BALDERSTON, Katharine C. "Johnson's Vile Melancholy." In 40, pp. 3–14.

1657 BALDERSTON, Katharine C. "Doctor Johnson and William Law." *PMLA,* 75 (1960), 382–94.

1658 BATE, Walter J. *The Achievement of Samuel Johnson.* New York, 1955.

1659 BATE, Walter J. "Johnson and Satire Manqué." In 22, pp. 145–60.

1660 BLOOM, Edward A. *Samuel Johnson in Grub Street.* Providence, R.I., 1957.

1661 BRONSON, Bertrand H. *Johnson Agonistes and Other Essays.* Berkeley, Cali., 1965.[†]

1662 CHAPIN, Chester F. *The Religious Thought of Samuel Johnson.* Ann Arbor, Mich., 1968.

1663 CHAPIN, Chester F. "Johnson and Pascal." In 43, pp. 3–16.

1664 CLIFFORD, James L. *Young Sam Johnson.* New York and London, 1955.

1665 CLIFFORD, James L. "Some Problems of Johnson's Obscure Middle Years." In 1647, pp. 99–110.

1666 CURTIS, Lewis P., and Herman W. LIEBERT. *Esto Perpetua: The Club of Dr. Johnson and his Friends, 1764–1784.* Hamden, Conn., 1963.

1667 EINBOND, Bernard L. *Samuel Johnson's Allegory.* The Hague, 1971.

1668 EMDEN, Cecil S. "Rhythmical Features in Dr. Johnson's Prose." *RES,* 25 (1949), 38–54.

1669 FLEEMAN, J. D. "Dr. Johnson and Henry Thrale, M.P." In 1647, pp. 170–89.

1670 FUSSELL, Paul. *Samuel Johnson and the Life of Writing.* New York, 1971.

1671 GREENE, Donald J. *The Politics of Samuel Johnson.* New Haven, Conn., 1960. Rpt. Port Washington, N.Y., 1973.

1672 GREENE, Donald J. "Samuel Johnson and 'Natural Law.'" *JBS,* 2 (1963), 59–75.

1673 GREENE, Donald J. "The Development of the Johnson Canon." In 27, pp. 407–27.

1674 GREENE, Donald J. " 'Pictures to the Mind': Johnson and Imagery." In 1647, pp. 137–58.

1675 GREENE, Donald J. *Samuel Johnson. (TEAS)* New York, 1970.

1676 GREENE, Donald J. "Samuel Johnson and the Great War for Empire." In 43, pp. 37–65.

1677 HALLIDAY, F. E. *Doctor Johnson and His World.* London, 1968.

1678 HARDY, John. "Johnson and Raphael's Counsel to Adam." In 1647, pp. 122–36.

1679 HART, Francis R. "Johnson as Philosophic Traveller: The Perfecting of an Idea." *ELH,* 36 (1969), 679–95.

1680 HOOVER, Benjamin B. *Samuel Johnson's Parliamentary Reporting: Debates in the Senate of Lilliput.* Berkeley, Cal., 1953.

1681 IRWIN, George. *Samuel Johnson: A Personality in Conflict.* Auckland and London, 1971.

1682 JEMIELITY, Thomas. "Dr. Johnson and the Uses of Travel." *PQ,* 51 (1972), 448–59.

1683 KETTON-CREMER, R. W. "Johnson and the Countryside." In 1647, pp. 65–75.

1684 KOLB, Gwin J. "More Attributions to Dr. Johnson." *SEL,* 1 (1961), 77–95. See p. 78, n. 6, for a list of articles (1939–59) concerned with new attributions.

1685 KORSHIN, Paul J. "Dr. Johnson and Jeremy Bentham: An Unnoticed Relationship." *MP,* 70 (1972), 38–45.

1686 KRUTCH, Joseph W. *Samuel Johnson.* New York, 1944.[*†]

1687 McADAM, E. L., Jr. *Dr. Johnson and the English Law.* Syracuse, N.Y., 1951.

1688 McADAM, E. L., Jr. *Johnson and Boswell: A Survey of their Writings.* Boston, 1969.

1689 MIDDENDORF, John H. "Johnson on Wealth and Commerce." In 1647, pp. 47–64.

1690 QUINLAN, Maurice J. *Samuel Johnson: A Layman's Religion.* Madison, Wis., 1964.

1691 QUINLAN, Maurice J. "Johnson's American Acquaintances." In 1647, pp. 190–207.

1692 READE, Aleyn Lyell. *Johnsonian Gleanings.* 11 Parts, 1909–52. Part 11: Consolidated Index of Persons to Parts 1–10.*

1693 ROBERTS, Sydney C. *Samuel Johnson.* (*WTW*) London, 1954.†

1694 SACHS, Arieh. *Passionate Intelligence: Imagination and Reason in the Work of Samuel Johnson.* Baltimore, 1967.

1695 SCHWARTZ, Richard B. *Samuel Johnson and the New Science.* Madison, Wisc., 1971.

1696 SHACKLETON, Robert. "Johnson and the Enlightenment." In 1647, pp. 76–92.

1697 SMITH, David Nichol, Robert W. CHAPMAN, and L. F. POWELL. *Johnson and Boswell Revised by Themselves and Others.* Oxford, 1928.

1698 SPITTAL, John Ker, ed. *Contemporary Criticisms of Dr. Samuel Johnson, His Works and His Biographers.* London, 1923.

1699 STANLIS, Peter J. "Dr. Johnson and Natural Law." *JBS,* 4 (1965), 149–57.

1700 STRUBLE, Mildred C. *A Johnson Handbook.* New York, 1933.

1701 VERBECK, Ernest. *The Measure and the Choice. A Pathographic Essay on Samuel Johnson.* Gent/Louvain, 1971.†

1702 VOITLE, Robert. *Samuel Johnson the Moralist.* Cambridge, Mass., 1961.

1703 VOITLE, Robert. "Stoicism and Samuel Johnson." In 49, pp. 107–27.

1703A WAIN, John. *Samuel Johnson: A Biography.* London, 1974.

1704 WARD, John Chapman. "Johnson's Conversation." *SEL,* 12 (1972), 519–33.

1705 WIMSATT, W. K., Jr. *The Prose Style of Samuel Johnson.* New Haven, Conn., 1941. Rpt. Hamden, Conn, 1972.

1706 WIMSATT, W. K., Jr. *Philosophick Words: A Study of Style and Meaning in the "Rambler" and "Dictionary" of Samuel Johnson.* New Haven, Conn., 1948.

Literary Criticism and the "Lives of the Poets"
(For the Life of Savage, see Richard Savage.)

Texts

1707 *Lives of the English Poets.* Introduction by Arthur Waugh. (WC) 2 vols. London, 1906.

1708 *Lives of the Poets.* (EL) 2 vols. London, 1925.

1709 *Lives of the Poets: A Selection.* Ed. J. P. Hardy. Oxford, 1971. [Cowley, Milton, Dryden, Pope, Thomson, Collins, and Gray.]

1710 *The Critical Opinions of Samuel Johnson.* Ed. Joseph Epes Brown. Princeton, N.J., 1926. [Excerpts, in dictionary form, with an introduction.]

Studies

1711 ALKON, Paul K. "Johnson's Conception of Admiration." *PQ*, 48 (1969), 59–81.

1712 BASNEY, Lionel. " 'Lucidus Ordo': Johnson and Generality." *ECS*, 5 (1971), 39–57.

1713 BATTERSBY, James L. "Patterns of Significant Action in the 'Life of Addison.' " *Genre,* 2 (1969), 28–42.

1714 BELL, Vereen M. "Johnson's Milton Criticism in Context." *ES*, 49 (1968), 127–32.

1715 DAMROSCH, Leopold. *Samuel Johnson and the Tragic Sense.* Princeton, N.J., 1972.

1716 EDINGER, William. "Johnson on Conceit: The Limits of Particularity." *ELH,* 39 (1972), 597–619.

1717 EVANS, Bergen. "Dr. Johnson's Theory of Biography." *RES,* 10 (1934), 301–10.

1718 FLEEMAN, J. D. "Some Proofs of Johnson's *Prefaces to the Poets.* " *The Library,* 5th ser., 17 (1963), 213–30.

1719 HAGSTRUM, Jean H. *Samuel Johnson's Literary Criticism.* Minneapolis, 1952; London, 1953. New ed., Chicago, 1967* [Includes "Studies of Johnson's Literary Criticism since 1952."]†

1720 HART, Edward. "Some New Sources of Johnson's *Lives.*" *PMLA,* 65 (1950), 1088–1111.

1721 HAVENS, Raymond D. "Johnson's Distrust of the Imagination." *ELH*, 10 (1948), 243–55.

1722 HORNE, Colin J. "An Emendation to Johnson's *Life of Pope.*" *The Library* 5th ser., 28 (1973), 156–57.

1723 INGHAM, Patricia. "Dr. Johnson's 'Elegance.' " *RES*, N.S., 19 (1968), 271–78.

1724 KEAST, William R. "Johnson's Criticism of the Metaphysical Poets." *ELH*, 17 (1950), 59–70. Rpt. in 29.

1725 KEAST, William R. "The Theoretical Foundations of Johnson's Criticism." *Critics and Criticism,* ed. R. S. Crane (Chicago, 1952), pp. 389–407.

1726 KEAST, William R. "Johnson and 'Cibber's' *Lives of the Poets*, 1753." In 27, pp. 89–101.

1727 KELLY, Richard. "Johnson Among the Sheep." *SEL*, 8 (1968), 475–85. [Criticism of the pastoral.]

1728 KORSHIN, Paul J. "Johnson and Swift: A Study in the Genesis of Literary Opinion." *PQ*, 48 (1969), 464–78.

1729 MISENHEIMER, James B., Jr. "Dr. Johnson's Concept of Literary Fiction." *MLR*, 62 (1967), 598–605.

1730 PERKINS, David. "Johnson on Wit and Metaphysical Poetry." *ELH*, 20 (1953), 200–17.

1731 REYNOLDS, W. Vaughan. "Johnson's Opinions on Prose Style." *RES*, 9 (1933), 433–46.

1732 SIGWORTH, Oliver F. "Johnson's *Lycidas:* The End of Renaissance Criticism." *ECS*, 1 (1967), 159–68. Comment by Victor J. Milne, *ibid.*, 2 (1969), 300–301; reply by Sigworth, pp. 301–302.

1733 TARBET, David W. "Lockean 'Intuition' and Johnson's Characterization of Aesthetic Response." *ECS*, 5 (1971), 58–79.

1734 TATE, Allen. "Johnson on the Metaphysicals." *Kenyon Rev.*, 11 (1949), 379–94.

1735 TILLOTSON, Geoffrey. "Imlac and the Business of a Poet." In 21, pp. 296–314.

1736 TURNAGE, Maxine. "Samuel Johnson's Criticism of the Works of Edmund Spenser." *SEL*, 10 (1970), 557–67.

1737 WARNCKE, Wayne. "Samuel Johnson on Swift: The *Life of Swift* and Johnson's Predecessors in Swiftian Biography." *JBS*, 7 (1968), 56–64.

1738 WATKINS, W. B. C. *Johnson and English Poetry Before 1660.* Princeton, N.J., 1936.

1739 WESLING, Donald. "An Ideal of Greatness: Ethical Implications in Johnson's Critical Vocabulary." *UTQ*, 34 (1965), 133–45.

1740 WILES, R. M. "Samuel Johnson's Response to Beauty." *SBHT*, 13 (1971–72), 2067–82.

1741 WIMSATT, W. K., Jr. "Samuel Johnson and Dryden's *Du Fresnoy.*" *SP*, 48 (1951), 26–39.

1742 WRIGHT, John W. "Samuel Johnson and Traditional Methodology." *PMLA*, 86 (1971), 40–50.

The "Dictionary"

Texts

1743 *Johnson's Dictionary: A Modern Selection.* Eds. E. L. McAdam, Jr., and George Milne. New York and London, 1963.†

Studies

1744 BALDERSTON, Katharine C. "Dr. Johnson's Use of William Law in the *Dictionary.*" *PQ*, 39 (1960), 379–88.

1745 BRAUDY, Leo. "Lexicography and Biography in the *Preface* to Johnson's *Dictionary.*" *SEL*, 10 (1970), 551–56.

1746 KEAST, William R. "The Preface to *A Dictionary . . . :* Johnson's Revision and the Establishment of the Text." *SB*, 5 (1952–53), 129–46.

1747 KEAST, William R. "Some Emendations in Johnson's Preface to the Dictionary." *RES*, N.S., 4 (1953), 52–57.

1748 KEAST, William R. "Johnson's *Plan of a Dictionary*: A Textual Crux." *PQ*, 33 (1954), 341–47.

1749 KEAST, William R. "The Two *Clarissas* in Johnson's *Dictionary.*" *SP*, 54 (1957), 429–39.

1750 KOLB, Gwin J. "Establishing the Text of Dr. Johnson's 'Plan of a Dictionary of the English Language.'" In 22, pp. 81–87.

1751 McCRACKEN, David. "The Drudgery of Defining: Johnson's Debt to Bailey's *Dictionarium Britannicum.*" *MP,* 66 (1969), 338–41.

1752 NOYES, Gertrude E. "The Critical Reception of Johnson's *Dictionary* in the Latter Eighteenth Century." *MP,* 52 (1955), 175–91.

1753 READ, Allen W. "The Contemporary Quotations in Johnson's *Dictionary.*" *ELH,* 2 (1935), 246–51.

1754 RYPINS, Stanley. "Johnson's *Dictionary* Reviewed by his Contemporaries." *PQ,* 4 (1925), 281–86.

1755 SAN JUAN, E., Jr. "The Actual and the Ideal in the Making of Samuel Johnson's *Dictionary.*" *UTQ,* 39 (1965), 148–58.

1756 SHERBO, Arthur. "Dr. Johnson's Revision of his *Dictionary.*" *PQ,* 31 (1952), 372–82.

1757 SLEDD, James H. and Gwin J. KOLB. *Dr. Johnson's Dictionary: Essays in the Biography of a Book.* Chicago, 1955.*

1758 TILLOTSON, Geoffrey. "Johnson's Dictionary." In his *Augustan Studies* (1961), pp. 224–28.

1759 WEINBROT, Howard D., ed. *New Aspects of Lexicography.* Carbondale, Ill., 1972. Contains three essays on "Samuel Johnson and the Eighteenth Century": Gwin J. Kolb and Ruth A. Kolb, "The Selection and Use of the Illustrative Quotations in Dr. Johnson's *Dictionary*"; H. D. Weinbrot, "Samuel Johnson's *Plan* and Preface to the Dictionary: The Growth of a Lexicographer's Mind"; David A. Hansen, "Redefinitions of Style, 1600–1800."

1760 WIMSATT, W. K., Jr., and Margaret H. WIMSATT. "Self-Quotations and Anonymous Quotations in Johnson's Dictionary." *ELH,* 15 (1948), 60–68.

"Rasselas"

Texts

1761 *The History of Rasselas, Prince of Abissinia.* Ed. Gwin J. Kolb. New York, 1962. Ed. John P. Hardy. 1968. Eds. Geoffrey Tillotson and Brian Jenkins. Oxford, 1971.

Studies

1762 BAKER, Sheridan. "*Rasselas*: Psychological Irony and Romance." *PQ,* 45 (1966), 249–61.

1763 BERNARD, F. V. "The Hermit of Paris and the Astronomer in *Rasselas.*" *JEGP,* 67 (1968), 272–78.

1764 HILLES, Frederick W. "*Rasselas,* an 'Uninstructive Tale.'" In 1647, pp. 111–21.

1765 JONES, Emrys. "The Artistic Form of *Rasselas.*" *RES,* N.S., 18 (1967), 387–401.

1766 KENNEY, William. "Johnson's *Rasselas* After Two Centuries." *Boston Univ. Studies in English,* 3 (1957), 88–96.

1767 KOLB, Gwin J. "Johnson's 'Dissertation on Flying' and John Wilkins' *Mathematical Magick.*" *MP,* 47 (1949), 24–31.

1768 KOLB, Gwin J. "The Structure of *Rasselas.*" *PMLA*, 66 (1951), 698–717.

1769 KOLB, Gwin J. "The Use of Stoical Doctrines in *Rasselas,* Chapter XVIII." *MLN*, 68 (1953), 439–47.

1770 KOLB, Gwin J. "Textual Cruces in *Rasselas.*" *ES*, 4 (1951), 37–52.

1771 LASCELLES, Mary. "*Rasselas* Reconsidered." *E&S*, 4 (1951), 37–52.

1772 LASCELLES, Mary. "*Rasselas*: A Rejoinder." *RES*, N.S., 21 (1970), 49–56.

1773 LOCKHART, Donald M. " 'The Fourth Son of the Mighty Emperor': The Ethiopian Background of Johnson's *Rasselas.*" *PMLA*, 78 (1963), 516–28.

1774 O'FLAHERTY, Patrick. "Dr. Johnson as Equivocator: The Meaning of *Rasselas.*" *MLQ*, 31 (1970), 195–208.

1775 PAGLIARO, Harold E. "Structural Patterns of Control in *Rasselas.*" In 43, pp. 208–29.

1776 PRESTON, Thomas R. "The Biblical Context of Johnson's *Rasselas.*" *PMLA*, 84 (1969), 274–81.

1777 SHERBURN, George. "Rasselas Returns—To What?" *PQ,* 28 (1959), 383–84.

1778 WAHBA, Magdi, ed. *Bicentenary Essays on Rasselas.* Cairo, 1959. Rev. by Gwin J. Kolb in *PQ*, 39 (1960), 336–39.

1779 WEINBROT, Howard D. "The Reader, the General, and the Particular: Johnson and Imlac in Chapter Ten of *Rasselas.*" *ECS*, 5 (1971), 80–96.

1780 WEITZMAN, Arthur J. "More Light on *Rasselas*: The Background of the Egyptian Episodes." *PQ*, 48 (1969), 42–58.

1781 WHITLEY, Alvin. "The Comedy of *Rasselas.*" *ELH*, 23 (1956), 48–70. Rev. by Gwin J. Kolb in *PQ*, 36 (1957), 379–81.

1782 WIMSATT, W. K. "In Praise of *Rasselas*: Four Notes (Converging)." In *Imagined Worlds: Essays . . . in Honour of John Butt,* eds. Maynard Mack and Ian Gregor (London, 1968), pp. 111–36.

Periodical Essays

Texts

1783 *The Rambler.* Ed. S. C. Roberts. (*EL*) London, 1953.

1784 *Essays from the Rambler, Adventurer, and Idler.* Ed. W. J. Bate. New Haven, Conn., 1968.

Studies

1785 BLOOM, Edward A. "Symbolic Names in Johnson's Periodical Essays." *MLQ,* 13 (1952), 333–52.

1786 BRADFORD, C. B. "Johnson's Revision of the *Rambler.*" *RES*, 15 (1939), 302–14.

1787 ELDER, A. T. "Irony and Humour in the *Rambler.*" *UTQ*, 30 (1960), 57–71.

1788 ELDER, A. T. "Thematic Patterning and Development in Johnson's Essays." *SP*, 62 (1965), 610–32.

1788A FAIRER, David. "Authorship Problems in *The Adventurer.*" *RES,* N.S. 25 (1974), 137–51.

1789 FLEEMAN, J. D. "Johnson's 'Rambler.' " *TLS,* May 21, 1971, p. 594.

1790 LEED, Jacob. "Patronage in the *Rambler.*" *SBHT,* 14 (1972), 5–21.

1791 McINTOSH, Carey. *The Choice of Life: Samuel Johnson and the World of Fiction.* New Haven, Conn., 1973.

1792 O'FLAHERTY, Patrick. "Johnson's *Idler*: The Equipment of a Satirist." *ELH,* (1970), 211–25.

1793 REWA, Michael P. "Aspects of Rhetoric in Johnson's 'Professedly Serious' *Rambler* Essays." *QJS,* 56 (1970), 75–84.

1794 RIELY, John C. "The Pattern of Imagery in Johnson's Periodical Essays." *ECS,* 3 (1970), 384–97.

1795 SHERBO, Arthur. "The Making of *Ramblers* 186 and 187." *PMLA,* 67 (1952), 575–80.

1796 WILES, Roy M. "The Contemporary Distribution of Johnson's *Rambler.*" *ECS,* 2 (1968), 155–71.

"A Journey to the Western Islands of Scotland"

1797 HART, Jeffrey. "Johnson's *A Journey* . . .: History as Art." *EIC,* 10 (1960), 44–59. Comment by Donald J. Greene, *Ibid.,* pp. 476–80.

1798 JEMIELITY, Thomas. "More in Notion than Facts: Samuel Johnson's *Journey* . . ." *Dalhousie Rev.,* 49 (1969), 319–30.

1799 JENKINS, Ralph E. " 'And I Travelled After Him': Johnson and Pennant in Scotland." *TSLL,* 14 (1972), 445–62.

1800 KAUL, R. K. "*A Journey* . . . Reconsidered." *EIC,* 13 (1961), 341–50.

1801 MEIER, T. K. "Pattern in Johnson's *A Journey. . . .*" *SSL,* 5 (1968), 185–93.

1802 O'FLAHERTY, Patrick. "Johnson in the Hebrides: Philosopher Becalmed." *SBHT,* 13 (1971), 1986–2001. Comment by Arthur Sherbo, *Ibid,* pp. 2119–27, and response by O'Flaherty, pp. 2229–33.

1803 PRESTON, Thomas R. "Homeric Allusion in *A Journey* . . ." *ECS,* 5 (1972), 545–58.

1804 SCHWARTZ, Richard B. "Johnson's *Journey.*" *JEGP,* 69 (1970), 292–303.

1805 SHERBO, Arthur. "Johnson's Intent in the *Journey* . . ." *EIC,* 16 (1966), 382–97. See also T. K. Meier, *Ibid.,* 18 (1968), 344–52.

1806 TODD, William B. "The Printing of Johnson's 'Journey' (1775)." *SB,* 6 (1954), 247–54.

1807 TRACY, Clarence. "Johnson's *Journey* . . .: A Reconsideration." *SVEC,* 58 (1967), 1593–1606.

Poems

Texts

1808 *Complete English Poems*. Ed. J. D. Fleeman. (Penguin) London, 1971. †

Concordance

1809 NAUGLE, Helen H. *A Concordance to the Poems of Samuel Johnson*. Ithaca, N.Y., 1973.

Studies

1810 BLOOM, Edward A. *"The Vanity of Human Wishes:* Reason's Images." *EIC*, 15 (1965), 181–92.

1811 BLOOM, Edward A., and Lillian D. BLOOM. "Johnson's *London* and Its Juvenalian Texts." *HLQ*, 34 (1970), 1–23; "Johnson's *London* and the Tools of Scholarship." *HLQ*, 34 (1971), 115–39.

1812 BLOOM, Edward A., and Lillian D. BLOOM. "Johnson's 'Mournful Narrative': The Rhetoric of 'London.' " In 22, pp. 107–44.

1813 BOYD, D. V. "Vanity and Vacuity: A Reading of Johnson's Verse Satires." *ELH*, 39 (1972), 387–403.

1814 EMSLIE, Macdonald. "Johnson's Satires and the 'Proper Wit of Poetry.' " *Camb. J.*, 7 (1954), 347–60.

1815 GIFFORD, Henry *"The Vanity of Human Wishes."* *RES*, N.S., 6 (1955), 157–65.

1816 HARDY, John P. "Johnson's *London*: The Country Versus the City." In 25, pp. 251–68. Rpt. with revisions in his *Reinterpretations: Essays on Poems by Milton, Pope and Johnson* (1971), pp. 103–23.

1817 HILLES, Frederick W. "Johnson's Poetic Fire." In 35, pp. 67–77. [*The Vanity of Human Wishes.*]

1818 KUPERSMITH, William. "Declamatory Grandeur: Johnson and Juvenal." *Arion*, 9 (1970), 52–72.

1819 MOODY, A. D. "Johnson's Poems: Textual Problems and Critical Readings." *The Library*, 5th ser., 26 (1971), 22–38.

1820 MOODY, A. D. "The Creative Critic: Johnson's Revisions of *London* and *The Vanity of Human Wishes."* *RES*, N.S., 22 (1971), 137–50.

1821 O'FLAHERTY, Patrick. "Johnson as Satirist: A New Look at *The Vanity of Human Wishes."* *ELH*, 34 (1967), 78–91.

1822 RICKS, Christopher. "Johnson's 'Battle of the Pygmies and Cranes.' " *EIC*, 16 (1966), 281–89.

1823 SELDEN, R. "Dr. Johnson and Juvenal: A Problem in Critical Method." *CL*, 32 (1970), 289–302.

1824 TUCKER, Susie I., and Henry GIFFORD. "Johnson's Poetic Imagination." *RES*, N.S., 8 (1957), 241–48.

The Edition of Shakespeare

Texts

1825 *Johnson's Notes to Shakespeare* [1773 text]. Ed. Arthur Sherbo. (*ARS*) 7 vols. Los Angeles, 1956–58.†

1826 *Samuel Johnson on Shakespeare.* Ed. W. K. Wimsatt, Jr. New York, 1960.

Studies

1827 CARNOCHAN, W. B. "Johnsonian Metaphor and the 'Adamant of Shakespeare.' " *SEL*, 10 (1970), 541–49.

1828 EASTMAN, Arthur M. "Johnson's Shakespeare and the Laity: A Textual Study." *PMLA*, 65 (1950), 1112–21.

1829 EASTMAN, Arthur M. "The Texts from Which Johnson Printed His Shakespeare." *JEGP*, 49 (1950), 182–91.

1830 EDDY, Donald D. "Samuel Johnson's Editions of Shakespeare." *PBSA*, 56 (1962), 428–44.

1831 FLEISCHMANN, Wolfgang B. "Shakespeare, Johnson, and the Dramatic 'Unities of Time and Place.' " In 49, 128–34.

1832 KRIEGER, Murray. "Fiction, Nature, and Literary Kinds in Johnson's Criticism of Shakespeare." *ECS*, 4 (1970–1), 184–98.

1833 MIDDENDORF, John H. "Ideas vs. Words: Johnson, Locke, and the Edition of Shakespeare." In 43, pp. 249–72.

1834 MONAGHAN, T. J. "Johnson's Additions to His *Shakespeare* for the Edition of 1773." *RES*, N.S. 4 (1953), 234–48.

1835 SCHOLES, Robert W. "Dr. Johnson and the Bibliographical Criticism of Shakespeare." *SQ*, 11 (1960), 163–71.

1836 SHERBO, Arthur. *Samuel Johnson, Editor of Shakespeare. With an Essay on "The Adventurer."* Urbana, Ill., 1956. See also Arthur M. Eastman. "In Defence of Dr. Johnson." *SQ*, 8 (1957), 493–500.

1837 STOCK, R. D. *Samuel Johnson and Neo-classical Dramatic Theory: The Intellectual Context of the Preface to Shakespeare.* Lincoln, Neb., 1973.

1838 TROWBRIDGE, Hoyt. "Scattered Atoms of Probability." *ECS*, 5 (1971), 1–38. [The Preface to Shakespeare.]

"Irene"

1839 BRONSON, Bertrand H. "Johnson's *Irene.*" In his *Johnson and Boswell: Three Essays* (Berkeley, Cal., 1944). Rpt. in his *Johnson Agonistes and Other Essays* (Berkeley, Cal., 1965).

1840 MORAN, Berna. "The Irene Story and Dr. Johnson's Sources." *MLN*, 71 (1956), 87–91.

1841 SMITH, David Nichol. *Samuel Johnson's "Irene."* Oxford, 1929.

1842 WAINGROW, Marshall. "The Mighty Moral of *Irene.*" In 35, pp. 79–92.

Other Writings

1843 FLEEMAN, J. D. "Some Notes on Johnson's Prayers and Meditations." *RES,* N.S., 19 (1968), 172–79.

1844 GRAY, James. *Johnson's Sermons: A Study.* Oxford, 1972.

1845 O'FLAHERTY, Patrick. "Johnson as Rhetorician: The Political Pamphlets of the 1770's." *SBHT,* 11 (1970), 1571–84. See also discussion by Donald J. Greene and O'Flaherty, *ibid.,* pp. 1585–91; 12 (1970), 1695–1703.

1846 SHERBO, Arthur. "Some Obervations on Johnson's Prefaces and Dedications." In 43, pp. 122–42.

Sir William Jones (1746–1794)

Works

1847 *Letters.* Ed. Garland Cannon. 2 vols. Oxford, 1970. See also Garland Cannon, "Five New Letters." *PQ,* 51 (1972), 951–55.

Bibliography

1848 CANNON, Garland. *Sir William Jones, Orientalist: An Annotated Bibliography of His Works.* Honolulu, 1952.

Studies

1849 CANNON, Garland. *Oriental Jones: A Biography of Sir William Jones (1746–1794).* New York and London, 1964.

1850 CANNON, Garland. "Sir William Jones and Dr. Johnson's Literary Club." *MP,* 63 (1965), 20–37.

1851 CANNON, Garland. "Sir William Jones's Indian Studies." *J. Amer. Oriental Soc.,* 91 (1971), 418–25.

1852 MUKHERJEE, S. N. *Sir William Jones: A Study in Eighteenth-Century British Attitudes to India.* Cambridge, Eng., 1968.

"Junius"

Works

1853 *The Letters of Junius.* Ed. C. W. Everett. London, 1927.

Studies

1854 BOWYER, T. H. *A Bibliographical Examination of the Earliest Editions of "The Letters of Junius."* Charlottesville, Va., 1957.

1855 ELLEGÅRD, Alvar. *Who Was Junius?* Stockholm, 1962.

1856 ELLEGÅRD, Alvar. *A Statistical Method for Determining Authorship: The Junius Letters, 1769–1772.* Stockholm, 1962.

Henry Home, Lord Kames (1696–1782)

1857 BEVILACQUA, Vincent M. "Rhetoric and Human Nature in Kames's *Elements of Criticism.*" *QJS,* 48 (1962), 46–50.

1858 BEVILACQUA, Vincent M. "Lord Kames's Theory of Rhetoric." *SM,* 30 (1963), 309–27.

1859 HORN, András. "Kames and the Anthropological Approach to Criticism." *PQ,* 44 (1965), 211–33.

1860 LEHMANN, William C. *Henry Home, Lord Kames, and the Scottish Enlightenment.* . . . The Hague, 1971.

1861 McGUINNESS, Arthur E. "Lord Kames on the Ossian Poems: Anthropology and Criticism." *TSLL,* 10 (1968), 65–75.

1862 McGUINNESS, Arthur E. *Henry Home, Lord Kames.* (TEAS.) New York, 1970.

1863 RANDALL, Helen W. *The Critical Theory of Lord Kames.* Northampton, Mass., 1944.

1864 ROSS, Ian Simpson. "Scots Law and Scots Criticism: The Case of Lord Kames." *PQ,* 45 (1966), 614–23.

1865 ROSS, Ian Simpson. *Lord Kames and the Scotland of His Day.* Oxford, 1972.

William Law (1686–1761)

Works

1866 *A Serious Call to a Devout and Holy Life.* Ed. G. W. Bromiley. Grand Rapids, Mich., 1966.

1867 *Selected Mystical Writings.* Ed. Stephen Hobhouse. 2d ed. rev. London, 1948.

Studies

1868 HOBHOUSE, Stephen. *William Law and Eighteenth-Century Quakerism, Including Some Unpublished Letters and Fragments of William Law and John Byrom.* London, 1927.

1869 HOBHOUSE, Stephen. "*Fides et Ratio,* the Book Which Introduced Jacob Boehme to William Law." *J. Theological Studies,* 37 (1936), 350–68.

1870 HOPKINSON, Arthur W. *About William Law: A Running Commentary on his Works.* London, 1948.

1871 MALEKIN, Peter. "Jacob Boehme's Influence on William Law." *SN,* 36 (1964), 245–60.

1872 MALEKIN, Peter. "William Law and John Wesley." *SN,* 37 (1965), 190–98.

1873 MALEKIN, Peter. "The Character Sketches in the *Serious Call.*" *SN,* 38 (1966), 314–22.

1874 MALEKIN, Peter, "William Law's Career, 1711–23." *N&Q,* 212 (1967), 405–06.

1875 TALON, Henri. *William Law: A Study in Literary Craftsmanship.* London, 1948; New York, 1949.

1876 WALKER, A. Keith. *William Law: His Life and Thought.* London, 1973.

George Lillo (1693–1739)

Works

1877 *The London Merchant.* Ed. William H. McBurney. Lincoln, Neb., 1965.[†]

1878 *Fatal Curiosity.* Ed. William H. McBurney. Lincoln, Neb., 1966.[†]

Studies

1879 BURGESS, C. F. "Further Notes for a Biography of George Lillo." *PQ,* 46 (1967), 424–28.

1880 BURGESS, C. F. "Lillo sans Barnwell, or the Playwright Revisited." *MP,* 66 (1968), 5–29.

1881 COHEN, Michael M. "Providence and Constraint in Two Lillo Tragedies." *ES,* 52 (1971), 231–36.

1882 JACKSON, Wallace. "Dryden's Emperor and Lillo's Merchant: The Relevant Bases of Action." *MLQ,* 26 (1965), 536–44.

1883 KEARFUL, Frank J. "Dramatic Rhetoric in Lillo's *London Merchant.*" *NM,* 73 (1972), 849–54.

1884 McBURNEY, William H. "What Lillo Read: A Speculation." *HLQ,* 29 (1966), 275–86. The sale catalogue of Lillo's library.

1885 PALLETTE, Drew B. "Notes for a Biography of George Lillo." *PQ,* 19 (1940), 261–67.

1886 PRICE, Lawrence M. "George Barnwell Abroad." *CL,* 2 (1950), 126–56.

1887 RODMAN, George B. "Sentimentalism in Lillo's 'The London Merchant.' " *ELH,* 12 (1945), 45–61. See also Raymond D. Havens, *ibid.*, pp. 183–87.

George, Lord Lyttelton (1709–1773)

1888 DAVIS, Rose Mary. *The Good Lord Lyttelton: A Study in Eighteenth Century Politics and Culture.* Bethlehem, Pa., 1939.

1889 ROBERTS, Sydney C. *An Eighteenth-Century Gentleman.* Cambridge, Eng., 1930.

Charles Macklin (1697?–1797)

Works

1890 *The Man of the World.* Ed. Dougald MacMillan. (*ARS*) Los Angeles, 1951.[†]

1891 *The Covent-Garden Theatre.* Ed. Jean B. Kern. (*ARS*) Los Angeles, 1965.†

1892 *A Will and No Will. The New Play Criticiz'd.* Ed. Jean B. Kern. (*ARS*) Los Angeles, 1967.†

1893 *Four Comedies.* Ed. J. O. Bartley. 1968. [*The True-Born Irishman, Love a la Mode, The Man of the World, The School for Husbands.*]

Studies

1894 APPLETON, William W. *Charles Macklin: An Actor's Life.* Cambridge, Mass., 1960.*

1895 FINDLAY, Robert R. "Charles Macklin and the Problem of 'Natural' Acting." *ETJ*, 19 (1967), 33–40.

1896 FINDLAY, Robert R. "The Comic Plays of Charles Macklin: Dark Satire at Mid-Eighteenth Century." *ETJ*, 20 (1968), 398–407.

1897 RAUSHENBUSH, Esther M. "Charles Macklin's Lost Play About Henry Fielding." *MLN*, 51 (1936), 505–14.

James Macpherson (1736–1796)

Works

1898 *James Macpherson's Ossian. Faksimile-Neudruck der Erstausgabe von 1762/63 mit Begleitband: die Varianten.* Ed. Otto L. Jiriczek. 3 vols. Heidelberg, 1940.

1899 *Fragments of Ancient Poetry.* Ed. John J. Dunn. (*ARS*) Los Angeles, 1966.

Studies

1900 BLACK, George F. "Macpherson's Ossian and the Ossianic Controversy: A Contribution Towards a Bibliography." *BNYPL*, 30 (1926), 424–39, 508–24. Supplement by John J. Dunn, *ibid.*, 75 (1971), 465–73.

1901 OKUN, Henry. "Ossian in Painting." *JWCI*, 30 (1967), 327–56.

1902 THOMSON, Derick S. *The Gaelic Sources of Macpherson's "Ossian."* Edinburgh, 1952.

1903 THOMSON, Derick S. " 'Ossian' Macpherson and the Gaelic World of the Eighteenth Century." *Aberdeen Univ. Rev.*, 40 (1963), 7–20.

Bernard Mandeville (1670–1733)

Works

1904 *The Fable of the Bees; or, Private Vices, Public Benefits.* Ed. F. B. Kaye. 2 vols. Oxford, 1924.

1905 *The Fable of the Bees.* Ed. Phillip Harth. (Penguin) London, 1970.†

1906 *A Letter to Dion.* Ed. Jacob Viner. (*ARS*) Los Angeles, 1953.†

1907 *An Enquiry into the Causes of the Frequent Executions at Tyburn*. Ed. Malvin R. Zirker, Jr. (*ARS*) Los Angeles, 1964.†

1908 *Aesop Dress'd, or a Collection of Fables Writ in Familiar Verse*. Ed. John S. Shea. (*ARS*) Los Angeles, 1966.†

Studies

1909 CHIASSON, Elias J. "Bernard Mandeville: A Reappraisal." *PQ*, 49 (1970), 489–519.

1910 EDWARDS, Thomas R., Jr. "Mandeville's Moral Prose." *ELH*, 31 (1964), 195–212.

1911 HARTH, Phillip. "The Satiric Purpose of *The Fable of the Bees*." *ECS*, 2 (1969), 321–40.*

1912 HAYEK, F. A. "Dr. Bernard Mandeville." *PBA*, 52 (1966), 125–41.

1913 HIND, George. "Mandeville's *Fable of the Bees* as Menippean Satire." *Genre*, 1 (1968), 307–15.

1914 NOXON, James. "Dr. Mandeville: 'A Thinking Man.' " In 36, pp. 233–52.

1915 ROSENBERG, Nathan. "Mandeville and Laissez-Faire." *JHI*, 24 (1963), 183–96.

1916 VICHERT, Gordon S. "Some Recent Mandeville Attributions." *PQ*, 45 (1966), 459–63.

William Mason (1725–1797)

Works

1917 *Satirical Poems Published Anonymously by William Mason, with Notes by Horace Walpole*. Ed. Paget Toynbee. Oxford, 1926.

Bibliography

1918 GASKELL, Philip. *The First Editions of William Mason*. Cambridge, Eng., 1951.

Studies

1919 CHASE, Isabel W. "William Mason and Sir William Chambers' *Dissertation on Oriental Gardening*." *JEGP*, 35 (1936), 517–29.

1920 DRAPER, John W. *William Mason: A Study in Eighteenth-Century Culture*. New York, 1924.*

1921 LOW, Donald A. "An Eighteenth-Century Imitation of Donne's First Satire." *RES*, N.S., 16 (1965), 291–98.

1922 LOW, Donald A. "William Mason's Notes on Shakespeare." *N&Q*, 215 (1970), 309–12.

1923 NABHOLTZ, John R. "Wordsworth and William Mason." *RES*, N.S., 15 (1964), 297–302.

Elizabeth Montagu (1720–1800)

Letters

1924 Elizabeth Montagu, the Queen of the Blue-Stockings: Her Correspondence from 1720 to 1761. Ed. Emily J. Climenson. 2 vols. London, 1906.

1925 Mrs. Montagu, "Queen of the Blues." Her Letters and Friendships from 1762 to 1800. Ed. Reginald Blunt. 2 vols. London, 1923.

Studies

1926 BUSSE, John. Mrs. Montagu, Queen of the Blues. London, 1928.

1927 HORNBEAK, Katherine G. "New Light on Mrs. Montagu." In 40, pp. 349–61.

1928 JONES, W. Powell. "The Romantic Bluestocking, Elizabeth Montagu." HLQ, 12 (1948), 85–98.

1929 PHILLIPS, George L. "Mrs. Montagu and the Climbing-Boys." RES, 25 (1949), 237–44.

1930 ROSS, Ian. "A Bluestocking over the Border: Mrs. Elizabeth Montagu's Aesthetic Adventures in Scotland, 1766." HLQ, 28 (1965), 213–33.

Lady Mary Wortley Montagu (1689–1762)

Works

1931 "The Nonsense of Common-Sense," 1737–1738. Ed. Robert Halsband. Evanston, Ill., 1947.

1932 Complete Letters. Ed. Robert Halsband. 3 vols. Oxford, 1965–67.

1933 Selected Letters. Ed. Robert Halsband. London, 1970.

Studies

1934 GRUNDY, Isobel. "Ovid and Eighteenth-Century Divorce: An Unpublished Poem by Lady Mary Wortley Montagu." RES, N.S. 23 (1972), 417–28.

1935 HALSBAND, Robert. The Life of Lady Mary Wortley Montagu. Oxford, 1956.*†

Edward Moore (1712–1757)

Works

1936 The Gamester. Eds. Charles H. Peake and Philip H. Wikelund. (ARS) Los Angeles, 1948.†

Studies

1937 CASKEY, John Homer. *The Life and Works of Edward Moore.* New Haven, Conn., 1927. Rpt. Hamden, Conn., 1973.

1938 COLLINS, Ralph L. "Moore's *The Foundling*—An Intermediary." *PQ,* 17 (1938), 139–43.

For *The World,* ed. by Moore as Adam Fitzadam, see "Periodicals."

Arthur Murphy (1727–1805)

Works

1939 *"The Way To Keep Him" and Five Other Plays by Arthur Murphy.* Ed. John P. Emery. New York, 1956.

1940 *The Englishman from Paris.* Ed. Simon Trefman. (*ARS*) Los Angeles, 1969.†

1941 *New Essays by Arthur Murphy.* Ed. Arthur Sherbo. East Lansing, Mich., 1963. Comment by Henry Knight Miller in *BNYPL,* 69 (1965), 459–70, and reply by Sherbo, *ibid.,* pp. 471–86.

1942 *The Lives of Henry Fielding and Samuel Johnson, Together with Essays from the Gray's-Inn Journal.* (*SF&R*) Gainesville, Fla., 1968.

Studies

1943 BOTTING, Roland B. 'The Textual History of Murphy's *Gray's-Inn Journal.*" *RS,* 25 (1957), 33–48.

1944 CASKEY, J. Homer. "Arthur Murphy and the War on Sentimental Comedy." *JEGP,* 30 (1931), 563–77.

1945 CASKEY, J. Homer. "Arthur Murphy's Commonplace-Book." *SP,* 37 (1940), 598–609.

1946 DUNBAR, Howard Hunter. *The Dramatic Career of Arthur Murphy.* New York, 1948.

1947 EMERY, John P. *Arthur Murphy, an Eminent English Dramatist of the Eighteenth Century.* Philadelphia, 1946.

Roger North (1653–1734)

Works

1948 *Roger North on Music: Being a Selection from his Essays Written . . . c. 1695–1728.* Ed. John Wilson, London, 1959.

Studies

1949 BIRRELL, T. A. "Roger North and Political Morality in the Later Stuart Period." *Scrutiny,* 17 (1951), 282–98.

1950 CLIFFORD, James L. "Roger North and the Art of Biography." In 27, pp. 275–85.

1951 KETTON-CREMER, R. W. "Roger North." *N&Q*, 204 (1959), 73–86.

1952 MILLARD, P. T. "The Chronology of Roger North's Main Works." *RES*, N.S. 24 (1973), 283–94.

1953 MORRIS, J. N. "North: A Brother's Life." In his *Versions of the Self* (New York, 1966).

1954 SCHWOERER, Lois G. "The Chronology of Roger North's Major Works." *History of Ideas Newsletter*, 3 (1957), 73–78.

1955 SCHWOERER, Lois G. "Roger North and his Notes on Legal Education." *HLQ,* 22 (1959), 323–43.

Thomas Percy (1729–1811)

Works

1956 *The Percy Letters.* Ed. D. Nichol Smith and Cleanth Brooks. Baton Rouge, La., and New Haven, Conn., 1944–61.
1. *With Edmond Malone.* Ed. Arthur Tillotson. 1944.
2. *With Richard Farmer.* Ed. Cleanth Brooks. 1946.
3. *With Thomas Warton.* Eds. M. G. Robinson and Leah Dennis. 1951.
4. *With David Dalrymple, Lord Hailes.* Ed. A. F. Falconer. 1954.
5. *With Evan Evans.* Ed. Aneirin Lewis. 1957.
6. *With George Paton.* Ed. A. F. Falconer. 1961.

Bibliography

1957 POWELL, L. F. "Percy's *Reliques.*" *The Library,* 4th ser., 9 (1928), 113–37.

1958 SMITH, D. Nichol. "The Constance Meade Collection and the University Press Museum." *Bodl. Lib. Record,* 6 (1958), 427–33.

Studies

1959 BATE, Walter J. "Percy's Use of His Folio-Manuscript." *JEGP,* 43 (1944), 337–48.

1960 BROOKS, Cleanth. "The History of Percy's Edition of Surrey's Poems." *Englische Studien,* 68 (1934), 424–30.

1961 BROOKS, Cleanth. "The Country Parson as Research Scholar: Thomas Percy, 1760–1770." *PBSA*, 53 (1959), 219–39.

1962 CHURCHILL, Irving L. "The Percy-Warton Letters—Additions and Corrections." *PMLA,* 48 (1933), 301–03.

1963 CHURCHILL, Irving L. "William Shenstone's Share in the Preparation of Percy's *Reliques.*" *PMLA,* 51 (1936), 960–74.

1964 DENNIS, Leah. "Percy's Essay *On the Ancient Metrical Romances.*" *PMLA*, 49 (1934), 81–97.

1965 DENNIS, Leah. "Thomas Percy: Antiquarian *vs.* Man of Taste." *PMLA*, 57 (1942), 140–54.

1966 FRIEDMAN, Albert B. *The Ballad Revival* (Chicago, 1961), Chap. 7.

1967 MacKENZIE, M. L. "The Great Ballad Collectors: Percy, Herd, Ritson." *SSL*, 2 (1965), 213–33.

1968 OGBURN, Vincent H. "Thomas Percy's Unfinished Collection, *Ancient English and Scottish Poems.*" *ELH*, 3 (1936), 183–89.

1969 OGBURN, Vincent H. "Further Notes on Thomas Percy." *PMLA*, 51 (1936), 449–58.

1970 OGBURN, Vincent H. "A Forgotten Chapter in the Life of Bishop Thomas Percy." *RES*, 12 (1936), 202–208.

Ambrose Philips (1674–1749)

1971 *Poems.* Ed. M. G. Segar. ("Percy Reprints.") Oxford, 1937.

Studies

1972 BUENO, Lillian de la Torre. "Was Ambrose Philips a Ballad Editor?" *Anglia,* 59 (1935), 252–70.

1973 CAMERON, W. J. "Ten New Poems by Ambrose Philips (1674–1749)." *N&Q,* 202 (1957), 469–70.

1974/5 FOGLE, S. F. "Notes on Ambrose Philips." *MLN,* 54 (1939), 354–59.

1976 GRIFFITH, R. H. "A Variorum Text of Four Pastorals by Ambrose Philips." *Univ. of Texas Bull. No. 12: Studies in English* (1932), 118–57.

1977 McCUE, Lillian Bueno. "The Canon of Ambrose Philips: Some Observations on Criteria." *PQ,* 19 (1940), 313–16.

1978 PARNELL, Paul E. *"The Distrest Mother,* Ambrose Philips' Morality Play." *CL,* 11 (1959), 111–23.

1979 WHEATLEY, Katherine E. "Andromaque as the 'Distrest Mother.'" *Romanic Rev.,* 39 (1948), 3–21.

1980 WINTON, Calhoun. "Some Manuscripts by and Concerning Ambrose Philips." *ELN,* 5 (1967), 99–101.

Hester Lynch Thrale, Later Piozzi (1741–1821)

Works

1981 *Anecdotes of the Late Samuel Johnson, LL.D., During the Last Twenty Years of His Life.* Ed S. C. Roberts. Cambridge, Eng., 1925.

1982 *Thraliana: The Diary . . . 1776–1809.* Ed. Katharine C. Balderston. 2 vols. Oxford, 1942. 2d ed., 1951.

1983 *Observations and Reflections Made in the Course of a Journey Through France, Italy, and Germany.* Ed. Herbert Barrows. Ann Arbor, Mich., 1967.

Studies

1984 CLIFFORD, James L. *Hester Lynch Piozzi (Mrs. Thrale).* Oxford, 1941. 2d ed., 1968.*

1985 CLIFFORD, James L. "Mrs. Piozzi's Letters." In 31, pp. 155–67.

1986 HYDE, Mary. *The Impossible Friendship: Boswell and Mrs. Thrale.* Cambridge, Mass., 1972.

1987 POTTLE, Frederick A. and Charles H. BENNETT. "Boswell and Mrs. Piozzi." *MP,* 39 (1942), 421–30.

1988 RIELY, J. C. "Lady Knight's Role in the Boswell-Piozzi Rivalry." *PQ,* 51 (1972), 961–65.

1989 SPACKS, Patricia M. "Scrapbook of a Self: Mrs. Piozzi's Late Journals." *HLB,* 18 (1970), 221–47.

Alexander Pope (1688–1744)

Works

1990 *Twickenham Edition of the Poems.* General editor, John Butt. 11 vols. in 12. London and New Haven, Conn., 1939–69.†
    1. *Pastoral Poetry and An Essay on Criticism.* Ed. E. Audra and Aubrey Williams. London, 1961.
    2. *The Rape of the Lock and Other Poems.* Ed. Geoffrey Tillotson. 3d ed. London, 1962.
    3. Part 1. *An Essay on Man.* Ed. Maynard Mack. London, 1950; New Haven, Conn., 1951.
    3. Part 2. *Epistles to Several Persons (Moral Essays).* Ed. F. W. Bateson. 2d ed. London, 1961.
    4. Imitations of Horace, with An Epistle to Dr. Arbuthnot and the Epilogue to the Satires. Ed. John Butt. London, 1939.
    5. *The Dunciad.* Ed. James Sutherland. 3d ed. London, 1963.
    6. *Minor Poems.* Eds. Norman Ault and John Butt. London, 1954. See Geoffrey Tillotson, "The Minor Poems in the Twickenham Pope," in his *Augustan Studies* (1961), pp. 147–54.
    7–8. *The Iliad.* Ed. Maynard Mack *et al.* London, 1967.
    9–10. *The Odyssey.* Ed. Maynard Mack *et al.* London, 1967.
    11. *Index.* London, 1969.

1991 *Poems.* Ed. John Butt. London, 1963. The Twickenham text, with some annotations.

1992 *Poetical Works.* Ed. Herberb Davis. (Oxford Standard Authors) London, 1966.

1993 *Prose Works.* Ed. Norman Ault. Vol. 1: *The Earlier Works, 1711–1720.* Oxford, 1936. No more published.

1994 *Pope's Own Miscellany. Being a Reprint of "Poems on Several Occasions," 1717.* Ed. Norman Ault. London, 1935. See Arthur E. Case in *MP,* 34 (1937), 305–13; and discussion between Ault and Case, *ibid.,* 35 (1937), 179–91.

1995 *The Art of Sinking in Poetry: Martinus Scriblerus'* πΕΡΙ ΒΑθΟγΣ: *A Critical Edition, with Bibliographical Notes on "The Last Volume" of the Swift-Pope Miscellanies,* by R. H. Griffith and E. L. Steeves. Ed. Edna L. Steeves. New York, 1952. Rpt. 1968.

1996 *Correspondence.* Ed. George Sherburn. 5 vols. Oxford, 1956. See also G. Sherburn, "Letters of Alexander Pope, Chiefly to Sir William Trumbull," *RES,* N.S. 9 (1958), 388–406. For reviews and comment on the *Correspondence* see John Butt, "Alexander Pope: A New View of His Character," *The Listener,* June 20, 1957, pp. 999, 1003 (rpt in 29); John Butt, "Pope's Letters: Some Notes and Corrections," *N&Q,* 202 (1957), 463–66; Maynard Mack in *PQ,* 36 (1957), 389–99; Donald F. Bond, "The Importance of Pope's Letters," *MP,* 56 (1958), 55–59 (rpt. in 2012); and Geoffrey Tillotson, "Pope's Letters in Professor Sherburn's Edition," in his *Augustan Studies* (1961), pp. 155–61.

1997 *Pope's Letters.* Sel. and ed. John Butt. (*WC*) London, 1960.

Bibliographies and Concordance

1998 BUTT, John. "Pope's Poetical Manuscripts." *PBA,* 40 (1954), 23–39. Rpt. in 2012.

1999 GRIFFITH, Reginald H. *Alexander Pope: A Bibliography.* 2 vols. Austin, Tex., 1922–27. Rpt. 1962. See also George Sherburn in *MP,* 22 (1925), 327–36.

2000 MACK, Maynard. "Two Variant Copies of *Pope's Works.* . . . *Volume II:* Further Light on Some Problems of Authorship, Bibliography, and Text." *The Library,* 5 ser., 12 (1957), 48–53.

2001 SHERBURN, George. "Notes on the Canon of Pope's Works, 1714–1720." *Manly Anniversary Studies* (Chicago, 1923), pp. 170–79.

2002 TODD, William B. "Concealed Pope Editions." *BC* 5 (1956), 48–52. See also D. F. Foxon, *ibid.,* pp. 277–79.

2003 WISE, Thomas J. *A Pope Library.* London, 1931.

2004 GUERINOT, Joseph V. *Pamphlet Attacks on Alexander Pope, 1711–1744: A Descriptive Bibliography.* London, 1969.

2005 LOPEZ, Cecilia L. *Alexander Pope: An Annotated Bibliography, 1945–1967.* Gainesville, Fla., 1970.

2006 TOBIN, James E. *Alexander Pope: A List of Critical Studies Published from 1895 to 1944.* New York, 1945.

2007 BEDFORD, Emmett G., and Robert J. DILLIGAN. *Concordance to the Poems of Alexander Pope.* 2 vols. Detroit, Mich., 1974.

Collected Studies

2008 BARNARD, John, ed. *Pope: The Critical Heritage.* London, 1973.

2009 DIXON, Peter, ed. *Alexander Pope.* "Writers and Their Background" London, 1972.†

2010 GUERINOT, Joseph V., ed. *Pope: A Collection of Critical Essays.* Englewood Cliffs, N.J., 1972.

2011 GURR, Elizabeth, ed. *Pope.* ("Writers and Critics") Edinburgh, 1971.

2012 MACK, Maynard ed. *Essential Articles for the Study of Alexander Pope.* Rev. and enl. ed. Hamden, Conn., 1968.

General Studies

2013 ADAMS, Percy G. "Pope's Concern with Assonance." *TSLL,* 9 (1968), 493–502.

2014 ADLER, Jacob H. *The Reach of Art: A Study in the Prosody of Pope.* Gainesville, Fla., 1964.

2015 ALLEN, Robert J. "Pope and the Sister Arts." In 28, pp. 78–88.

2016 ALTENBERND, A. L. "On Pope's 'Horticultural Romanticism.'" *JEGP,* 54 (1955), 470–77. Rpt. in 2012.

2017 ATKINS, G. Douglas. "Pope and Deism: A New Analysis." *HLQ,* 35 (1972), 257–78.

2018 AUDEN, W. H. "Pope." *EIC,* 1 (1951), 208–24. Rpt. in 2012.

2019 AUDRA, Emile. *L'Influence française dans l'oeuvre de Pope.* Paris, 1931.*

2020 AULT, Norman. *New Light on Pope, with Some Additions to His Poetry Hitherto Unknown.* London, 1949. See also A. E. Case in 23.

2021 BLUESTONE, Max. "The Suppressed Metaphor in Pope." *EIC,* 8 (1958), 347–54. Comment and discussion by Aubrey L. Williams *et al., Ibid.,* 9 (1959), 197–201, 437–43; 10 (1960), 114–16.

2022 BOYCE, Benjamin. *The Character Sketches in Pope's Poems.* Durham, N.C., 1962.

2023 BOYCE, Benjamin. "Mr. Pope, in Bath, Improves the Design of his Grotto." In 27, pp. 143–53.

2024 BOYCE, Benjamin. "The Poet and the Postmaster: The Friendship of Alexander Pope and Ralph Allen." *PQ,* 45 (1966), 114–22. See also his *The Benevolent Man: A Life of Ralph Allen* (Cambridge, Mass., 1967).

2025 BRACHER, Frederick. "Pope's Grotto: The Maze of Fancy." *HLQ,* 12 (1949), 141–62. Rpt. in 2012.

2026 BROWER, Reuben A. *Alexander Pope: The Poetry of Allusion.* Oxford, 1959.*†

2027 BUTT, John. "Pope: The Man and the Poet." In 26, pp. 69–79.

2028 BUTT, John. "Pope and the Opposition to Walpole's Government." In his *Pope, Dickens, and Others: Essays and Addresses* (Edinburgh, 1969), pp. 111–26.

2029 CLARK, Donald B. *Alexander Pope.* (*TEAS*) London, 1967.

2030 DEARING, Vinton A. "Pope, Theobald, and Wycherley's *Posthumous Works.*" *PMLA,* 68 (1953), 223–36.

2031 DIXON, Peter. " 'Talking upon Paper': Pope and Eighteenth-Century Conversation." *ES,* 46 (1965), 36–44.

2032 EDWARDS, Thomas R., Jr. *This Dark Estate: A Reading of Pope.* Berkeley, Cal., 1963.

2033 EDWARDS, Thomas R., Jr. "Visible Poetry: Pope and Modern Criticism." *Harvard Eng. Studies,* 2 (1971), 299–321.

2034 EHRENPREIS, Irvin. "The Style of Sound: The Literary Value of Pope's Versification." In 45, pp. 232–46.

2035 FAIRCLOUGH, G. Thomas. "Pope and Boileau: A Supplementary Note." *NM,* 64 (1963), 232–43.

2036 GOLDSTEIN, Malcolm. *Pope and the Augustan Stage.* Stanford, Cal., 1958.

2037 GREENE, Donald J. " 'Dramatic Texture' in Pope." In 35, pp. 31–53.

2038 GRIFFITH, R. H. "Pope Editing Pope." Texas *Studies in English 1944* (Austin, 1945), pp. 5–108.

2039 HUSEBOE, Arthur R. "Pope's Critical Views of the London Stage." *RECTR,* 3 (1964), 25–37.

2040 JACK, Ian. *Pope.* (*WTW*) London, 1954.

2041 JONES, John A. *Pope's Couplet Art.* Athens, Ohio, 1969.

2042 KNIGHT, G. Wilson. *Laureate of Peace: On the Genius of Alexander Pope.* London, 1955.

2043 KOON, Helene. "Pope's First Editors." *HLQ,* 35 (1971), 19–27.

2044 KRIEGER, Murray. *The Classic Vision: The Retreat from Extremity in Modern Literature.* Baltimore, 1971. Includes studies of "Eloisa to Abelard" and "The Rape of the Lock."

2045 LEAVIS, F. R. "Pope." *Scrutiny,* 2 (1933–34), 268–84. Rpt. in 2012.

2046 MacDONALD, W. L. *Pope and His Critics: A Study in Eighteenth-Century Personalities.* Seattle, Wash., 1951.

2047 MACK, Maynard. "On Reading Pope." *College English,* 7 (1946), 263–73.

2048 MACK, Maynard. " 'Wit and Poetry and Pope': Some Observations on his Imagery." In 28, pp. 20–40. Rpt. in 29.*

2049 MACK, Maynard. " 'The Shadowy Cave': Some Speculations on a Twickenham Grotto." In 27, pp. 69–88.

2050 MACK, Maynard. "A Poet in His Landscape: Pope at Twickenham." In 35, pp. 3–29.

2051 MACK, Maynard. *"Secretum Iter:* Some Uses of Retirement Literature in the Poetry of Pope." In 52, pp. 207–43.

2052 MACK, Maynard. *The Garden and the City. Retirement and Politics in the Later Poetry of Pope, 1731–1743.* Toronto, 1969.*

2053 MILLER, John H. "Pope and the Principle of Reconciliation." *TSLL,* 9 (1967), 165–92.

2054 MONK, Samuel H. " 'A Grace Beyond the Reach of Art.' " *JHI,* 5 (1944), 131–50. Rpt. in 2012.

2055 NICOLSON, Marjorie, and G. S. ROUSSEAU. *"This Long Disease, My Life": Alexander Pope and the Sciences.* Princeton, N.J., 1968.

2056 PARKIN, Rebecca P. *The Poetic Workmanship of Alexander Pope.* Minneapolis, 1955.

2057 PIPER, William B. "The Conversational Poetry of Pope." *SEL,* 10 (1970), 505–24.

2058 RIVERS, Isabel. *The Poetry of Conservatism, 1600–1745: A Study of Poets and Public Affairs from Jonson to Pope.* Cambridge, Eng., 1973.

2059 ROGERS, Pat. "Pope and the Syntax of Satire." *Literary English since Shakespeare,* ed. G. Watson (New York, 1970), pp. 236–65.

2060 ROGERS, Pat. "A Pope Family Scandal." *TLS,* Aug. 31, 1973, p. 1005. See also E. P. Thompson, "Alexander Pope and the Windsor Blacks," *ibid.,* Sept. 7, pp. 1031–33, and further comment by Howard Erskine-Hill and Andrew Varnay, *ibid.,* Sept. 14 and 21, pp. 1056, 1084. [*Windsor-Forest* and Pope's attitude toward current political and social conditions.]

2061 ROGERS, Robert W. *The Major Satires of Alexander Pope.* Urbana, Ill., 1955.*

2062 ROGERS, Robert W. "Notes on Alexander Pope's Early Education." *SAQ,* 70 (1971), 236–47.

2063 ROOT, Robert K. *The Poetical Career of Alexander Pope.* Princeton, N.J., 1938.*

2064 RUSSO, John Paul. *Alexander Pope: Tradition and Identity.* Cambridge, Mass., 1972.

2065 SAMBROOK, A. J. "The Shape and Size of Pope's Garden." *ECS,* 5 (1972), 450–55.

2066 SHERBURN, George. *The Early Career of Alexander Pope.* Oxford, 1934. Rpt. 1968.*

2067 SHERBURN, George. "Pope at Work." In 31, pp. 49–64.

2068 SHERBURN, George. "Pope and 'the Great Shew of Nature.'" In 37, pp. 306–15.

2069 SHERBURN, George. "Pope on the Threshold of His Career." *HLB,* 13 (1959), 29–46.

2070 SIBLEY, Agnes M. *Alexander Pope's Prestige in America, 1725–1835.* New York, 1949.

2071 SITWELL, Edith. *Alexander Pope.* London, 1930.†

2072 SPACKS, Patricia M. *An Argument of Images: The Poetry of Alexander Pope.* Cambridge, Mass., 1971.*

2073 TILLOTSON, Geoffrey. *On the Poetry of Pope.* Oxford, 1938. 2d ed., Oxford, 1950.*

2074 TILLOTSON, Geoffrey. *Pope and Human Nature.* Oxford, 1958. See also J. M. Cameron, "Mr. Tillotson and Mr. Pope," *Dublin Rev.,* 233 (1959), 153–70.

2075 TORCHIANA, Donald T. "Brutus: Pope's Last Hero." *JEGP,* 61 (1962), 853–67. Rpt. in 2012.

2076 WARREN, Austin. *Alexander Pope as Critic and Humanist.* Princeton, N.J., 1929.

2077 WELLINGTON, James E. "Pope and Charity." *PQ,* 46 (1967), 225–35.

2078 WIMSATT, W. K., Jr. "One Relation of Rhyme to Reason: Alexander Pope." *MLQ,* 5 (1944), 323–38. Rpt. in 23 and 2012.

2079 WIMSATT, W. K., Jr. "An Image of Pope." In 35, pp. 55–65.

2080 WIMSATT, W. K., Jr. *The Portraits of Alexander Pope.* New Haven, Conn., 1965. See also *The Scriblerian,* 6 (1974), 62–63.

"An Essay on Criticism"

2081 ADEN, John M. "'*First* Follow Nature': Strategy and Stratification in *An Essay on Criticism.*" *JEGP,* 55 (1956), 604–17.

2082 EMPSON, William. "Wit in the Essay on Criticism." *Hudson Rev.*, 2 (1950), 559–77. Rpt. in his *Structure of Complex Words* (1951), pp. 84–100. Rpt. in 2012.

2083 FENNER, Arthur, Jr. "The Unity of Pope's *Essay on Criticism.*" *PQ*, 39 (1960), 435–46. Rpt. in 2012.

2084 FISHER, Alan S. "Cheerful Noonday, 'Gloomy' Twilight: Pope's *Essay on Criticism.*" *PQ*, 51 (1972), 832–44.

2085 HOOKER, E. N. "Pope on Wit: The *Essay on Criticism.*" In 37, pp. 225–46. Rpt. in 29 and 2012.

2086 HOTCH, Ripley. "Pope Surveys His Kingdom: *An Essay on Criticism.*" *SEL*, 13 (1973), 474–87.

2087 MARKS, Emerson R. "Pope on Poetry and the Poet." *Criticism*, 12 (1970), 271–80.

2088 RAMSEY, Paul. "The Watch of Judgment: Relativism and *An Essay on Criticism.*" In 21, pp. 128–39.

2089 SCHMITZ, Robert M. *Pope's Essay on Criticism, 1709: A Study of the Bodleian Manuscript Text, with Facsimiles, Transcripts, and Variants.* St. Louis, 1962.*

"Pastorals" and "Windsor-Forest"

2090 BATTESTIN, Martin C. "The Transforming Power: Nature and Art in Pope's Pastorals." *ECS*, 2 (1969), 183–204.

2091 CLEMENTS, Frances M. "Lansdowne, Pope, and the Unity of *Windsor-Forest.*" *MLQ*, 33 (1972), 44–53.

2092 DURANT, David S. "Man and Nature in Alexander Pope's *Pastorals.*" *SEL*, 11 (1971), 469–85.

2093 HAUSER, David R. "Pope's Lodona and the Uses of Mythology." *SEL*, 6 (1966), 465–82.

2094 MELCHIORI, Georgio. "Pope in Arcady: The Theme of *Et in Arcadia Ego* in his Pastorals." *Eng. Miscellany*, 14 (1963), 83–93. Rpt. in 2012.

2095 MOORE, John Robert. "*Windsor-Forest* and William III." *MLN*, 66 (1951), 451–54. Rpt. in 2012.

2096 MORRIS, David B. "Virgilian Attitudes in Pope's *Windsor-Forest.*" *TSLL*, 15 (1973), 231–50.

2097 PROVOST, Foster. *Pope's Pastorals: An Exercise in Poetical Technique.* Baton Rouge, La., 1954.

2098 SCHMITZ, Robert M. *Pope's "Windsor Forest," 1712: A Study of the Washington University Holograph.* St. Louis, 1952.*

2099 WASSERMAN, Earl R. *The Subtler Language.* Baltimore, 1959. Rpt. 1968. Chap. 4: "Pope, Windsor Forest."*†

"The Rape of the Lock"

2100 BROOKS, Cleanth. "The Case of Miss Arabella Fermor: A Re-examination." *Sewanee Rev.*, 51 (1943), 505–24. Rpt. in his *The Well Wrought Urn: Studies in the Structure of Poetry* (New York, 1947), pp. 74–95. Rpt. in 2012.

2101/2 COHEN, Ralph. "Transformation in *The Rape of the Lock.*" *ECS,* 2 (1969), 205–24.

2103 CUNNINGHAM, J. S. *Pope's "The Rape of the Lock."* London and Woodbury, N.Y., 1961.[†]

2104 DYSON, A. E., and Julian LOVELOCK. "In Spite of All Her Art: Pope's 'The Rape of the Lock.'" *Crit. Survey,* 5 (1971), 197–210.

2105 FROST, William. "*The Rape of the Lock* and Pope's Homer." *MLQ,* 8 (1947), 342–54. Rpt. in 2012.

2106 GOGGIN, L. P. "La Caverne aux vapeurs." *PQ,* 42 (1963), 404–11.

2107 HARDY, J. P. *Reinterpretations: Essays on Poems by Milton, Pope and Johnson* (London, 1971), pp. 50–80.

2108 HOFFMAN, Arthur J. "Spenser and *The Rape of the Lock.*" *PQ,* 49 (1970), 530–46.

2109 HUNT, John Dixon, ed. *The Rape of the Lock: A Casebook.* London, 1968.

2110 HYMAN, Stanley E. "The Rape of the Lock." *Hudson Rev.,* 13 (1960), 406–12.

2111 JACKSON, James L. "Pope's *The Rape of the Lock* Considered as a Five-Act Epic." *PMLA,* 65 (1950), 1283–87.

2112 KRIEGER, Murray. "The 'Frail China Jar' and the Rude Hand of Chaos." *Centennial Rev. of Arts and Sciences,* 5 (1961), 176–94. Rpt. in his *The Play and Place of Criticism* (Baltimore, 1967), and in 2012.

2113 PRESTON, John. " 'Th' Informing Soul': Creative Irony in *The Rape of the Lock.*" *DUJ,* N.S. 27 (1966), 125–30.

2114 ROGERS, Pat. "Faery Lore and *The Rape of the Lock.*" *RES,* N.S. 25 (1974), 25–38.

2114A ROGERS, Pat. "Wit and Grammar in *The Rape of the Lock.*" *JEGP,* 72 (1973), 17–31.

2115 ROUSSEAU, G. S., ed. *Twentieth-Century Interpretations of "The Rape of the Lock."* Englewood Cliffs, N.J., 1969.[†]

2116 WASSERMAN, Earl R. "The Limits of Allusion in *The Rape of the Lock.*" *JEGP,* 65 (1966), 425–44.

2117 WILLIAMS, Aubrey. "The 'Fall' of China and *The Rape of the Lock.*" *PQ,* 41 (1962), 412–25. Rpt. in 2012.

2118 WIMSATT, W. K., Jr. "The Game of Ombre in *The Rape of the Lock.*" *RES,* N.S., 1 (1950), 136–43.

2119 WIMSATT, W. K., Jr. "Belinda Ludens: Strife and Play in *The Rape of the Lock.*" *New Literary History,* 4 (1973), 357–74.

"Eloisa to Abelard" and "Elegy to the Memory of an Unfortunate Lady"

2120 *Alexander Pope: Eloisa to Abelard: With the Letters of Heloise to Abelard in the Version by J. Hughes (1713).* Ed. James E. Wellington. Miami, 1965.

Studies

2121 ANDERSON, David L. "Abélard and Heloïse: Eighteenth-Century Motif." *SVEC,* 84 (1971), 7–51.

2122 BARRETT, John M. "Pope's Eloisa to Abelard." *TSLL,* 9 (1967), 57–68.

2123 GILLIE, Christopher. "Alexander Pope: 'Elegy to the Memory of an Unfortunate Lady.' " *Interpretations,* ed. John Wain (London, 1955), pp. 75–85.

2124 KALMEY, Robert P. "Pope's *Eloisa to Abelard* and 'Those Celebrated Letters.' " *PQ,* 47 (1968), 164–78.

2125 KRIEGER, Murray. " 'Eloisa to Abelard': The Escape from Body or the Embrace of Body." *ECS,* 3 (1969), 28–47. Comment by Robert P. Kalmey, *ibid.,* 5 (1971), 315–18, and reply by Krieger, pp. 318–20.

2126 MANDEL, Barrett J. "Pope's 'Eloisa to Abelard.' " *TSLL,* 9 (1967), 57–68.

2127 MELL, Donald C., Jr. "Pope's Idea of the Imagination and the Design of 'Elegy to the Memory of an Unfortunate Lady.' " *MLQ,* 29 (1968), 395–406.

2128 MORRIS, David B. " 'The Visionary Maid': Tragic Passion and Redemptive Sympathy in Pope's 'Eloisa to Abelard.' " *MLQ,* 14 (1973), 247–71.

2129 O HEHIR, Brendan P. "Virtue and Passion: The Dialectic of *Eloisa to Abelard.* " *TSLL,* 2 (1960), 219–32. Rpt. in 2102.

2130 PETTIT, Henry. "Pope's *Eloisa to Abelard:* An Interpretation." *Univ. of Colorado Studies, Series in Language and Literature,* No. 4 (1953), 67–74. Rpt. in 2012.

2131 WEINBROT, Howard D. "Pope's 'Elegy to the Memory of an Unfortunate Lady.' " *MLQ,* 32 (1971), 255–67.

2132 WRIGHT, Lawrence S. "Eighteenth-Century Replies to Pope's Eloisa." *SP,* 31 (1954), 519–33.

"The Dunciad"

Texts

2133 *The Dunciad Variorum with the Prolegomena of Scriblerus. Reproduced in Facsimile from the First Issue of the Original Edition of 1729.* Introduction by Robert K. Root. Princeton, N.J., 1929.

Studies

2134 EDWARDS, Thomas R., Jr. "Light and Nature: A Reading of the *Dunciad.*" *PQ,* 39 (1960), 447–63. Rpt. in 2012.

2135 ERSKINE-HILL, Howard H. "The 'New World' of Pope's *Dunciad.*" *RMS,* 6 (1962), 47–67. Rpt. in 2012.

2136 ERSKINE-HILL, Howard H. *Pope: The Dunciad.* London, 1972.

2137 FRIEDMAN, Arthur. "Pope and Deism (*The Dunciad,* IV, 459–92)." In 28, pp. 87–95.

2138 HIGHET, Gilbert. " 'The Dunciad.' " *MLR,* 36 (1941), 320–43.

2139 HOPKINS, Robert H. " 'The Good Old Cause' in Pope, Addison, and Steele." *RES,* N.S., 17 (1966), 62–68.

2140 HOWARD, William J. "The Mystery of the Cibberian *Dunciad.*" *SEL,* 8 (1968), 463–74.

2141 JONES, Emrys. "Pope and Dulness." *PBA.,* 54 (1968), 231–63.

2142 KERNAN, Alvin B. "*The Dunciad* and the Plot of Satire." *SEL,* 2 (1962), 255–66. Rpt. in 2012.

2143 KINSLEY, William. "The *Dunciad* as Mock-Book." *HLQ,* 35 (1971), 29–47.

2144 KROPF, C. R. "Education and the Neoplatonic Idea of Wisdom in Pope's *Dunciad.*" *TSLL,* 15 (1973), 593–604.

2145 MENGEL, Elias F., Jr. "The *Dunciad* Illustrations." *ECS,* 7 (1973–74), 161–78.

2146 MORRIS, David B. "The Kinship of Madness in Pope's *Dunciad.*" *PQ,* 51 (1972), 813–31.

2147 PEAVY, Charles D. "The Pope-Cibber Controversy: A Bibliography." *RECTR,* 3 (1964), 51–55.

2148 REICHARD, Hugo M. "Pope's Social Satire: Belles-Lettres and Business." *PMLA,* 67 (1952), 420–34. Rpt. in 2012.

2149 SHERBO, Arthur. "No Single Scholiast: Pope's 'The Dunciad.'" *MLR,* 65 (1970), 503–16.

2150 SHERBURN, George. "The *Dunciad, Book IV.*" Texas *Studies in English 1944.* (Austin, Tex., 1945), pp. 174–90. Rpt. in 2012.

2151 SITTER, John E. *The Poetry of Pope's Dunciad.* Minneapolis, 1971.

2152 TANNER, Tony. "Reason and the Grotesque: Pope's *Dunciad.*" *Crit. Quarterly,* 7 (1965), 145–60. Rpt. in 2012.

2153 WILLIAMS, Aubrey L. *Pope's Dunciad: A Study of Its Meaning.* Baton Rouge, La., 1955.*

2154 WILLIAMS, Robert W. "Some Baroque Influences in Pope's *Dunciad.*" *BJA,* 9 (1969), 186–94.

"An Essay on Man"

Texts

2155 *An Essay on Man. Reproduction of the MSS in the Pierpont Morgan Library and the Houghton Library, with the Printed Text of the Original Edition.* Ed. Maynard Mack. (Roxburgh Club.) London, 1962.

Studies

2156 ALDERMAN, William E. "Pope's *Essay on Man* and Shaftesbury's *The Moralists.*" *PBSA,* 67 (1973), 131–40.

2157 BOYCE, Benjamin. "Baroque into Satire: Pope's Frontispiece for the 'Essay on Man.'" *Criticism,* 4 (1962), 14–27.

2158 BRETT, R. L. "Pope's *Essay on Man.*" In his *Reason and Imagination: A Study of Form and Meaning in Four Poems* (1960), pp. 51–77.

2159 CAMERON, J. M. "Doctrinal to an Age: Notes Towards a Revaluation of Pope's *Essay on Man.*" *Dublin Rev.,* 225 (1951), 54–67. Rpt. in 2012.

2160 FRENCH, David P. "Pope, Milton, and the *Essay on Man.*" *Bucknell Rev.,* 16 (1968), 103–11.

2161 GOLDGAR, Bertrand A. "Pope's Theory of the Passions: The Background of Epistle II of the *Essay on Man.*" *PQ,* 41 (1962), 730–43.

2162 HUGHES, R. E. "Pope's *Essay on Man:* The Rhetorical Structure of Epistle I." *MLN,* 70 (1955), 177–81. Rpt. in 2012.

2163 KALLICH, Martin. *"Heav'n's First Law: Rhetoric and Order in Pope's 'Essay on Man.' "* De Kalb, Ill., 1967.

2164/5 KNAPP, Richard G. *The Fortunes of Pope's "Essay on Man" in Eighteenth-Century France.* Geneva, 1971.

2166 LITZ, Francis E. "Pope's Use of Derham." *JEGP,* 60 (1961), 65–74.

2167 MASLEN, K. I. D. "New Editions of Pope's *Essay on Man,* 1745–48." *PBSA,* 62 (1968), 177–88.

2168 PRIESTLEY, F. E. L. " 'Order, Union, Full Consent of Things!' " *UTQ,* 42 (1972), 1–13.

2169 PRIESTLEY, F. E. L. "Pope and the Great Chain of Being." In 41, pp. 213–28.

2170 ROGERS, Robert W. "Notes on Pope's Collaboration with Warburton in Preparing a Final Edition of the *Essay on Man.*" *PQ,* 26 (1947), 358–66.

2171 ROGERS, Robert W. "Critiques of the 'Essay on Man' in France and Germany, 1736–1755." *ELH,* 15 (1948), 176–93.

2172 ROGERS, Robert W. "Alexander Pope's *Universal Prayer.*" *JEGP,* 54 (1955), 612–24. Rpt. in 2012.

2173 TUVESON, Ernest. *"An Essay on Man* and 'The Way of Ideas.' " *ELH,* 26 (1959), 368–86. Comment by Robert Marsh in *PQ,* 39 (1960), 349–51; reply by Tuveson, *ibid.,* 40 (1961), 262–69.

2174 WHITE, Douglas H. *Pope and the Context of Controversy: The Manipulation of Ideas in "An Essay on Man."* Chicago, 1970.

Imitations of Horace and Donne, with the "Epistle to Dr. Arbuthnot" and the Epilogue to the Satires

2175 ADEN, John M. *Something Like Horace: Studies in the Art and Allusion of Pope's Horation Satires.* Nashville, Tenn., 1969.

2176 BLOOM, Lillian D. "Pope as Textual Critic: A Bibliographical Study of His Horatian Text." *JEGP,* 47 (1948), 150–55. Rpt. in 2012.

2177 DIXON, Peter. "The Theme of Friendship in the 'Epistle to Dr. Arbuthnot.' " *ES,* 44 (1963), 191–97.

2178 DIXON, Peter. *The World of Pope's Satires: An Introduction to the 'Epistles' and 'Imitations of Horace.'* London, 1968. Rpt. 1973.*

2179 DOUGLASS, Richard H. "More on the Rhetoric and Imagery of Pope's *'Arbuthnot.'* " *SEL,* 13 (1973), 488–502.

2180 FEDER, Lillian. "Sermo or Satire: Pope's Defence of his Art." In 21, pp. 140–55.

2181 HALSBAND, Robert. *Lord Hervey: Eighteenth-Century Courtier.* Oxford, 1973.

ALEXANDER POPE

2182 HARDY, J. P. *Reinterpretations: Essays on Poems by Milton, Pope and Johnson* (1971), pp. 81–102. [The "Epistle to Dr. Arbuthnot."]

2183 HUNTER, G. K. "The 'Romanticism' of Pope's Horace." *EIC,* 10 (1960), 390–404. [Pope's "Imitation of the First Satire of the Second Book."]

2184 HUNTER, J. Paul. "Satiric Apology as Satiric Instance: Pope's *Arbuthnot.*" *JEGP,* 68 (1969), 625–47.

2185 JACK, Ian. "Pope and 'the Weighty Bullion of Dr. Donne's Satires.'" *PMLA,* 66 (1951), 1009–22. Rpt. in 2012.

2186 KNOEPFLMACHER, U. C. "The Poet as Physician: Pope's *Epistle to Dr. Arbuthnot.*" *MLQ,* 31 (1970), 440–49.

2187 KUPERSMITH, William. "Pope's Horace and the Critics: Some Reconsiderations." *Arion,* 9 (1970), 205–19.

2188 MACK, Maynard. "The Muse of Satire." *Yale Rev.,* 41 (1951), 80–92. Rpt. in 23.

2189 MACK, Maynard. "Some Annotations in the Second Earl of Oxford's Copies of Pope's *Epistle to Dr. Arbuthnot* and *Sober Advice from Horace.*" *RES,* N.S. 8 (1957), 48–53.

2190 MARESCA, Thomas E. *Pope's Horatian Poems.* Columbus, Ohio, 1966.

2191 MENGEL, Elias F., Jr. "Patterns of Imagery in Pope's *Arbuthnot.*" *PMLA,* 69 (1954), 189–97.

2192 MOSKOVIT, Leonard. "Pope's Purposes in *Sober Advice.*" *PQ,* 44 (1965), 195–99.

2193 MOSKOVIT, Leonard. "Pope and the Tradition of the Neoclassical Imitation." *SEL,* 8 (1968), 445–62.

2194 OSBORN, James M. "Pope, the Byzantine Empress, and Walpole's Whore." *RES,* N.S. 6 (1955), 372–82. [The Epilogue to the Satires.] Rpt. in 2012. See also John M. Aden, "Another Analogue to Pope's Vice Triumphant," *MP,* 66 (1968), 151–52.

2195 PAGLIA, Camille A. "Lord Hervey and Pope." *ECS,* 6 (1973), 348–71.

2196 SCHONHORN, Manuel. "The Audacious Contemporaneity of Pope's *Epistle to Augustus.*" *SEL,* 8 (1968), 431–43.

2197 SCHONHORN, Manuel. "Pope's *Epistle to Augustus:* Notes toward a Mythology." *TSL,* 16 (1971), 15–33.

2198 WILLIAMS, Aubrey L. "Pope and Horace: The Second Epistle of the Second Book." In 27, pp. 309–21.

2199 WILLIAMS, Aubrey L. "The 'Angel, Goddess, Montague' of Pope's *Sober Advice from Horace.*" *MP,* 71 (1973), 56–58.

Moral Essays (Epistles to Several Persons)

2200 ALPERS, Paul J. "Pope's *To Bathurst* and the Mandevillian State." *ELH,* 25 (1958), 23–42. Rpt. in 2012.

2201 BAKER, H. C. Collins, and Muriel I. BAKER. *The Life and Circumstances of James Brydges, First Duke of Chandos: Patron of the Liberal Arts.* Oxford, 1949.

2202 BRADY, Frank. "The History and Structure of Pope's *To a Lady.*" *SEL,* 9 (1969), 439–62.

115

2203 BUTT, John. " 'A Master Key to Popery.' " In 28, pp. 41–57. [Pope's defence of the Epistle to Burlington.]

2204 DEARING, V. A. "The Prince of Wales's Set of Pope's Works." *HLB,* 4 (1950), 325–36. [Epistle II.] Rpt. in 2012.

2205 EDWARDS, Thomas R., Jr. " 'Reconcil'd Extremes': Pope's *Epistle to Bathurst.*" *EIC,* 11 (1961), 290–308.

2206 EHRENPREIS, Irvin. "The Cistern and the Fountain: Art and Reality in Pope and Gray." In 21, pp. 156–75. [*To a Lady* and *The Bard.*]

2207 GIBSON, William A. "Three Principles of Renaissance Architectural Theory in Pope's *Epistle to Burlington.*" *SEL,* 11 (1971), 487–505.

2208 GRUNDY, Isobel. "Pope, Peterborough, and the Characters of Women." *RES,* N.S. 20 (1969), 461–68. See also 2213.

2209 HENRY, Avril, and Peter DIXON. "Pope and the Architects: A Note on the Epistle to Burlington." *ES,* 51 (1970), 437–41.

2210 MAHAFFEY, Kathleen. "Timon's Villa: Walpole's Houghton." *TSLL,* 9 (1967), 193–222.

2211 OSBORN, James M. "Pope, the 'Apollo of the Arts,' and His Countess." In 51, pp. 101–43. [Epistle IV.]

2212 PARKIN, Rebecca P. "The Role of Time in Alexander Pope's *Epistle to a Lady.*" *ELH,* 32 (1965), 490–501. Rpt. in 2012.

2213 SCHMITZ, Robert M. "Peterborough's and Pope's Nymphs: Pope at Work." *PQ,* 48 (1969), 192–200. See also "Pope's Nymphs in Manuscript." *Scriblerian,* 2 (1970), 37–39.

2214 SHERBURN, George. " 'Timon's Villa' and Cannons." *Huntington Lib. Bull.,* No. 8 (1935), 131–52.

2215 STUMPF, Thomas A. "Pope's *To Cobham, To a Lady,* and the Traditions of Inconstancy." *SP,* 67 (1970), 339–58.

2216 WASSERMAN, Earl R. *Pope's "Epistle to Bathurst": A Critical Reading with an Edition of the Manuscripts.* Baltimore, 1960.*

The Translation of Homer

2217 *The Illiad. Translated by Alexander Pope.* Eds. Reuben A. Brower and W. H. Bond. New York, 1965.†

Studies

2218 CALLAN, Norman. "Pope's *Iliad:* a New Document." *RES,* N.S., 4 (1953), 109–21. [The proof sheets of Books 1–8, with Pope's corrections.] Rpt. in 2012.

2219 FARNHAM, Fern. "Achilles' Shield: Some Observations on Pope's *Iliad.*" *PMLA,* 84 (1969), 1571–81.

2220 KNIGHT, Douglas. *Pope and the Heroic Tradition: A Critical Study of his "Iliad,"* New Haven, Conn., 1951.*

2221 KNIGHT, Douglas. "The Development of Pope's *Iliad* Preface: A Study of the Manuscript." *MLQ,* 16 (1955), 237–46. Rpt. in 2012.

2222 MASON, H. A. *To Homer through Pope: An Introduction to Homer's Iliad and Pope's Translation.* 1972.

2223 SCHMITZ, Robert M. "The 'Arsenal' Proof Sheets of Pope's *Iliad:* A Third Report." *MLN,* 74 (1959), 486–89.

2224 ZIMMERMAN, N. Hans-Joachim. *Alexander Popes Noten zu Homer: Eine Manuskrit- und Quellenstudie.* Heidelberg, 1966.

The Edition of Shakespeare

2225 BUTT, John. *Pope's Taste in Shakespeare.* London, 1936.

2226 DIXON, P. "Pope's Shakespeare." *JEGP,* 63 (1964), 191–203.

2227 HART, John A. "Pope as Scholar-Editor." *SB,* 23 (1970), 45–59.

2228 McKERROW, Ronald B. *The Treatment of Shakespeare's Text by His Earlier Editors, 1709–1768.* London, 1933.

2229 SUTHERLAND, James R. " 'The Dull Duty of an Editor.' " *RES,* 21 (1945), 202–15. Rpt. in 2012.

2230 THEOBALD, Lewis. *Preface to the Works of Shakespeare (1734).* Ed. Hugh G. Dick. (*ARS*) Los Angeles, 1949.†

Minor Poems

2231 ERSKINE-HILL, Howard. "The Medal Against Time: A Study of Pope's Epistle *To Mr. Addison." JWCI,* 28 (1965), 274–98.

2232 ERSKINE-HILL, Howard. "Alexander Pope at Fifteen: A New Manuscript." *RES,* N.S., 17 (1966), 268–77.

2233 FULLER, John. "A New Epilogue by Pope?" *RES,* N.S., 17 (1966), 409–13. [To Gay's *Wife of Bath.*]

2234 HALSBAND, Robert. "Pope, Lady Mary, and the *Court Poems* (1716)." *PMLA,* 68 (1953), 237–50.

2235 MAHAFFEY, Kathleen. "Pope's 'Artimesia' and 'Phryne' as Personal Satire." *RES,* N.S., 21 (1970), 466–71.

2236 RYLEY, Robert M. "A Note on the Authenticity of Some Lines from Pope." *PQ,* 46 (1967), 417–21.

2237 SCHMITZ, Robert M. "Two New Holographs of Pope's Birthday Lines to Martha Blount." *RES,* N.S. 8 (1957), 234–40.

2238 TILLOTSON, Geoffrey. "Pope's 'Epistle to Harley': An Introduction and Analysis." In 28, pp. 58–77. Rpt. in his *Augustan Studies* (1961), pp. 162–83.

2239 WASSERMAN, Earl R. "Pope's *Ode for Musick." ELH,* 28 (1961), 163–86. Rpt. in 2012.

Richard Price (1723–1791)

Works

2240 *A Review of the Principal Questions in Morals.* Ed. D. Daiches Raphael. Oxford, 1948.

Studies

2241 ÅQVIST, Lennart. *The Moral Philosophy of Richard Price.* Lund, 1960.

2242 CONE, Carl B. *Torchbearer of Freedom: The Influence of Richard Price on Eighteenth-Century Thought.* Lexington, Ky., 1952.

2243 HUDSON, William D. *Reason and Right: A Critical Examination of Richard Price's Moral Philosophy.* London, 1970.

2244 LABOUCHEIX, Henri. *Richard Price, Théoricien de la Révolution américaine: Le Philosophe et le sociologue, le pamphlétaire, et l'orateur.* Paris, 1970.

2245 THOMAS, D. O. "Richard Price, Apostle of Candour." *EA,* 25 (1972), 290–98.

Joseph Priestley (1733–1804)

Works

2246 *Autobiography.* Introduction by Jack Lindsay, Bath, 1970.

2247 *A Course of Lectures on Oratory and Criticism.* Eds. Vincent M. Bevilacqua and Richard Murphy. Carbondale, Ill., 1965.

2248 *Writings on Philosophy, Science, and Politics.* Ed. John A. Passmore. New York, 1965.

Bibliography

2249 CROOK, Ronald E. *A Bibliography of Joseph Priestley, 1733–1804.* London, 1966.

Studies

2250 GIBBS, F. W. *Joseph Priestley, Adventurer in Science and Champion of Truth.* London, 1965.

2251 GILLIAM, John G. *The Crucible: The Story of Joseph Priestley, LL.D., F.R.S.* London, 1954.

Matthew Prior (1664–1721)

Works

2252 *Literary Works.* Eds. H. Bunker Wright and Monroe K. Spears. 2 vols. 2d ed., Oxford, 1971.

Studies

2253 BARRETT, W. P. "Matthew Prior's *Alma.*" *MLR,* 27 (1932), 454–58.

2254 EVES, Charles K. *Matthew Prior, Poet and Diplomatist.* New York, 1939. Rpt. 1973.*

2255 EWING, Majl. "Musical Settings of Prior's Lyrics in the 18th Century." *ELH,* 10 (1943), 159–71.

2256 FELLOWS, Otis. "Prior's 'Pritty Spanish Conceit.' " *MLN,* 87 (1972), 3–11.

2257 JACK, Ian. "The 'Choice of Life' in Johnson and Prior." *JEGP,* 49 (1950), 523–30.

2258 KLINE, Richard B. "Matthew Prior and 'Dear Will Nuttley': An Addition to the Canon." *PQ,* 47 (1968), 157–63.

2259 KLINE, Richard B. "Prior to Southwell: Two Unpublished Letters." *The Scriblerian,* 6 (1974), 64–68.

2260 LEGG, L. G. Wickham. *Matthew Prior: A Study of His Public Career and Correspondence.* Cambridge, Eng., 1921. Rpt. New York, 1972.

2261 SPEARS, Monroe K. "The Meaning of Matthew Prior's 'Alma.' " *ELH,* 13 (1946), 266–90.

2262 SPEARS, Monroe K. "Matthew Prior's Attitude Toward Natural Science." *PMLA,* 63 (1948), 485–507.

2263 SPEARS, Monroe K. "Matthew Prior's Religion." *PQ,* 27 (1948), 159–80.

2264 SPEARS, Monroe K. "Some Ethical Aspects of Matthew Prior's Poetry." *SP,* 45 (1948), 606–29.

2265 WRIGHT, H. Bunker. "Ideal Copy and Authoritative Text: The Problem of Prior's *Poems on Several Occasions* (1718)." *MP,* 49 (1952), 234–41.

2266 WRIGHT, H. Bunker. "Prior Knowledge." *The Scriblerian,* 6 (1974), 68–70.

James Ralph (1705?–1762)

2267 BASTIAN, J. M. "James Ralph's Second Adaptation from John Banks." *HLQ,* 25 (1962), 181–88. [A Ms draft of *Anna Bullen.*]

2268 KENNY, Robert W. "Ralph's *Case of Authors:* Its Influence on Goldsmith and Isaac D'Israeli." *PMLA,* 52 (1937), 104–13.

2269 KENNY, Robert W. "James Ralph: An Eighteenth-Century Philadelphian in Grub Street." *Penn. Mag. of History and Biography,* 64 (1940), 218–42.

2270 MCKILLOP, Alan D. "James Ralph in Berkshire." *SEL,* 1 (1961), 43–51. [Texts of three letters.]

2271 SHIPLEY, John B. "Franklin Attends a Book Auction." *Penn. Mag. of History and Biography,* 80 (1956), 37–45. [The sale of Ralph's library in 1762.]

2272 SHIPLEY, John B. "David Garrick and James Ralph: Remarks on a Correspondence." *N&Q,* 203 (1958), 403–08.

2273 SHIPLEY, John B. "James Ralph's Pamphlets." *The Library,* 5th ser., 19 (1964), 130–46.

2274/5 SHIPLEY, John B. "James Ralph, Prince Titi, and the Black Box of Frederick, Prince of Wales." *BNYPL,* 71 (1967), 143–57.

2276 SHIPLEY, John B. "The Authorship of *The Touch-Stone* (1728)." *PBSA,* 62 (1968), 189–98.

Allan Ramsay (1686–1758)

Works

2277 *Works.* 5 vols. (Vols. 1–2. Eds. Burns Martin and John W. Oliver. Vols. 3–5. Eds. Alexander M. Kinghorn and Alexander Law.) Edinburgh, 1951–72.

Bibliography

2278 MARTIN, Burns. *Bibliography of Allan Ramsay.* Glasgow, 1931.

Studies

2279 MacLAINE, Allan H. "The *Christus Kirk* Tradition: The Evolution in Scots Poetry to Burns." *SSL,* 2 (1965), 3–18.

2280 MARTIN, Burns. *Allan Ramsay: A Study of His Life and Works.* Cambridge, Mass., 1931. Rpt. Westport, Conn., 1973.*

2281 YEO, Elspeth. "The MS of Ramsay's *Gentle Shepherd." SSL,* 4 (1966), 47–48.

Thomas Reid (1710–1796)

Works

2282 *Philosophical Orations.* Ed. Wallace R. Humphries. Aberdeen, 1937.

2283 *Essays on the Intellectual Powers of Man.* Ed. and abridged A. D. Woozley. London, 1941. Ed. Baruch A. Brody. Cambridge, Mass., 1969.†

2284 *Essays on the Active Powers of the Human Mind.* Ed. Baruch A. Brody. Cambridge, Mass., 1969.

2285 *An Inquiry into the Human Mind.* Ed. Timothy J. Duggan. Chicago, 1970.

Studies

2286 CALDWELL, R. L. "Another Look at Thomas Reid." *JHI,* 23 (1962), 545–59.

2287 FAUROT, J. H. "The Development of Reid's Theory of Knowledge." *UTQ,* 21 (1952), 224–31.

2288 JONES, Olin McKendree. *Empiricism and Intuitionism in Reid's Common Sense Philosophy.* Princeton, N.J., 1927.

2289 KIVEY, Peter. "Lectures on the Fine Arts: An Unpublished Manuscript of Thomas Reid's." *JHI,* 31 (1970), 17–32.

2290 ROBBINS, David O. "The Aesthetics of Thomas Reid." *JAAC,* 5 (1942), 30–41.

2291 ROSS, Ian. "Unpublished Letters of Thomas Reid to Lord Kames, 1762–1782." *TSLL,* 7 (1965), 17–65.

2292 TODD, D. D. "Reid Redivivus?" *TSLL,* 14 (1972), 303–12.

Sir Joshua Reynolds (1723–1792)

Works

2293 *Discourses on Art.* Ed. Robert R. Wark. San Marino, Cal., 1959.

2294 *Letters.* Ed. Frederick W. Hilles. Cambridge, Eng., 1929.

2295 *Portraits by Sir Joshua Reynolds: Character Sketches of Oliver Goldsmith, Samuel Johnson, and David Garrick.* . . . Ed. Frederick W. Hilles. New York and London, 1952. [Boswell Private Papers.]

Studies

2296 BEVILACQUA, Vincent M. "*Ut Rhetorica Pictura:* Sir Joshua Reynolds' Rhetorical Conception of Art." *HLQ,* 34 (1970), 59–78.

2297 GERBER, Helmut E. "Reynolds' Pendulum Figure and the Watch-Maker." *PQ,* 38 (1959), 66–83.

2298 GOLDSTEIN, Harvey D. "*Ut Poesis Pictura:* Reynolds on Imitation and Imagination." *ECS,* 1 (1968), 213–35.

2299 GOMBRICH, E. H. *Norm and Form: Studies in the Art of the Renaissance.* London, 1966. Pp. 129–36: "Reynolds's Theory and Practice of Imitation."

2300 HILLES, Frederick W. *The Literary Career of Sir Joshua Reynolds.* Cambridge, Eng., 1936.*

2301 HILLES, Frederick W. "Sir Joshua's Prose." In 40, pp. 49–60.

2302 HUDSON, Derek. *Sir Joshua Reynolds: A Personal Study. With Reynolds' 'Journey from London to Brentford' Now First Published.* London, 1958.

2303 MACKLEM, Michael. "Reynolds and the Ambiguities of Neo-Classical Criticism." *PQ,* 31 (1952), 383–98.

2304 MOORE, Robert E. "Reynolds and the Art of Characterization." In 21, pp. 332–57.

Elizabeth Singer Rowe (1674–1737)

2305 HUGHES, Helen Sard. *The Gentle Hertford: Her Life and Letters.* New York, 1940.

2306 HUGHES, Helen Sard. "Elizabeth Rowe and the Countess of Hertford." *PMLA,* 59 (1944), 726–46.

2307 WRIGHT, H. Bunker. "Matthew Prior and Elizabeth Singer." *PQ,* 24 (1945), 71–82.

Nicholas Rowe (1674–1718)

Works

2308 *Three Plays by Nicholas Rowe.* Ed. J. R. Sutherland. London, 1929. [*Tamerlane, The Fair Penitent, Jane Shore.*]

2309 *The Fair Penitent.* Ed. J. H. Wilson. Boston, 1963. Ed. Malcolm Goldstein. Lincoln, Neb., 1969.†

2310 *Tamerlane.* Ed. Landon C. Burnes. London, 1966.

Studies

2311 CLARK, Donald B. "The Source and Characterization of Nicholas Rowe's 'Tamerlane.' " *MLN,* 65 (1950), 145–52.

2312 CLARK, Donald B. "An Eighteenth-Century Adaptation of Massinger." *MLQ,* 13 (1952), 239–52. [*The Fair Penitent.*]

2313 DUSSINGER, John A. "Richardson and Johnson: Critical Agreement on Rowe's 'The Fair Penitent.' " *ES,* 49 (1968), 45–47.

2314 GOLDSTEIN, Malcolm. "Pathos and Personality in the Tragedies of Nicholas Rowe," In 43, pp. 172–85.

2315 HESSE, Alfred W. *Nicholas Rowe's Translation of Lucan's Pharsalia, 1703–18.* . . . Philadelphia, 1950.

2316 JACKSON, Alfred. "Rowe's Edition of Shakespeare." *The Library,* 4th ser., 10 (1930), 455–73.

2317 JACKSON, Alfred. "Rowe's Historical Tragedies." *Anglia,* 54 (1930), 307–30.

2318 KEARFUL, Frank J. "The Nature of Tragedy in Rowe's *The Fair Penitent.*" *PLL,* 2 (1966), 351–60.

2319 ROWAN, D. F. "Shore's Wife." *SEL,* 6 (1966), 447–64.

2320 SCHWARZ, Alfred. "An Example of Eighteenth-Century Pathetic Tragedy: Rowe's *Jane Shore.*" *MLQ,* 22 (1961), 236–47.

2321 THORP, Willard. "A Key to Rowe's *Tamerlane.*" *JEGP,* 39 (1940), 124–27.

2322 WHITING, George W. "Rowe's Debt to *Paradise Lost.*" *MP,* 32 (1935), 271–79.

2323 WYMAN, Lindley A. "The Tradition of the Formal Meditation in Rowe's *The Fair Penitent.*" *PQ,* 42 (1963), 412–16.

Richard Savage (1697?–1743)

Works

2324 *Poetical Works.* Ed. Clarence Tracy. Cambridge, Eng., 1962.

2325 *An Author To Be Let.* Ed. James Sutherland. (*ARS*) Los Angeles, 1960.†

Studies

2326 BOYCE, Benjamin. "Johnson's *Life of Savage* and Its Literary Background." *SP,* 53 (1956), 576–98.

2327 DUSSINGER, John A. "Style and Intention in Johnson's *Life of Savage.*" *ELH,* 37 (1970), 564–80.

2328 FLEEMAN, J. D. "The Making of Johnson's *Life of Savage,* 1744." *The Library,* 5th ser., 22 (1967), 346–52.

2329 HOGAN, Floriana T. "Notes on Savage's *Love in a Veil* and Calderón's *Peor Está Que Estaba.*" *RECTR,* 8, i (1969), 23–29.

2330 JOHNSON, Samuel. *An Account of the Life of Mr. Richard Savage.* Ed. Clarence Tracy. Oxford, 1971.

2331 TRACY, Clarence. *The Artificial Bastard: A Biography of Richard Savage.* Toronto and Cambridge, Mass., 1953.*

2332 TRACY, Clarence. "Some Uncollected Authors. XXXVI. Richard Savage, d. 1743." *BC,* 12 (1963), 340–49.

2333 TRACY, Clarence. "More Poems by Richard Savage." *N&Q,* 210 (1965), 452–53.

2334 VESTERMAN, William. "Johnson and the *Life of Savage.*" *ELH,* 36 (1969), 659–78.

Anna Seward (1742–1809)

Letters

2335 *The Swan of Lichfield: . . . A Selection from the Correspondence. . . .* Ed. Hesketh Pearson. London, 1936.

Studies

2336 ADDLESHAW, S. "The Swan of Lichfield: Anna Seward and Her Circle." *Church Quarterly Rev.,* 124 (1937), 1–34.

2337 ASHMUN, Margaret. *The Singing Swan: An Account of Anna Seward and Her Acquaintance with Dr. Johnson, Boswell and Others of Their Time.* New Haven, Conn., 1931.*

2338 CLIFFORD, James L. "The Authenticity of Anna Seward's Published Correspondence." *MP,* 39 (1941), 113–22. Rpt. in 23.

2339 HANFORD, James Holly. "A Letter from the Swan of Lichfield." *Newberry Lib. Bull.,* 4 (1957), 201–10.

2340 MONK, Samuel H. "Anna Seward and the Romantic Poets: A Study in Taste." *Wordsworth and Coleridge: Studies in Honor of George McLean Harper* (Princeton, N.J., 1939), pp. 118–34. •

2341 MYERS, Robert M. *Anna Seward: An Eighteenth-Century Handelian.* Williamsburg, Va., 1947.

2342 ROUSSEAU, G. S. "Anna Seward to William Hayley: A Letter from the Swan of Lichfield." *HLB,* 15 (1967), 273–80.

Anthony Ashley Cooper, 3d Earl of Shaftesbury (1671-1713)

Works

2343 *Characteristicks of Men, Manners, Opinions, Times.* Ed. John M. Robertson. 2 vols. London, 1900.

2344 *Life, Unpublished Letters, and Philosophical Regimen.* Ed. Benjamin Rand. London, 1900.

2345 *Second Characters.* Ed. Benjamin Rand. Cambridge, Eng., 1914.

Studies

2346 ALDERMAN, William E. "The Style of Shaftesbury." *MLN,* 38 (1923), 209–15.

2347 ALDERMAN, William E. "Shaftesbury and the Doctrine of Benevolence in the Eighteenth Century." *TWA,* 26 (1931), 137–59.

2348 ALDERMAN, William E. "Shaftesbury and the Doctrine of Moral Sense in the Eighteenth Century." *PMLA,* 46 (1931), 1087–94.

2349 ALDERMAN, William E. "Shaftesbury and the Doctrine of Optimism in the Eighteenth Century." *TWA,* 28 (1933), 297–305.

2350 ALDERMAN, William E. "English Editions of Shaftesbury's *Characteristics.*" *PBSA,* 61 (1967), 315–34.

2351 ALDRIDGE, Alfred Owen. "Lord Shaftesbury's Literary Theories." *PQ,* 24 (1945), 46–64.

2352 ALDRIDGE, Alfred Owen. "Shaftesbury and the Test of Truth." *PMLA,* 60 (1945), 129–56.

2353 ALDRIDGE, Alfred Owen. "Shaftesbury's Earliest Critic." *MP,* 44 (1946), 10–22. [Robert Day, *Free Thoughts in Defence of a Future State,* 1700.]

2354 ALDRIDGE, Alfred Owen. "Shaftesbury, Christianity, and Friendship." *Anglican Theological Rev.,* 32 (1950), 121–36.

2355 ALDRIDGE, Alfred Owen. "Two Versions of Shaftesbury's *Inquiry Concerning Virtue.*" *HLQ,* 13 (1950), 207–14.

2356 ALDRIDGE, Alfred Owen. "Shaftesbury and the Deist Manifesto." *Trans. Amer. Philos. Soc.,* 41 (1951), 297–385.

2357 ALDRIDGE, Alfred Owen. "Shaftesbury and Bolingbroke." *PQ,* 31 (1952), 1–16.

2358 BRETT, R. L. *The Third Earl of Shaftesbury: A Study in Eighteenth-Century Literary Theory.* London, 1951.*

2359 BROADBENT, J. B. "Shaftesbury's Horses of Instruction." In 30, pp. 79–89.

2360/1 GREAN, Stanley. *Shaftesbury's Philosophy of Religion and Ethics: A Study in Enthusiasm.* Athens, Ohio, 1967.

2362 HAYMAN, John G. "The Evolution of 'The Moralists.'" *MLR,* 64 (1969), 728–33.

2363/4 HAYMAN, John G. "Shaftesbury and the Search for a Persona." *SEL,* 10 (1970), 491–504.

2365 MOORE, Cecil A. "Shaftesbury and the Ethical Poets in England, 1700–1760." *PMLA,* 31 (1916), 264–325. Rpt. in his *Backgrounds of English Literature, 1700– 1760* (Minneapolis, 1953). See also Herbert Drennon, "Henry Needler and Shaftesbury," *PMLA,* 46 (1931), 1095–1106; and Alfred Owen Aldridge, "Henry Needler's Knowledge of Shaftesbury," *MLN,* 62 (1947), 264–67.

2366 ROGERS, Pat. "Shaftesbury and the Aesthetics of Rhapsody." *BJA,* 12 (1972), 244–57.

2367 SCHLEGEL, Dorothy B. *Shaftesbury and the French Deists.* Chapel Hill, N.C., 1956.

2368 SCHLEGEL, Dorothy B. "Shaftesbury's Hermetic Symbolism." *Proc. IVth Congress International Comparative Lit. Assn.* (The Hague, 1966), 2, 1128–33.

2369 STOLNITZ, Jerome. "On the Significance of Lord Shaftesbury in Modern Aesthetic Theory." *Philos. Quarterly,* 11 (1961), 97–113.

2370 TUVESON, Ernest. "The Importance of Shaftesbury." *ELH,* 20 (1053), 267–99.

2371 TUVESON, Ernest. "Shaftesbury on the Not So Simple Plan of Human Nature." *SEL,* 5 (1965), 403–34.

2372 TUVESON, Ernest. "Shaftesbury and the Age of Sensibility." In 21, pp. 73–93.

2373 UPHAUS, Robert W. "Shaftesbury on Art: The Rhapsodic Aesthetic." *JAAC,* 27 (1969), 341–48.

2374 VOITLE, Robert B. "Shaftesbury's Moral Sense." *SP,* 52 (1955), 17–38.

2375 WHITAKER, S. F. "The First Edition of Shaftesbury's *Moralists.*" *The Library,* 5th ser., 7 (1952), 235–41.

2376 WOLFF, Erwin. *Shaftesbury und seine Bedeutung für die englische Literatur des 18. Jahrhunderts: Der Moralist und die literarische Form.* Tübingen, 1960.* See rev. by Irène Simon in *Revue des Langues Vivantes,* 27 (1961), 200–15.

William Shenstone (1714–1763)

Letters and "Miscellany"

2377 *Letters.* Ed. Duncan Mallam. Minneapolis, 1939.

2378 *Letters.* Ed. Marjorie Williams. Oxford, 1939.

2379 *Shenstone's Miscellany, 1759–1763.* Ed. Ian A. Gordon. Oxford, 1952.

Bibliography

2380 WILLIAMS, Iolo A. *Seven XVIIIth Century Bibliographies* (London, 1924), pp. 41–71.

Studies

2381 FISHER, J. "Shenstone, Gray, and the 'Moral Elegy.'" *MP,* 34 (1937), 273–94.

2382 HILL, Charles J. "Shenstone and Richard Graves's *Columella.*" *PMLA,* 49 (1934), 566–76.

2383 HUGHES, Helen S. "Shenstone and the Countess of Hertford." *PMLA*, 46 (1931), 1113–27.

2384 HUMPHREYS, A. R. *William Shenstone: An Eighteenth-Century Portrait.* Cambridge, Eng. 1937.

2385 LEWIS, Roy. "William Shenstone and Edward Knight: Some New Letters." *MLR*, 42 (1947), 422–33.

2386 MALLAM, Duncan. "Some Inter-Relationships of Shenstone's Essays, Letters, and Poems." *PQ*, 28 (1949), 458–64.

2387 SAMBROOK, A. J. "Another Early Version of Shenstone's *Pastoral Ballad.*" *RES*, N.S., 18 (1967), 169–73.

2388 WILLIAMS, Marjorie. *William Shenstone: A Chapter in Eighteenth-Century Taste.* Birmingham, Eng., 1935.

Richard Brinsley Sheridan (1751–1816)

Works

2389 *Dramatic Works.* Ed. Cecil Price. 2 vols. Oxford, 1973.

2390 *Plays and Poems.* Ed. R. Crompton Rhodes. 3 vols. Oxford, 1928.

2391 *Letters.* Ed. Cecil Price. 3 vols. Oxford, 1966.

Bibliography

2392 WILLIAMS, Iolo A. *Seven XVIIIth Century Bibliographies* (London, 1924), pp. 209–39.

Studies

2393 DARLINGTON, W. A. *Sheridan, 1751–1816.* (*WTW*) 1951.

2394 DEELMAN, Christian. "The Original Cast of *The School for Scandal.*" *RES*, N.S. 13 (1962), 257–66.

2395 DULCK, Jean. *Les Comédies de R. B. Sheridan: Etude littéraire.* Paris, 1962.

2396 JACKSON, J. R. de J. "The Importance of Witty Dialogue in *The School for Scandal.*" *MLN*, 76 (1961), 601–07.

2397 LANDFIELD, Jerome. "The Triumph and Failure of Sheridan's Speeches Against Hastings." *SM*, 28 (1961), 143–56.

2398 MAHONEY, John L. "Sheridan on Hastings: The Classical Oration and Eighteenth-Century Politics." *Burke Newsletter*, 6 (1965), 414–22.

2399 MATLAW, Myron. "English Versions of *Die Spanier in Peru.*" *MLQ*, 16 (1955), 63–67.

2400 MATLAW, Myron. "Adultery Analyzed: The History of *The Stranger.*" *QJS*, 43 (1957), 22–28.

2401 MATLAW, Myron. " 'This is Tragedy!!!': The History of *Pizarro.*" *QJS*, 43 (1957), 288–94.

2402 NETTLETON, George H. "Sheridan's Introduction to the American Stage." *PMLA*, 65 (1950), 163–82.

2403 PRICE, Cecil. "The Completion of 'The School for Scandal.'" *TLS*, Dec. 28, 1967, p. 1265.

2404 PRICE, Cecil. "The First Prologue to *The Rivals.*" *RES*, N.S. 20 (1969), 192–95.

2405 RHODES, R. Crompton. *Harlequin Sheridan: The Man and the Legends.* Oxford, 1933. Rpt. New York, 1972.

2406 SCHILLER, Andrew. "*The School for Scandal:* The Restoration Unrestored." *PMLA*, 62 (1956), 694–704.

2407 SPRAGUE, Arthur C. "In Defence of a Masterpiece: 'The School for Scandal' Re-examined." *English Studies To-day*, 3d ser. (Edinburgh, 1964), pp. 125–35.

2408 WILLIAMS, George W. "A New Source of Evidence for Sheridan's Authorship of *The Camp* and *The Wonders of Derbyshire.*" *SP*, 47 (1950), 619–28.

Christopher Smart (1722–1771)

Works

2409 *Collected Poems.* Ed. Norman Callan. 2 vols. (Muses' Library) London, 1949.

2410 *Poems.* Ed. Robert Brittain. Princeton, N.J., 1950. A selection.

2411 *Jubilate Agno.* Re-edited from the Original Manuscript by W. H. Bond. Cambridge, Mass., 1954.

Studies

2412 ABBOTT, Charles D. "Christopher Smart's Madness." *PMLA*, 45 (1930), 25–34.

2413 ADAMS, Francis D. "Wordplay in the D Fragment of *Jubilate Agno.*" *PQ*, 48 (1969), 82–91.

2414 AINSWORTH, Edward G., and Charles E. NOYES. *Christopher Smart: A Biographical and Critical Study.* Columbia, Mo., 1943.*

2415 BLAYDES, Sophia B. *Christopher Smart as a Poet of his Time: A Re-appraisal.* The Hague, 1966.

2416 CHRISTENSEN, Allan C. "Liturgical Order in Smart's *Jubilate Agno:* A Study of Fragment C." *PLL*, 6 (1970), 366–73.

2417 DAVIE, Donald. "Christopher Smart: Some Neglected Poems." *ECS*, 3 (1969), 242–64.

2418 DEARNLEY, Moira. *The Poetry of Christopher Smart.* London, 1968; New York, 1969.

2419 DEVLIN, Christopher. *Poor Kit Smart.* London, 1961.

2420 FITZGERALD, Robert P. "The Form of Christopher Smart's *Jubilate Agno.*" *SEL*, 8 (1968), 487–99.

2421 FRIEDMAN, John B. "The Cosmology of Praise: Smart's *Jubilate Agno.*" *PMLA*, 82 (1967), 250–56.

2422 GREENE, D. J. "Smart, Berkeley, the Scientists and the Poets: A Note on Eighteenth-Century Anti-Newtonism." *JHI,* 14 (1953), 327–52.

2423 GRIGSON, Geoffrey. *Christopher Smart. (WTW)* London, 1961.†

2424 HART, Edward. "Christopher Smart's Verse Satire." *Satire Newsletter,* 6 (1968), 29–34.

2425 HAVENS, Raymond D. "The Structure of Smart's *Song to David." RES,* 14 (1938), 178–82.

2426 KUHN, Albert J. "Christopher Smart: The Poet as Patriot of the Lord." *ELH,* 30 (1963), 121–36.

2427 MERCHANT, W. Moelwyn. "Patterns of Reference in Smart's *Jubilate Agno." HLB,* 14 (1960), 20–26.

2428 PARISH, Charles. "Christopher Smart's Knowledge of Hebrew." *SP,* 58 (1961), 516–32.

2429 PARISH, Charles. "Christopher Smart's 'Pillars of the Lord.' " *MLQ,* 24 (1963), 158–63.

2430 PARKIN, Rebecca P. "Christopher Smart's Sacramental Cat." *TSLL,* 11 (1969), 1191–96.

2431 PRICE, Cecil. "Six Letters by Christopher Smart." *RES,* N.S., 8 (1957), 144–48.

2432 RIZZO, Betty W. "Christopher Smart's 'Chaucerian' Poems." *The Library,* 5th ser., 28 (1973), 124–30.

2433 ROGERS, K. M. "The Pillars of the Lord: Some Sources of 'A Song to David.' " *PQ,* 40 (1961), 525–34.

2434 RYSKAMP, Charles. "Problems in the Text of Smart." *The Library,* 5th ser., 14 (1959), 293–98.

2435 SALTZ, Robert D. "Reason in Madness: Christopher Smart's Poetic Development." *Southern Humanities Rev.,* 4 (1970), 57–68.

2436 SHERBO, Arthur. *Christopher Smart: Scholar of the University.* East Lansing Mich., 1967.

2437 SHERBO, Arthur. "Two Pieces Newly Ascribed to Christopher Smart." *MLR,* 62 (1967), 214–20.

2438 SHERBO, Arthur. "Christopher Smart's Three Translations of Horace." *JEGP,* 66 (1967), 347–58.

2439 WILKINSON, Jean. "Three Sets of Religious Poems." *HLQ,* 36 (1973), 203–26.

2440 WILLIAMSON, Karina. "Christopher Smart's *Hymns and Spiritual Songs." PQ,* 38 (1959), 413–24.

2441 WILLIAMSON, Karina. "Christopher Smart: Problems of Attribution Reconsidered." *The Library,* 5th ser., 28 (1973), 116–23.

Adam Smith (1723–1790)

Works

2442 *Adam Smith's Moral and Political Philosophy.* Ed. Herbert W. Schneider. New York, 1948.†

2443 *Lectures on Rhetoric and Belles-Lettres.* Ed. John M. Lothian. London, 1963.

2444 *Early Writings.* Ed. J. Ralph Lindgren. New York, 1967.

Bibliography

2445 BULLOCK, Charles J. *The Vanderblue Memorial Collection of Smithiana and a Catalogue of the Collection.* Boston, 1939.

2446 SCOTT, W. R. "Studies Relating to Adam Smith During the Last Fifty Years." *PBA,* 26 (1940), 249–74.

Studies

2447 BEVILACQUA, Vincent M. "Adam Smith's Lectures on Rhetoric and Belles Lettres." *SSL,* 3 (1964), 41–60.

2448 BEVILACQUA, Vincent M. "Adam Smith and Some Philosophical Origins of Eighteenth-Century Rhetorical Theory." *MLR,* 63 (1968), 559–68.

2449 BONAR, James. *A Catalogue of the Library of Adam Smith.* 1894. 2d ed., 1932. Additions by Claude Jones in *Economic History,* 4 (1940), 326–28. See also Hiroshi Mizuta, *Adam Smith's Library: A Supplement to Bonar's Catalogue, with a Check List of the Whole Library* (Cambridge, Eng., 1967).

2450 BRISSENDEN, R. F. "Authority, Guilt and Anxiety in *The Theory of Moral Sentiments.*" *TSLL,* 11 (1969), 945–62.

2451 CAMPBELL, Thomas D. *Adam Smith's Science of Morals.* London, 1971.

2452 COATS, A. W. "Adam Smith: The Modern Re-appraisal." *RMS,* 6 (1962), 25–48.

2453 DANKERT, Clyde E. "Adam Smith, Educator." *Dalhousie Rev.,* 47 (1967), 13–27.

2454 FAY, Charles R. *Adam Smith and the Scotland of His Day.* Cambridge, Eng., 1958.

2455 FAY, Charles R. *The World of Adam Smith.* Cambridge, Eng., 1960.

2456 GOLDEN, James L. "Adam Smith as a Rhetorical Theorist and Literary Critic." *Costerus,* 1 (1972), 89–113.

2457 HOLLANDER, Samuel. *The Economics of Adam Smith.* London, 1973.

2458 HOWELL, Wilbur S. "Adam Smith's Lecture on Rhetoric: An Historical Assessment." *SM,* 36 (1969), 393–418.

2459 MACFIE, A. L. *The Individual in Society: Papers on Adam Smith.* New York, 1968.

2460 MacLEAN, Kenneth. "Imagination and Sympathy: Sterne and Adam Smith." *JHI,* 10 (1949), 399–410.

2461 MALEK, James S. "Adam Smith's Contribution to Eighteenth-Century British Aesthetics." *JAAC,* 31 (1972), 49–54.

2462 MIDDENDORF, John H. "Dr. Johnson and Adam Smith." *PQ,* 40 (1961), 281–96.

2463 RAE, John. *Life of Adam Smith.* London, 1895. Rpt. with Introduction by Jacob Viner. New York, 1965.

2464 SCOTT, W[illiam] R[obert]. *Adam Smith as Student and Professor. With Unpublished Documents.* ... Glasgow, 1937.

2465 TAYLOR, W. L. *Francis Hutcheson and David Hume as Predecessors of Adam Smith.* Durham, N.C., 1965.

Joseph Spence (1699–1768)

Works

2466 *Observations, Anecdotes and Characters of Books and Men, Collected from Conversation.* Ed. James M. Osborn. 2 vols. Oxford, 1966.

2467 *Letters from the Grand Tour.* Ed. Slava Klima. Montreal, 1974.

Studies

2468 OSBORN, James M. "The First History of English Poetry." In 28, pp. 230–50.

2469 OSBORN, James M. "Spence, Natural Genius, and Pope." *PQ,* 45 (1966), 123–44.

2470 OSBORN, James M. "Joseph Spence's Collections Relating to the 'Lives of the Poets'." *HLB,* 16 (1968), 129–38.

2471 WRIGHT, Austin. *Joseph Spence: A Critical Biography.* Chicago, 1950.

Sir Richard Steele (1672–1729)

Works

2472 *The Christian Hero.* Ed. Rae Blanchard. Oxford, 1932.

2473 *Tracts and Pamphlets.* Ed. Rae Blanchard. Baltimore, 1944. Rpt. 1967.

2474 *Occasional Verse.* Ed. Rae Blanchard. Oxford, 1952.

2475 *The Englishman: A Political Journal.* Ed. Rae Blanchard. Oxford, 1955.

2476 *Periodical Journalism, 1714–16.* Ed. Rae Blanchard. Oxford, 1959. [*The Lover, The Reader, Town-Talk,* and *Chit-Chat.*]

2477 *The Theatre, 1720.* Ed. John Loftis. Oxford, 1962. See also a "continuation" by "Sir John Falstaffe" (1720). Ed. John Loftis. (*ARS*) Los Angeles, 1948.†

2478 *Plays.* Ed. Shirley Strum Kenny. Oxford, 1971.

2479 *The Tender Husband.* Ed. Calhoun Winton. Lincoln, Neb., 1967.†

2480 *The Conscious Lovers.* Ed. Shirley S. Kenny. Lincoln, Neb., 1968.†

2481 *Correspondence.* Ed. Rae Blanchard. Oxford, 1941. Rpt., with Appendix of 17 additional letters, 1968.

Bibliography

2482 RAU, Fritz. "Die Steele-Literatur seit 1930." *GRM,* N.F., 3 (1953), 214–30.

2483 KENNY, Shirley S. "Recent Scholarship on Richard Steele." *British Studies Monitor*, 6 (1973), 12–24.

Studies

2484 AITKEN, George A. *The Life of Richard Steele.* 2 vols. London, 1889. Rpt. New York, 1968.*

2485 AUBIN, Robert A. "Behind Steele's Satire on Undertakers." *PMLA*, 64 (1949), 1008–26.

2486 BAINE, Rodney M. "The Publication of Steele's *Conscious Lovers.*" *SB*, 2 (1949–50), 169–73.

2487 BATESON, F. W. "The Errata in *The Tatler.*" *RES*, 5 (1929), 155–66. See also Rae Blanchard, *Ibid.*, 6 (1930), 183–85.

2488 BLANCHARD, Rae. "Richard Steele and the Status of Women." *SP*, 26 (1929), 325–55.

2489 BLANCHARD, Rae. "Was Sir Richard Steele a Freemason?" *PMLA*, 63 (1948), 903–17.

2490 BLANCHARD, Rae. "The Songs in Steele's Plays." In 28, pp. 185–200.

2491 BLANCHARD, Rae. "Steele, Charles King, and the Dunkirk Pamphlets." *HLQ*, 14 (1951), 423–29.

2492 BLANCHARD, Rae. "Richard Steele's Maryland Story." *Amer. Quarterly*, 10 (1958), 78–82. [*The Lover*, No. 36.]

2493 BLANCHARD, Rae. "Richard Steele and the Secretary of the S.P.C.K." In 27, pp. 287–95.

2494 BLOOM, Edward A., and Lillian D. BLOOM. "Steele in 1719: Additions to the Canon." *HLQ*, 31 (1968), 123–51. [Three pieces against the Peerage Bill.]

2495 BOND, Donald F. "Armand de la Chapelle and the First French Version of the *Tatler.*" In 27, pp. 161–84.

2496 BOND, Richmond P. *New Letters to the Tatler and Spectator.* Austin, Tex., 1959.

2497 BOND, Richmond P. *The Tatler: The Making of a Literary Journal.* Cambridge, Mass., 1971.

2498 CONNELY, Willard. *Sir Richard Steele.* London, 1934.

2499 DUST, Alvin I. "An Aspect of the Addison-Steele Literary Relationship." *ELN*, 1 (1964), 196–200.

2500 ELLIOTT, Robert C. "Swift's 'Little' Harrison, Poet and Continuator of the *Tatler.*" *SP*, 44 (1949), 544–59.

2501 GRAHAM, Walter. "Some Predecessors of the *Tatler.*" *JEGP*, 24 (1925), 548–54.

2502 GRAHAM, Walter. "Defoe's *Review* and Steele's *Tatler*—the Question of Influence." *JEGP*, 33 (1934), 250–54.

2503 GREENE, Elvena M. "Three Aspects of Richard Steele's Theory of Comedy." *ETJ*, 20 (1968), 141–46.

2504 GREENOUGH, C. N. "The Development of the *Tatler*, Particularly in Regard to News." *PMLA*, 31 (1916), 633–63. See also Robert W. Achurch, "Richard Steele, Gazetteer and Bickerstaff," in 702, pp. 49–72.

2505 HAZARD, Paul. "Une Source anglaise de l'Abbé Prévost." *MP,* 27 (1930), 339–44. [*The Conscious Lovers.*]

2506 HOPKINS, Robert H. "The Issue of Anonymity and the Beginning of the Steele-Swift Controversy of 1713–14: A New Interpretation." *ELN,* 2 (1964), 15–21. [*Guardian* 53.]

2507 HOPKINS, Robert H. "A Further Note on Richard Steele's Authorship of the Dedication to Bickerstaff's 'Almanack' (1709)." *N&Q,* 210 (1965), 448–49.

2508 KELSALL, Malcolm. "Terence and Steele." In 524, pp. 11–27.

2509 KENNY, Shirley S. "Richard Steele and the 'Pattern of Genteel Comedy.' " *MP,* 70 (1972), 22–37.

2510 KLINE, Richard B. "Tory Prior and Whig Steele: A Measure of Respect?" *SEL,* 9 (1969), 43–66.

2511 LOFTIS, John. "Richard Steele's Censorium." *HLQ,* 14 (1950), 43–66.

2512 LOFTIS, John. "The Blenheim Papers and Steele's Journalism, 1715–1718." *PMLA,* 66 (1951), 197–210.

2513 LOFTIS, John. *Steele at Drury Lane.* Berkeley, Cal., 1952.*

2514 Moore, John Robert. "Steele's Unassigned Tract Against the Earl of Oxford." *PQ,* 28 (1949), 413–18.

2515 MOORE, John Robert. "Defoe, Steele, and the Demolition of Dunkirk." *HLQ,* 13 (1950), 279–302.

2516 RAU, Fritz. "Texte, Ausgaben und Verfasser des 'Tatler' und 'Spectator': Forschungsbericht." *GRM,* N.F., 8 (1958), 126–44.

2517 RAU, Fritz. "Zur Gestalt des 'Tatler' und 'Spectator': Kritischer Bericht." *GRM,* N.F., 10 (1960), 401–19.

2518 SNYDER, Henry L. "The Identity of Monoculus in *The Tatler.*" *PQ,* 48 (1969), 20–26. See also Patricia Köster, " 'Monoculus' and Party Satire." *Ibid.,* 49 (1970), 259–62.

2519 SNYDER, Henry L. "Arthur Maynwaring, Richard Steele, and *The Lives of Two Illustrious Generals.*" *SB,* 24 (1971), 152–62.

2520 STEPHENS, John C., Jr. "Mr. Crab, the Librarian." *N&Q,* 201 (1956), 105–06. [*The Guardian.*]

2521 TODD, William B. "Early Editions of *The Tatler.*" *SB,* 15 (1962), 121–33.

2522 WINTON, Calhoun. "Steele, the Junto, and *The Tatler,* No. 4." *MLN,* 72 (1957), 178–82.

2523 WINTON, Calhoun. "Steele, Mrs. Manley, and John Lacy." *PQ,* 62 (1963), 272–75.

2524 WINTON, Calhoun. *Captain Steele: The Early Career of Richard Steele.* Baltimore, 1964.*

2525 WINTON, Calhoun. *Sir Richard Steele, M.P.: The Later Career.* Baltimore, 1970.

Jonathan Swift (1667–1745)

Works

2526 *Prose Works* Ed. Herbert Davis. 14 vols. Oxford, 1939–68.

2527 *Poems.* Ed. Harold Williams. 2d ed. 3 vols. Oxford, 1958.

2528 *Poetical Works.* Ed. Herbert Davis. Oxford, 1967.

2529 *Correspondence.* Ed. F. Elrington Ball. 6 vols. London, 1910–14. Ed. Harold Williams. 5 vols. Oxford, 1963–65. Vols. 4–5, rev. by David Woolley. Oxford, 1972.

2530 *A Discourse of the Contests and Dissentions Between the Nobles and the Commons in Athens and Rome.* Ed. Frank H. Ellis. Oxford, 1967. Rev. by Edward Rosenheim, Jr. in *MP,* 66 (1968), 59–74.

2531 *The Drapier's Letters to the People of Ireland.* Ed. Herbert Davis. Oxford, 1935.

2532 *An Enquiry into the Behaviour of the Queen's Last Ministry.* Ed. Irvin Ehrenpreis. Bloomington, Ind., 1956.

2533 *Gulliver's Travels.* Ed. Harold Williams. London, 1926. Ed. Arthur E. Case. New York, 1938.

2534 *Journal to Stella.* Ed. Harold Williams. 2 vols. Oxford, 1948.

2535 *Polite Conversation.* Ed. Eric Partridge. New York, 1963.

2536 *"A Tale of a Tub." To Which Is Added "The Battle of the Books" and the "Mechanical Operation of the Spirit."* Ed. A. C. Guthkelch and D. Nichol Smith. 2d rev. ed. Oxford, 1958.

Collected Studies

2537 FRENCH, David P., *et al.,* eds. *Jonathan Swift: Tercentenary Essays.* Tulsa, Okla., 1967.

2538 JEFFARES, A. Norman, ed. *Fair Liberty Was All His Cry: A Tercentenary Tribute. . . .* London, 1967.

2539 JEFFARES, A. Norman. *Swift.* ("Modern Judgements") London, 1968.†

2540 McHUGH, Roger, and Philip EDWARDS, eds. *Jonathan Swift, 1667–1967: A Dublin Tercentenary Tribute.* Dublin, 1968.

2541 RAWSON, C. J., ed. *Focus: Swift.* London, 1971.

2542 TUVESON, Ernest, ed. *Swift: A Collection of Critical Essays.* Englewood Cliffs, N.J., 1964.

2543 VICKERS, Brian, ed. *The World of Jonathan Swift: Essays for the Tercentenary.* Cambridge, Mass., 1968.

2544 WILLIAMS, Kathleen. *Swift: The Critical Heritage.* London, 1970.

Bibliography

2545 DAVIS, Herbert. "The Canon of Swift." *Eng. Institute Annual 1942* (New York, 1943), pp. 119–36.

2546 MAYHEW, George P. *"Rage or Raillery": The Swift Manuscripts at the Huntington Library.* San Marino, Cal., 1967.

2547 OSBORN, James M. "Swiftiana in the Osborn Collection at Yale." *University Rev.* (Dublin), 4 (1967), 72–83.

2548 TEERINK, H. *A Bibliography of the Writings of Jonathan Swift,* 2d ed., rev. by Arthur H. Scouten. Philadelphia, 1963.*

2549 LAMONT, Claire. "A Checklist of Critical and Biographical Writings on Jonathan Swift, 1945–65." In 2538, pp. 356–91.

2550 LANDA, Louis A., and James E. TOBIN. *Jonathan Swift: A List of Critical Studies . . . 1895 to 1945. . . .* New York, 1945.

2551 MAYHEW, George P. "Recent Swift Scholarship." In 2540, pp. 187–98.

2552 QUINTANA, R. "A Modest Appraisal: Swift Scholarship and Criticism, 1945–65." In 2538, pp. 342–55.

2553 SHERBURN, George. "Methods in Books about Swift." *SP,* 35 (1938), 635–56.

2554 STATHIS, James J. *A Bibliography of Swift Studies, 1945–1965.* Nashville, Tenn., 1967. Additions by Peter J. Schakel in *PQ,* 47 (1968), 436–38.

2555 VOIGT, Milton. *Swift and the Twentieth Century.* Detroit, 1964. Contains an introductory chapter, "Nineteenth-Century Views."

General Studies

2556 ADEN, John M. "Swift, Pope, and 'the Sin of Wit.' " *PBSA,* 62 (1968), 80–85.

2557 BEAUMONT, Charles A. *Swift's Classical Rhetoric.* Athens, Ga., 1961.†

2558 BEAUMONT, Charles A. *Swift's Use of the Bible: A Documentation and a Study in Allusion.* Athens, Ga., 1965.†

2559 BULLITT, John M. *Jonathan Swift and the Anatomy of Satire: A Study of Satiric Technique.* Cambridge, Mass., 1953.*

2560 DAVIS, Herbert. *Jonathan Swift: Essays on His Satire and Other Studies.* New York, 1964.

2561 DONAGHUE, Denis. *Jonathan Swift: A Critical Introduction.* Cambridge, Eng., 1969.

2562 EHRENPREIS, Irvin. *The Personality of Jonathan Swift.* London, 1958.

2563 EHRENPREIS, Irwin. *Swift: The Man, His Works, and the Age.* 2 vols. London, 1962–67.* Vol. 1: *Mr. Swift and His Contemporaries.* Vol. 2: *Dr. Swift.* Vol. 3 in progress.

2564 EWALD, William B., Jr. *The Masks of Jonathan Swift.* Cambridge, Mass., 1954.

2565 FERGUSON, Oliver W. *Jonathan Swift and Ireland.* Urbana, Ill., 1962.

2566 GILBERT, Jack G. *Jonathan Swift: Romantic and Cynic Moralist.* Austin, Tex., 1966. Rpt, New York, 1973.

2567 GOLDGAR, Bertrand A. *The Curse of Party: Swift's Relations with Addison and Steele.* Lincoln, Neb., 1961.

2568 HUNTING, Robert. *Jonathan Swift. (TEAS)* New York, 1967.

2569 JOHNSON, Maurice. "A Literary Chestnut: Dryden's Cousin Swift." *PMLA,* 67 (1952), 1024–34. Discussion by John Robert Moore and Johnson, *ibid.,* 68 (1953), 1232–40.

2570 KIERNAN, Colm. "Swift and Science." *Historical Journal,* 14 (1971), 709–22.

2571 LANDA, Louis A. "Swift's Economic Views and Mercantilism." *ELH,* 10 (1943), 310–35.

2572 LANDA, Louis A. "Jonathan Swift and Charity." *JEGP,* 44 (1945), 337–50.

2573 LANDA, Louis A. "Swift, the Mysteries and Deism." *Texas Studies in English 1944* (Austin, 1945), 239–56.

2574 LANDA, Louis A. *Swift and the Church of Ireland.* Oxford, 1954.

2575 LEYBURN, Ellen D. "Swift's View of the Dutch." *PMLA,* 66 (1951), 734–45.

2576 LEYBURN, Ellen D. "Swift's Language Trifles." *HLQ,* 15 (1952), 195–200.

2577 MAYHEW, George P. "Swift's Games with Language in Rylands English MS 659." *BJRL,* 37 (1954), 413–48.

2578 MAYHEW, George P. "Swift and the Tripos Tradition." *PQ,* 45 (1966), 85–101.

2579 MAYHEW, George P. "A Portrait of Jonathan Swift." *HLQ,* 29 (1966), 287–94.

2580 MILIC, Louis T. *A Quantitative Approach to the Style of Jonathan Swift.* The Hague, 1967.

2581 MOORE, John Robert. "Swift as Historian." *SP,* 49 (1952), 583–604.

2582 PEAKE, Charles. "Swift and the Passions." *MLR,* 55 (1960), 169–80.

2583 PONS, Emile. *Swift: Les Années de jeunesse et le "Conte du Tonneau."* Strasbourg, 1925.*

2584 PRICE, Martin. *Swift's Rhetorical Art: A Study in Structure and Meaning.* New Haven, Conn., 1953. Rpt, Carbondale, Ill., 1973.*

2585 QUINLAN, Maurice J. "Swift's Use of Literalization as a Rhetorical Device." *PMLA,* 82 (1967), 516–21.

2586 QUINTANA, Ricardo. *The Mind and Art of Jonathan Swift.* Rev. ed. New York, 1953.*

2587 QUINTANA, Ricardo. *Swift: An Introduction.* New York, 1955.

2588/9 ROSENHEIM, Edward W., Jr. *Swift and the Satirist's Art.* Chicago, 1963.*

2590 ROSENHEIM, Edward W., Jr. "Swift and the Atterbury Case." In 45, pp. 174–204.

2591 SAID, Edward W. "Swift's Tory Anarchy." *ECS,* 3 (1969), 48–66.

2592 SAMS, Henry W. "Swift's Satire of the Second Person." *ELH,* 26 (1959), 36–44.

2593 SCRUGGS, Charles. "Swift's Views on Language: The Basis of His Attack on Poetic Diction." *TSLL,* 13 (1972), 581–92.

2594 SMITH, Roland M. "Swift's Little Language and Nonsense Names." *JEGP,* 53 (1954), 178–96. See also *ibid.,* 56 (1957), 154–62.

2595 SPECK, W. A. *Swift.* ("Literature in Perspective") London, 1969.

2595A SPILLER, Michael R. G. "The Idol of the Store: The Background of Swift's Critique of Descartes." *RES,* N.S. 25 (1974), 15–24.

2596 ULMAN, Craig H. *Satire and the Correspondence of Swift.* Cambridge, Mass., 1973.

2597 WARD, David. *Jonathan Swift: An Introductory Essay.* London, 1973.†

2598 WILLIAMS, Harold. *Dean Swift's Library.* Cambridge, Eng., 1932.

2599 WILLIAMS, Harold. "Swift's Early Biographers." In 28, pp. 114–28.

2600 WILLIAMS, Kathleen. *Jonathan Swift and the Age of Compromise.* Lawrence, Kans., 1958.†

2601 WILLIAMS, Kathleen. "Restoration Themes in the Major Satires of Swift." *RES,* N.S., 16 (1965), 258–71.

2602 WILLIAMS, Kathleen *Jonathan Swift.* ("Profiles in Literature") London, 1968.

"A Tale of a Tub" and "The Battle of the Books"

2603 ADAMS, Robert M. "Jonathan Swift, Thomas Swift, and the Authorship of *A Tale of a Tub.*" *MP,* 64 (1967), 198–232. Comment by Dipak Nandy, *ibid.,* 66 (1969), 333–37.

2604 ADAMS, Robert M. "The Mood of the Church and *A Tale of a Tub.*" In 51, pp. 71–99.

2605 ANDREASEN, N. J. C. "Swift's Satire on the Occult in *A Tale of a Tub.*" *TSLL,* 5 (1963), 410–21.

2606 CARNOCHAN, W. B. "Swift's *Tale:* On Satire, Negation, and the Uses of Irony." *ECS,* 5 (1971), 122–44.

2607 CHIASSON, Elias J. "Swift's Clothes Philosophy in the *Tale* and Hooker's Concept of Law." *SP,* 59 (1962), 64–82.

2608 CLARK, John R. *Form and Frenzy in Swift's "Tale of a Tub."* Ithaca, N.Y., 1970.

2609 CLARK, John R. "Further *Iliads* in Swift's Nut-Shell." *PQ,* 51 (1972), 945–50.

2610 CLIFFORD, James L. "Swift's *Mechanical Operation of the Spirit.*" In 28, pp. 135–46.

2611 DEPORTE, Michael V. *Nightmares and Hobbyhorses: Swift, Sterne, and Augustan Ideas of Madness.* San Marino, Cal., 1974.

2612 ELLIOTT, Robert C. "Swift's *Tale of a Tub:* An Essay in Problems of Structure." *PMLA,* 66 (1951), 441–55.

2613 FRENCH, David P. "Swift, Temple, and 'A Digression on Madness.' " *TSLL,* 5 (1963), 42–57.

2614 HARTH, Phillip. *Swift and Anglican Rationalism: The Religious Background of "A Tale of a Tub."* Chicago, 1961.*

2615 HOPKINS, Robert H. "The Personation of Hobbism in Swift's *Tale of a Tub* and *Mechanical Operation of the Spirit.*" *PQ,* 45 (1966), 372–78.

2616 IRVING, William H. "Boccalini and Swift." *ECS,* 7 (1973–74), 143–60.

2617 JONES, Richard F. *Ancients and Moderns: A Study of the Background of the "Battle of the Books."* St. Louis, 1936. 2d ed., 1961.* See also Felix Morrison in *PQ,* 13 (1934), 16–20.

2618 KELLING, Harold D. "Reason in Madness: *A Tale of a Tub.*" *PMLA,* 69 (1954), 198–222.

2619 KORSHIN, Paul J. "Swift and Typological Narrative in *A Tale of a Tub.*" *Harvard Eng. Studies,* 1 (1970), 67–91. [On Section VII.]

2620 LEVINE, Jay Arnold. "The Design of *A Tale of a Tub.* . . . *ELH,* 33 (1966), 198–227.

2621 OLSON, R. C. "Swift's Use of the *Philosophical Transactions* in Section V of *A Tale of a Tub.*" *SP,* 49 (1952), 459–67.

2622 PAULSON, Ronald. *Theme and Structure in Swift's "Tale of a Tub."* New Haven, Conn., 1960. Rpt. Hamden, Conn., 1972.*

2623 PINKUS, Philip. "The Upside-down World of *A Tale of a Tub.*" *ES,* 44 (1963), 161–75.

2624 PONS, Emile. See 2583 above. See R. Quintana, "Emile Pons and the Modern Study of Swift's *Tale of a Tub.*" *EA,* 18 (1965), 5–17.

2625 RAWSON, C. J. "Order and Cruelty: A Reading of Swift (with Some Comments on Pope and Johnson)." *EIC,* 20 (1970), 24–56. Comment by G. K. Holzknecht, *ibid.,* pp. 496–97; by Philip Drew, *ibid.,* 21 (1971), 417–18; reply by Rawson, pp. 115–16.

2626 ROGERS, Pat. "Form in *A Tale of a Tub.*" *EIC,* 22 (1972), 142–60.

2627 ROSCELLI, William J. "*A Tale of a Tub* and the 'Cavils of the Sour.' " *JEGP,* 64 (1965), 41–56.

2628 SCRUGGS, Charles. "Swift's Use of Lucretius in *A Tale of a Tub.*" *TSLL,* 15 (1973), 39–49.

2629 STARKMAN, Miriam K. *Swift's Satire on Learning in "A Tale of a Tub."* Princeton, N.J., 1950. Rpt. 1968.*

2630 STOUT, Gardner D., Jr. "Speaker and Satiric Vision in Swift's *Tale of a Tub.*" *ECS,* 3 (1969), 175–99.

Bickerstaff Pamphlets

2631 BOND, Richmond P. "John Partridge and the Company of Stationers." *SB,* 16 (1963), 61–80.

2632 BOND, Richmond P. "Isaac Bickerstaff, Esq." In 27, pp. 103–24.

2633 MAYHEW, George P. "The Early Life of John Partridge." *SEL,* 1 (1961), 31–42.

2634 MAYHEW, George P. "Swift's Bickerstaff Hoax as an April Fool's Joke." *MP,* 61 (1964), 270–80.

"Journal to Stella"

2635 EHRENPREIS, Irvin. "Swift's 'Little Language' in the *Journal to Stella.*" *SP,* 45 (1948), 80–88.

2636 ENGLAND, A. B. "Private and Public Rhetoric in the *Journal to Stella.*" *EIC,* 22 (1972), 131–41.

2737 SMITH, Frederik N. "Dramatic Elements in Swift's *Journal to Stella.*" *ECS,* 1 (1968), 332–52.

2638 WOOLF, Virginia. "Swift's *Journal to Stella.*" *The Second Common Reader* (New York, 1932), pp. 68–79.

"Drapier's Letters"

2639 DAVIES, Godfrey. "Swift's *The Story of the Injured Lady*." *HLQ,* 6 (1943), 473–89.

2640 GOODWIN, A. "Wood's Halfpence." *EHR,* 51 (1936), 647–74.

2641 WOODRING, Carl R. "The Aims, Audience, and Structure of the Drapier's Fourth Letter." *MLQ,* 17 (1956), 50–59.

"Gulliver's Travels"

2642 BARROLL, J. Leeds, III. "Gulliver and the Struldbruggs." *PMLA,* 73 (1958), 43–50.

2643 BENTMAN, Raymond. "Satiric Structure and Tone in the Conclusion of *Gulliver's Travels.*" *SEL,* 11 (1971), 535–45.

2644 BRACHER, Frederick. "The Maps in *Gulliver's Travels.*" *HLQ,* 7 (1944), 59–74.

2645 BRADY, Frank. *Twentieth-Century Interpretations of "Gulliver's Travels."* Englewood Cliffs, N.J., 1968.

2646 CARNOCHAN, W. B. *Lemuel Gulliver's Mirror for Man.* Berkeley, Cal., 1968.

2647 CASE, Arthur E. *Four Essays on "Gulliver's Travels."* Princeton, N.J., 1945.*

2648 CLARK, Paul O. "A *Gulliver* Dictionary." *SP,* 50 (1953), 592–624.

2649 CLUBB, Merrel D. "The Criticism of Gulliver's 'Voyage to the Houyhnhnms,' 1726–1914." *Stanford Studies in Language and Literature* (1941), pp. 203–32.

2650 CRANE, R. S. "The Houyhnhnms, the Yahoos, and the History of Ideas." In 42, pp. 231–53. Rpt. in his *The Idea of the Humanities* (Chicago, 1967), II, 261–82.*

2651 DANCHIN, Pierre. "The Text of *Gulliver's Travels.*" *TSLL,* 2 (1960), 233–50.

2652 EDDY, William A. *Gulliver's Travels: A Critical Study.* Princeton, N.J., 1923.

2653 ELLIOTT, Robert C. *The Shape of Utopia: Studies in a Literary Genre* (Chicago, 1970), chap. 3.

2654 FINK, Z. S. "Political Theory in *Gulliver's Travels.*" *ELH,* 14 (1947), 151–61.

2655 FITZGERALD, Robert P. "The Allegory of Luggnagg and the Struldbruggs in *Gulliver's Travels.*" *SP,* 65 (1968), 657–76.

2656 GOLDGAR, Bertrand A. "A Contemporary Reaction to *Gulliver's Travels.*" *Scriblerian,* 5 (1972), 1–3.

2657 GREENE, Donald J. "The Sin of Pride: A Sketch for a Literary Exploration." *New Mexico Quarterly,* 34 (1964), 8–30.

2658 GREENE, Donald J. "The Education of Lemuel Gulliver." In 36, pp. 3–20.

2659 HUBBARD, Lucius L. *Contributions Towards a Bibliography of "Gulliver's Travels."* Chicago, 1922.

2660 JENKINS, Clauston. "The Ford Changes and the Text of *Gulliver's Travels.*" *PBSA,* 62 (1968), 1–23.

2661 KALLICH, Martin. *The Other End of the Egg: Religious Satire in "Gulliver's Travels."* New York, 1970.

2662 KELSALL, M. M. "*Iterum* Houyhnhnms: Swift's Sextumvirate and the Horses." *EIC,* 19 (1969), 35–45.

2663 KORSHIN, Paul J. "The Intellectual Context of Swift's Flying Island." *PQ,* 50 (1971), 630–46.

2664 LAWLIS, Merritt. "Swift's Uses of Narrative: The Third Chapter of the Voyage to Lilliput." *JEGP,* 72 (1973), 1–16.

2665 LAWRY, Jon S. "Dr. Lemuel Gulliver and 'the Thing Which Was Not.' " *JEGP,* 67 (1968), 212–34.

2666 LENFEST, David S. "A Checklist of Illustrated Editions of *Gulliver's Travels,* 1727–1914." *PBSA,* 62 (1968), 85–123.

2667 MONK, Samuel H. "The Pride of Lemuel Gulliver." *SR,* 63 (1955), 48–71. Rpt. in 29.*

2668 NICOLSON, Marjorie, and Nora M. MOHLER. "The Scientific Background of Swift's *Voyage to Laputa.* " *Annals of Science,* 2 (1937), 299–334. Rpt. in Miss Nicolson's *Science and Imagination* (Ithaca, N.Y. 1956).

2669 NICOLSON, Marjorie, and Nora M. MOHLER. "Swift's 'Flying Island' in the *Voyage to Laputa.* " *Annals of Science,* 2 (1937), 405–30.

2670 ORWELL, George. "Politics vs. Literature: An Examination of *Gulliver's Travels.* " *Shooting an Elephant and Other Essays* (New York, 1945), pp. 53–76.

2671 PHILMUS, Robert M. "Swift, Gulliver, and 'The Thing Which Was Not.' " *ELH,* 38 (1971), 62–79.

2672 RAWSON, C. J. *Gulliver and the Gentle Reader: Studies in Swift and Our Time.* London, 1973.

2673 REICHERT, John F. "Plato, Swift, and the Houyhnhnms." *PQ,* 47 (1968), 179–92.

2674 ROSENHEIM, Edward, Jr. "The Fifth Voyage of Lemuel Gulliver: A Footnote." *MP,* 60 (1962), 103–19.*

2675 ROSS, Angus. *Swift: "Gulliver's Travels."* ("Studies in English Literature") London, 1968.

2676 SHERBURN, George. "Errors Concerning the Houyhnhnms." *MP,* 56 (1958), 92–97.*

2677 TRAUGOTT, John. "A Voyage to Nowhere with Thomas More and Jonathan Swift: *Utopia* and *The Voyage to the Houyhnhnms.* " *SR.,* 69 (1961), 534–65.

2678 TRAUGOTT, John. "Swift's Allegory: The Yahoo and the Man-of-Mode." *UTQ,* 33 (1963), 1–18.

2679 WALTON, J. K. "The Unity of the *Travels.* " *Hermathena,* 104 (1967), 5–50.

2680 WILLIAMS, Harold. *The Text of "Gulliver's Travels."* Cambridge, Eng., 1952.*

Poems

2681 ADEN, John M. "Corinna and the Sterner Muse of Swift." *ELN,* 4 (1966), 21–31.

2682 BALL, F. Elrington. *Swift's Verse, an Essay.* London, 1929.

2683 DAVIS, Herbert. "Swift's View of Poetry." *Studies in English by Members of University College, Toronto* (Toronto, 1931), pp. 9–58.

2684 DAVIS, Herbert. "A Modest Defence of 'The Lady's Dressing Room.' " In 27, pp. 39–48.

2685 ENGLAND, A. B. "World Without Order: Some Thoughts on the Poetry of Swift." *EIC,* 16 (1966), 32–43.

2686 FERGUSON, Oliver W. "The Authorship of 'Apollo's Edict.' " *PMLA,* 70 (1955), 433–40. [By Mrs. Barber?]

2687 FISCHER, John I. "The Uses of Virtue: Swift's Last Poem to Stella." *Essays in Honor of E. L. Marilla* (Baton Rouge, La. 1970), pp. 201–09.

2688 FISHER, John I. "How To Die: *Verses on the Death of Dr. Swift.*" *RES,* N.S. 21 (1970), 422–41.

2689 GREENE, Donald. "On Swift's Scatalogical Poems." *SR,* 75 (1967), 672–89.

2690 GULICK, Sidney L., Jr. "Jonathan Swift's 'The Day of Judgment.' " *PMLA,* 48 (1933), 850–55.

2691 HARRIS, Kathryn M. " 'Occasions So Few': Satire as a Strategy of Praise in Swift's Early Odes." *MLQ,* 31 (1970), 22–37.

2692 JOHNSON, Maurice. *The Sin of Wit: Jonathan Swift as a Poet.* Syracuse, N.Y., 1950.

2693 JOHNSON, Maurice, "Text and Possible Occasion for Swift's 'Day of Judgment.' " *PMLA,* 86 (1971), 210–17. Comment by W. B. Carnochan, *ibid.,* 87 (1972), 518–20, and Charles R. Sleeth, *ibid.,* 88 (1973), 144–45.

2694 JOHNSON, Maurice. "Swift's Poetry Reconsidered." In 43, pp. 233–48.

2695 JONES, Gareth. "Swift's *Cadenus and Vanessa:* A Question of 'Positives.' " *EIC,* 20 (1970), 424–40.

2696 LEE, Jae Num. *Swift and Scatalogical Satire.* Albuquerque, N.M., 1971.

2697 MAYHEW, George P. " 'Rage or Raillery': Swift's *Epistle to a Lady* and *On Poetry: A Rhapsody.*" *HLQ,* 33 (1960), 159–80. Rpt. in 2546.

2698 MAYHEW, George P. "Jonathan Swift's 'On the Burning of Whitehall in 1697' Re-examined." *HLB,* 19 (1971), 399–411.

2699 MAYHEW, George P. "Swift's Political 'Conversion' and His 'Lost' Ballad on the Westminster Election of 1710." *BJRL,* 53 (1971), 397–427.

2700 O HEHIR, Brendan. "Meaning in Swift's 'Description of a City Shower.' " *ELH,* 27 (1960), 194–207.

2701 OHLIN, Peter. " 'Cadenus and Vanessa': Reason and Passion." *SEL,* 4 (1964), 485–96.

2702 PEAKE, Charles. "Swift's 'Satirical Elegy on a Late Famous General.' " *Rev. of Eng. Lit.,* 3 (1962), 80–89.

2703 RAWSON, C. J. " 'The Only Infinite Below': Speculations on Swift, Wallace Stevens, R. D. Laing and Others." *EIC,* 22 (1972), 161–81.

2704 REES, Christine. "Gay, Swift, and the Nymphs of Drury Lane." *EIC,* 23 (1973), 1–21.

2705 ROBERTS, Philip. "Swift, Queen Anne, and *The Windsor Prophecy.*" *PQ,* 49 (1970), 254–58.

2706 ROTHSTEIN, Eric. "Jonathan Swift as Jupiter: 'Baucis and Philemon.' " In 45, pp. 205–24.

2707 SAN JUAN, E., Jr. "The Anti-Poetry of Jonathan Swift." *PQ,* 44 (1965), 387–96.

2708 SCHAKEL, Peter J. "Virgil and the Dean: Christian and Classical Allusion in *The Legion Club.*" *SP,* 70 (1973), 427–38.

2709 SCOUTEN, Arthur H., and Robert D. HUME. "Pope and Swift: Text and Interpretation of Swift's Verses on His Death." *PQ,* 52 (1973), 205–31.

2710 SHINAGEL, Michael. *A Concordance to the Poems of Jonathan Swift.* Ithaca, N.Y., 1972.

2711 SLEPIAN, Barry. "The Ironic Intention of Swift's Verses on His Own Death." *RES,* N.S. 14 (1963), 249–56.

2712 TYNE, James L., S. J. "Vanessa and the Houyhnhnms: A Reading of 'Cadenus and Vanessa.'" *SEL,* 11 (1971), 517–34.

2713 UPHAUS, Robert W. "From Panegyric to Satire: Swift's Early Odes and *A Tale of a Tub.*" *TSLL,* 13 (1971), 55–70.

2714 UPHAUS, Robert W. "Swift's Poetry: The Making of Meaning." *ECS,* 5 (1972), 569–86.

2715 UPHAUS, Robert W. "Swift's 'Whole Character': The Delany Poems and 'Verses on the Death of Dr. Swift.'" *MLQ,* 34 (1973), 406–16.

2716 WAINGROW, Marshall. *"Verses on the Death of Dr. Swift."* *SEL,* 5 (1965), 513–18.

2717 WEEDON, Margaret. "An Uncancelled Copy of the First Collected Edition of Swift's Poems." *The Library,* 5th ser., 22 (1967), 44–56.

Other Works

2718 BÉRANGER, J. "Swift en 1714: position politique et sentiments personnels." *EA,* 15 (1962), 222–47.

2719 COOK, Richard I. *Jonathan Swift as a Tory Pamphleteer.* Seattle, Wash., 1967.

2720 FERGUSON, Oliver W. "Swift's *Saeva Indignatio* and *A Modest Proposal.* " *PQ,* 38 (1959), 473–79.

2721 HAMILTON, David. "Swift, Wagstaff, and the Composition of *Polite Conversation.*" *HLQ,* 30 (1967), 281–95.

2722 JARRELL, Mackie L. "The Proverbs in Swift's *Polite Conversation.*" *HLQ,* 20 (1956), 15–38.

2723 LANDA, Louis A. *"A Modest Proposal* and Populousness." *MP,* 40 (1942), 161–70. Rpt. in 29.

2724 McKENZIE, Alan T. "Proper Words in Proper Places: Syntax and Substantive in *The Conduct of the Allies.*" *ECS,* 1 (1968), 253–60.

2725 MAYHEW, George P. "Swift's Anglo-Latin Games and a Fragment of *Polite Conversation* in Manuscript." *HLQ,* 17 (1954), 133–59.

2726 MAYHEW, George P. "Swift's Notes for His *History of the Last Four Years,* Book IV." *HLQ,* 24 (1961), 311–22.

2727 PETERSON, Leland D. "Swift's *Project:* A Religious and Political Satire." *PMLA,* 82 (1967), 54–63. Discussion by Phillip Harth and Peterson, *ibid.,* 84 (1969), 336–43; by John R. Van Meter, *ibid.,* 86 (1971), 1017–25; by Donald Greene, *ibid.,* 87 (1972), 520.

2728 QUINLAN, Maurice J. "Swift's *Project for the Advancement of Religion. . . .*" *PMLA,* 71 (1956), 201–12.

2729 SAMS, Henry W. "Jonathan Swift's Proposal Concerning the English Language: A Reconsideration." In 49, pp. 76–87.

2730 WITTKOWSKY, George. "Swift's *Modest Proposal:* The Biography of an Early Georgian Pamphlet." *JHI,* 4 (1943), 75–104.

James Thomson (1700–1748)

Works

2731 *Complete Poetical Works.* Ed. J. Logie Robertson. Oxford, 1908, 1951.

2732 *The Castle of Indolence and Other Poems.* Ed. Alan D. McKILLOP. Lawrence, Kans., 1961.

2733 *The Seasons and The Castle of Indolence.* Ed. James Sambrook. Oxford, 1972.

2734 *Letters and Documents.* Ed. Alan D. McKILLOP. Lawrence, Kans., 1958. See also McKILLOP, "Two More Thomson Letters." *MP,* 60 (1962), 128–30.

Bibliography

2735 CAMPBELL, Hilbert H. "A Bibliography of Twentieth-Century Criticism and Commentary on James Thomson (1700–1748), with Selected Eighteenth and Nineteenth Century Items." *Bull. of Bibliography,* 31 (1974), 9–72.

Studies

2736 CAMERON, Margaret M. *L'Influence des Saisons de Thomson sur la poésie descriptive en France, 1759–1810.* Paris, 1927.

2737 CAMPBELL, Hilbert H. "Shiels and Johnson: Biographers of Thomson." *SEL,* 12 (1972), 535–44.

2738 CHALKER, John. "Thomson's *Seasons* and Virgil's *Georgics:* The Problem of Primitivism and Progress." *SN,* 35 (1963), 41–56.

2739 COHEN, Ralph. "Literary Criticism and Artistic Interpretation: Eighteenth-Century English Illustrations of *The Seasons.*" In 42, pp. 279–306.

2740 COHEN, Ralph. *The Art of Discrimination: Thomson's "The Seasons" and the Language of Criticism.* Berkeley, Calif., 1964.* See Robert L. Marsh, "The Seasons of Discrimination." *MP,* 64 (1967), 238–52.

2741 COHEN, Ralph. "Thomson's Poetry of Space and Time." In 21, pp. 176–92.

2742 COHEN, Ralph. *The Unfolding of "The Seasons": A Study of Thomson's Poem.* Baltimore, 1970.* See also Hilbert H. Campbell, "Thomson's *Seasons,* the Countess of Hertford, and Elizabeth Young. . . ." *TSLL,* 14 (1972), 435–44.

2743 COOKE, Arthur L. "James Thomson and William Hinchcliffe." *JEGP,* 57 (1958), 755–61.

2744 DRENNON, Herbert. "James Thomson's Contact with Newtonianism and His Interest in Natural Philosophy." *PMLA,* 49 (1934), 71–80. Other articles by Drennon on this subject in *MP,* 32 (1934), 33–36; in *SP,* 31 (1934), 453–71; in *PQ,* 14 (1935), 70–82; in *Englische Studien,* 70 (1936), 358–72. On these see *PQ,* 14 (1935), 175–76.

2745 DRENNON, Herbert. "James Thomson and John Norris." *PMLA,* 53 (1938), 1094–1101.

2746 FOXON, D. F. " 'Oh! *Sophonisba! Sophonisba!* Oh!' " *SB,* 12 (1959), 204–13. [On the publication of Thomson's play.]

2747 FRANCIS, T. R. [Editions of *Tancred and Sigismunda.*] *BC,* 7 (1958), 190; 8 (1959), 181–82. See also Carl J. Stratman, *ibid.,* 9 (1960), 188.

2748 GRANT, Douglas. *James Thomson; Poet of "The Seasons."* London, 1951.*

2749 HAVENS, Raymond D. "Primitivism and the Idea of Progress in Thomson." *SP,* 29 (1932), 41–52.

2750 HUGHES, Helen Sard. "Thomson and the Countess of Hertford." *MP,* 25 (1928), 439–68; 28 (1931), 468–70. See also Hilbert H. Campbell, *ibid.,* 67 (1970), 367–69.

2751 JOHNSON, Walter Gilbert. *James Thomson's Influence on Swedish Literature in the Eighteenth Century.* Urbana, Ill., 1936.

2752 KERN, Jean B. "James Thomson's Revisions of *Agamemnon.*" *PQ,* 45 (1966), 289–303.

2753 McKILLOP, Alan D. *The Background of Thomson's Seasons.* Minneapolis, 1942.*

2754 McKILLOP, Alan D. "Thomson and the Jail Committee." *SP,* 47 (1950), 62–71.

2755 McKILLOP, Alan D. *The Background of Thomson's "Liberty."* Houston, Tex., 1951.

2756 McKILLOP, Alan D. "James Thomson's Juvenile Poems." *Newberry Lib. Bull.,* 4 (1955), 13–23.

2757 McKILLOP, Alan D. "Thomson and the Licensers of the Stage." *PQ,* 37 (1958), 448–53.

2758 McKILLOP, Alan D. "The Early History of *Alfred.*" *PQ,* 41 (1962), 311–24.

2759 MARCUS, Hans. "Die Entstehung von 'Rule Britannia.' " *Anglia Beiblatt,* 36 (1925), 21–32, 54–64, 78–89, 155–59. See also A. H. Krappe, *ibid.,* 43 (1932), 256–60.

2760 MOREL, Léon. *James Thomson, sa vie et ses oeuvres.* Paris, 1895.*

2761 POTTER, G. R. "James Thomson and the Evolution of Spirits." *Englische Studien,* 61 (1926), 57–65.

2762 SPACKS, Patricia M. *The Varied God: A Critical Study of Thomson's "The Seasons."* Berkeley, Cal., 1959.

2763 SPACKS, Patricia M. "Vision and Meaning in James Thomson." *Studies in Romanticism,* 4 (1965), 206–19.

2764 [TAYLOR, Eric S.] "James Thomson's Library." *TLS,* June 20, 1942, p. 312. See Alan D. McKILLOP in *PQ,* 22 (1943), 179–80.

2765 TODD, William B. "Unauthorized Readings in the First Edition of Thomson's 'Coriolanus.' " *PBSA,* 46 (1952), 62–66.

2766 TODD, William B. "The Text of *The Castle of Indolence.*" *ES,* 34 (1953), 115–21.

2767 WELLS, John Edwin. "Thomson's *Britannia:* Issues, Attribution, Date, Variants." *MP,* 40 (1942), 43–56.

2768 WELLS, John Edwin. "Thomson's *Seasons* 'Corrected and Amended.' " *JEGP,* 42 (1943), 104–14.

2769 WERKMEISTER, Lucyle. "Thomson and the London Daily Press, 1789–97." *MP,* 62 (1965), 237–40.

2770 WILLIAMS, George G. "Did Thomson Write the Poem *To the Memory of Mr. Congreve?*" *PMLA,* 45 (1930), 1010–13. See also John Edwin Wells in *TLS,* Oct. 3, 1936, p. 701.

2771 WILLIAMS, Ralph M. "Thomson and Dyer: Poet and Painter." In 40, pp. 209–16.

2772 WILLIAMS, Ralph M. "Thomson's 'Ode on the Winter Solstice.'" *MLN,* 70 (1955), 256–57.

John Toland (1670–1722)

2773 HEINEMANN, F. H. "Prolegomena to a Toland Bibliography." *N&Q,* 185 (1943), 182–86. Other articles by Heinemann in *RES,* 20 (1944), 125–46, and 25 (1949), 346–49; in *Philos. Rev.,* 54 (1945), 437–57; in *Archiv für Philosophie,* 4 (1950), 35–66 (with unpublished material).

2774 JACOB, Margaret C. "John Toland and the Newtonian Ideology." *JWCI,* 32 (1969), 307–36.

2775 NICHOLL, H. F. "John Toland: Religion Without Mystery." *Hermathena,* 100 (1965), 54–65.

2776 SIMMS, J. G. "John Toland (1670–1722), a Donegal Heretic." *Irish Hist. Studies,* 16 (1969), 304–20.

Horace Walpole (1711–1797)

Works

2777 *Correspondence.* Ed. W. S. Lewis *et al.* New Haven, Conn., 1937– . In progress.

2778 *Selected Letters.* Ed. W. S. Lewis. New Haven, Conn., 1973.†

2779 *Memories and Portraits.* Ed. Matthew Hodgart. London, 1963.

Bibliography

2780 HAZEN, Allen T. *A Bibliography of the Strawberry Hill Press.* . . . New Haven, Conn., 1942. Rpt. with Supplement, 1973.

2781 HAZEN, Allen T. *A Bibliography of Horace Walpole.* New Haven, Conn., 1948.

2782 HAZEN, Allen T. *A Catalogue of Horace Walpole's Library. With "Horace Walpole's library" by W. S. Lewis. 3 vols. New Haven, Conn., 1969.*

Studies

2783 CHASE, Isabel W. U. *Horace Walpole, Gardenist: An Edition of Walpole's "The History of Modern Taste in Gardening" with an Estimate of Walpole's Contribution to Landscape Architecture.* Princeton, N.J., 1943.

2784 DOBRÉE, Bonamy. "Horace Walpole." In 27, pp. 185–200.

2785 GWYNN, Stephen. *The Life of Horace Walpole.* London, 1932.

2786 HONOUR, Hugh. *Horace Walpole.* (*WTW*) London, 1958.†

2787 KALLICH, Martin. *Horace Walpole.* (*TEAS*) New York, 1971.

2788 KETTON-CREMER, R. W. *Horace Walpole: A Biography.* London, 1940, 1964; Ithaca, N.Y., 1966.

2789 LEWIS, W. S. *Horace Walpole.* New York and London, 1961.*

2790 LEWIS, W. S. *A Guide to the Life of Horace Walpole . . . as Illustrated by an Exhibition Based on the Yale Edition of His Correspondence.* New Haven, Conn., 1973.

2791 SMITH, Warren H. "Horace Walpole and Two Frenchwomen." In 40, pp. 341–49. [Mme de Sévigné and Mme du Deffand.]

2792 SMITH, Warren H., ed. *Horace Walpole: Writer, Politician, and Connoisseur.* New Haven, Conn., 1967.

2793 STEIN, Jess M. "Horace Walpole and Shakespeare." *SP,* 31 (1934), 51–68.

2794 STUART, Dorothy M. *Horace Walpole.* London, 1927.

William Warburton (1698–1779)

2795 CHERPACK, Clifton. "Warburton and the *Encyclopédie.*" *CL,* 7 (1955), 226–39.

2796 CHERPACK, Clifton. "Warburton and Some Aspects of the Search for the Primitive in Eighteenth-Century France." *PQ,* 36 (1957), 221–33.

2797 CURRY, Stephen J. "The Literary Criticism of William Warburton." *ES,* 48 (1967), 398–408.

2798 EVANS, A. W. *Warburton and the Warburtonians: A Study in Some Eighteenth-Century Controversies.* London, 1932.

2799 RYLEY, Robert M. "William Warburton as 'New Critic.' " In 21, pp. 249–65.

2800 RYLEY, Robert M. "Warburton, Warton, and Ruffhead's *Life of Pope.*" *PLL,* 4 (1968), 51–62.

Edward Ward (1667–1731)

2801 *The London Spy, Compleat in Eighteen Parts.* Introduction by Ralph Straus. London, 1924.

2802 *The London Spy.* Ed. Kenneth Fenwick. London and New York, 1955.

2803 *Five Travel Scripts Commonly Attributed to Edward Ward.* Ed. Howard W. Troyer. New York, 1933.

Bibliography

2804 CAMERON, W. J. "Bibliography of Ned Ward (1667–1731)." *N&Q,* 198 (1953), 284–86. See also S. H. Ward, *ibid.,* pp. 436–38.

2805 JONES, Claude E. "Short-Title Checklist of Works Attributed to Edward Ward (1667–1731)." *N&Q,* 190 (1948), 135–39.

Studies

2806 ALLEN, Robert J. "Ned Ward and *The Weekly Comedy.*" *HSNPL,* 17 (1935), 1–13.

2807 TROYER, Howard W. *Ned Ward of Grubstreet: A Study of Sub-Literary London in the Eighteenth Century.* Cambridge, Mass., 1946, 1968.*

The Wartons

2808 *The Three Wartons: A Choice of their Verse.* Ed. Eric Partridge. London, 1927.

2809 FENNER, Arthur, Jr. "The Wartons 'Romanticize' their Verse." *SP,* 53 (1956), 501–08.

2810 MARTIN, Burns. "Some Unpublished *Wartoniana.*" *SP,* 29 (1932), 53–67.

2811 PITTOCK, Joan. *The Ascendancy of Taste: The Achievement of Joseph and Thomas Warton.* London, 1973.

Thomas Warton (the Elder) (c. 1688–1745)

Works

2812 *Poems on Several Occasions (1748).* (Facsimile Text Soc.) New York, 1930.

Studies

2813 KIRSCHBAUM, Leo. "The Imitations of Thomas Warton the Elder." *PQ,* 22 (1943), 119–24; 24 (1945), 89–90.

2814 WILLOUGHBY, Edwin E. "The Chronology of the Poems of Thomas Warton, the Elder." *JEGP,* 30 (1931), 87–89.

Joseph Warton (1722–1800)

Studies

2815 ALLISON, James. "Joseph Warton's Reply to Dr. Johnson's *Lives.*" *JEGP,* 51 (1952), 181–91.

2816 ALLISON, James. "Mrs. Thrale's Marginalia in Joseph Warton's *Essay.*" *HLQ,* 19 (1956), 155–64.

2817 GRIFFITH, Philip M. "Joseph Warton's Criticism of Shakespeare." *Tulane Studies in Eng.,* 14 (1965), 17–56.

2818 HYSHAM, Julia. "Joseph Warton's Reputation as a Poet." *Studies in Romanticism,* 1 (1962), 220–29.

2819 KINSLEY, J. "The Publication of Warton's 'Essay on Pope.' " *MLR,* 44 (1949), 91–93.

2820 LEEDY, Paul F. "Genres Criticism and the Significance of Warton's Essay on Pope." *JEGP,* 45 (1946), 140–46.

2821 MacCLINTOCK, William D. *Joseph Warton's Essay on Pope: A History of the Five Editions.* Chapel Hill, N.C., 1933.

2822 McKILLOP, Alan D. "Shaftesbury in Joseph Warton's *Enthusiast.*" *MLN,* 70 (1955), 337–39.

2823 MORLEY, Edith J. "Joseph Warton's Criticism of Pope." *MLN,* 36 (1921), 276–81.

2824 MORRIS, David B. "Joseph Warton's Figure of Virtue: Poetic Indirection in 'The Enthusiast.' " *PQ,* 50 (1971), 678–83.

2825 PITTOCK, Joan. "Joseph Warton and His Second Volume of the *Essay on Pope.*" *RES,* N.S. 18 (1967), 264–73.

2826 SCHICK, George B. "Joseph Warton's Conceptions of the Qualities of a True Poet." *Boston Univ. Studies in Eng.,* 3 (1957), 77–87.

2827 SCHICK, George B. "Joseph Warton's Critical Essays in his 'Virgil.' " *N&Q,* 206 (1961), 255–56.

2828 SMITH, Audley L. "The Primitivism of Joseph Warton." *MLN,* 42 (1927), 501–04.

2829 TROWBRIDGE, Hoyt. "Joseph Warton's Classification of English Poets." *MLN,* 51 (1936), 515–18.

2830 TROWBRIDGE, Hoyt. "Joseph Warton on the Imagination." *MP,* 35 (1937), 73–87.

Thomas Warton (the Younger) (1728–1790)

Works

2831 *A History of English Poetry: An Unpublished Continuation.* Ed. Rodney M. Baine. (*ARS*) Los Angeles, 1953.[†]

Studies

2832 HAVENS, Raymond D. "Thomas Warton and the Eighteenth-Century Dilemma." *SP,* 25 (1928), 36–50. Rpt. in 23.

2833 KINGHORN, A. M. "Warton's *History* and Early English Poetry." ES, 44 (1963), 197–204.

2834 MILLER, Frances S. "The Historic Sense of Thomas Warton, Junior." *ELH,* 5 (1938), 430–49.

2835 RINAKER, Clarissa. *Thomas Warton: A Biographical and Critical Study.* Urbana, Ill., 1916.*

2836 SMITH, David Nichol. *Warton's History of English Poetry.* London, 1929.

2837 SMITH, David Nichol. "Thomas Warton's Miscellany: *The Union.*" *RES,* 19 (1943), 263–75.

2838 WELLEK, René. *The Rise of English Literary History* (rev. ed., New York, 1966),[†] chap. 6.

Isaac Watts (1674–1748)

Works

2839 *Reliquiae Juveniles: Miscellaneous Thoughts in Prose and Verse (1734). (SF&R.)* Ed. S. J. Rogal. Gainesville, Fla., 1968.

2840 *Divine Songs.* Facsimile Reproductions of the First Edition of 1735 and an Illustrated Edition of 1840. With Introduction and Bibliography by J. H. P. Pafford. London, 1971.

Bibliography

2841 ROGAL, Samuel J. "A Checklist of Works by and about Isaac Watts (1674–1748)." *BNYPL,* 71 (1967), 207–15.

Studies

2842 DAVIS, Arthur P. *Isaac Watts: His Life and Works.* New York, 1943.

2843 ESCOTT, Harry. *Isaac Watts, Hymnographer: A Study of the Beginnings, Development, and Philosophy of the English Hymn.* London, 1962.

2844 RUPP, E. G. *Six Makers of English Religion, 1500–1700.* New York, 1957.

2845 STEESE, Peter D. "Dennis's Influence on Watts's Preface to *Horae Lyricae.*" *PQ,* 42 (1963), 275–77.

John Wesley (1703–1791)

Works

2846 *Works.* 14 vols. London, 1872. Rpt. Grand Rapids, Mich., 1958–59.

2847 *John Wesley: A Representative Collection of His Writings.* Ed. Albert C. Outler. New York, 1964.

2848 *Journal.* Abridged by Nehemiah Curnock. New York, 1963.

2849 *Letters.* Ed. John Telford. 8 vols. 1931, 1956.

Bibliography

2850 GREEN, Richard. *The Works of John and Charles Wesley: A Bibliography.* ... London, 1896, 1906.

2851 ROGAL, Samuel J. "The Wesleys: A Checklist of Critical Commentary." *Bull. of Bibliography,* 28, no. 1 (1971), 22–34.

Studies

2852 BRAILSFORD, Mabel R. *A Tale of Two Brothers: John and Charles Wesley.* London, 1954.

2853 GOLDEN, James L. "John Wesley on Rhetoric and Belles Lettres." *SM,* 28 (1961), 250–64.

2854 HERBERT, Thomas W. *John Wesley as Editor and Author.* Princeton, N.J., 1940.

2855/6 LAWTON, George. *John Wesley's English: A Study of His Literary Style.* London, 1962.

2857 MONK, Robert C. *John Wesley: His Puritan Heritage.* Nashville, Tenn., 1966.

2858 WRIGHT, Louis B. "John Wesley: Scholar and Critic." *SAQ,* 29 (1930), 262–81.

Gilbert White (1720–1793)

Works

2859 *Writings.* Selected and ed. by H. J. Massingham. 2 vols. London, 1938.

2860 *The Natural History of Selborne.* Ed. R. M. Lockley. (EL). London, 1909, 1950. Ed. James Fisher. New York, 1960.

2861 *The Antiquities of Selborne.* Ed. W. Sidney Scott. 1950.

2862 *Journals.* Ed. Walter Johnson. 1931.†

Bibliography

2863 MARTIN, Edward A. *A Bibliography of Gilbert White.* . . . Rev. ed. London, 1934.

2864 PRANCE, Claude A. "Some Uncollected Authors. XLIV: Gilbert White, 1720–1793." *BC,* 17 (1968), 300–21.

Studies

2865 EMDEN, Cecil S. *Gilbert White in His Village.* London, 1956.

2866 JOHNSON, Walter. *Gilbert White, Pioneer, Poet, and Stylist.* London, 1928.

2867 SCOTT, Walter Sidney. *White of Selborne.* London, 1950.

John Wilkes (1727–1797)

2868/9 BREDVOLD, Louis I. *The Contributions of John Wilkes to the "Gazette littéraire de l'Europe."* Ann Arbor, Mich., 1950.

2870 CHRISTIE, Ian R. *Wilkes, Wyvill and Reform: The Parliamentary Reform Movement in British Politics, 1760–1785.* London, 1962.

2871 HAMILTON, Adrian. *The Infamous "Essay on Woman"; or, John Wilkes Seated Between Vice and Virtue*. London, 1972. [Facsimile rpt. of the *Essay*, with related documents.]

2872 KRONENBERGER, Louis. *The Extraordinary Mr. Wilkes: His Life and Times*. New York, 1974.

2873 McCRACKEN, George. "John Wilkes, Humanist." *PQ*, 11 (1932), 109–34.

2874 NOBBE, George. *The North Briton: A Study in Political Propaganda*. New York, 1939.

2875 POSTGATE, Raymond. *"That Devil Wilkes."* Rev. ed., London, 1956.

2876 RUDÉ, George. *Wilkes and Liberty: A Social Study of 1763 to 1774*. Oxford, 1962.

2877 TRENCH, Charles C. *Portrait of a Patriot: A Biography of John Wilkes*. Edinburgh, 1962.

Anne Finch, Countess of Winchilsea (1661–1720)

Works

2878 *Poems.* Ed. Myra Reynolds. Chicago, 1903.

2879 *Minor Poets of the Eighteenth Century.* Ed. Hugh I'Anson Fausset. (*EL*) London, 1930.

Studies

2880 ANDERSON, Paul B. "Mrs. Manley's Text of Three of Lady Winchilsea's Poems." *MLN*, 45 (1930), 95–99.

2881 BROWER, Reuben A. "Lady Winchilsea and the Poetic Tradition of the Seventeenth Century." *SP*, 42 (1945), 61–80.

2882 BUXTON, John. *A Tradition of Poetry* (London, 1967), chap. 8.

2883 HUGHES, Helen Sard. "Lady Winchilsea and Her Friends." *London Mercury*, 19 (1929), 624–35.

Mary Wollstonecraft (1759–1797)

Letters

2884 *Four New Letters of Mary Wollstonecraft and Helen Maria Williams.* Eds. Benjamin P. Kurtz and Carrie C. Antrey. Berkeley, Cal., 1937.

Studies

2885/6 GEORGE, Margaret. *One Woman's 'Situation': A Study of Mary Wollstonecraft.* Urbana, Ill., 1970.

2887 GODWIN, William. *Memoirs of Mary Wollstonecraft.* Ed. W. Clarke Durant. London, 1927.

2888 JAMES, H. R. *Mary Wollstonecraft: A Sketch.* London, 1932.

2889 NITCHIE, Elizabeth. "An Early Suitor of Mary Wollstonecraft." *PMLA,* 58 (1943), 163–69.

2890 PREEDY, George R. *This Shining Woman: Mary Wollstonecraft Godwin, 1759–1797.* London, 1937.

2891 WARDLE, Ralph M. "Mary Wollstonecraft, *Analytical Reviewer.*" *PMLA,* 62 (1947), 1000–09. See also Derek Roper in *N&Q,* 203 (1958), 37–38.

Arthur Young (1741–1820)

Works

2892 *Autobiography. With Selections from His Correspondence.* Ed. M. Betham-Edwards. London, 1898. Rpt. New York, 1968.

2893 *Travels in France During the Years 1787, 1788, and 1789.* Ed. Constantia Maxwell. Cambridge, Eng., 1929.

Studies

2894 DEFRIES, Amelia. *Sheep and Turnips: Being the Life and Times of Arthur Young, F.R.S., First Secretary to the Board of Agriculture.* London, 1938.

2895 GAZLEY, John G. *The Life of Arthur Young, 1741–1820.* Philadelphia, 1973.

2896 HASLAM, C. S. *The Biography of Arthur Young, F.R.S., from His Birth Until 1787.* Rugby, 1930.

Edward Young (1683–1765)

2897 *Conjectures on Original Composition.* Ed. Edith J. Morley. Manchester, 1918. (Scholar Press Facsimile.) Leeds, 1966.

2898 *Correspondence.* Ed. Henry Pettit. Oxford, 1971.

Bibliography

2899 FORSTER, Harold. "Some Uncollected Authors. XLV: Edward Young in Translation." *BC,* 19 (1970), 481–500; 20 (1971), 47–67, 209–24.

2900 PETTIT, Henry. *A Bibliography of Young's Night Thoughts.* Boulder, Col., 1954.

Studies

2901 BLISS, Isabel St. John. "Young's *Night-Thoughts* in Relation to Contemporary Christian Apologetics." *PMLA,* 49 (1934), 37–70.

2902 BLISS, Isabel St. John. *Edward Young. (TEAS)* New York, 1969.*

EDWARD YOUNG

2903 CLARK, Harry H. "The Romanticism of Edward Young." *TWA,* 24 (1929), 1–45. Rev. by R. S. Crane in *PQ,* 9 (1930), 203–05.

2904 HALL, Mary S. "On Light in Young's *Night Thoughts."* *PQ,* 48 (1969), 452–63.

2905 KELLY, Richard M. "Imitation of Nature: Edward Young's Attack upon Alexander Pope." *Xavier Univ. Studies,* 4 (1965), 168–76.

2906 LEEK, Helen. "The Edward Young — Edmund Curll Quarrel: A Review." *PBSA,* 62 (1969), 321–35.

2907 McKILLOP, Alan D. "Richardson, Young, and the *Conjectures." MP,* 22 (1925), 391–404.*

2908 ODELL, Daniel W. "Locke, Cudworth, and Young's *Night* Thoughts." *ELN,* 4 (1967), 188–93.

2909 ODELL, Daniel W. "Young's *Night Thoughts* as an Answer to Pope's *Essay on Man." SEL,* 12 (1972), 481–501.

2910 PETTIT, Henry. *The English Rejection of Young's Night Thoughts.* Boulder, Col., 1957.

2911 PETTIT, Henry, "The Occasion of Young's *Night Thoughts." ES,* 49 (1969), *Anglo-American Supp.,* pp. xi–xx.

2912 SHELLEY, Henry C. *The Life and Letters of Edward Young.* London, 1914.

2913 STEINKE, Martin W. *Edward Young's 'Conjectures on Original Composition' in England and Germany.* New York, 1917.

2914 SWEDENBERG, H. T., Jr. "Letters of Edward Young to Mrs. Judith Reynolds." *HLQ,* 2 (1938), 89–100.

2915 THOMAS, Walter. *Le Poète Edward Young (1683–1765). Etude sur sa vie et ses oeuvres.* Paris, 1901.

2916 WICKER, C. V. *Edward Young and the Fear of Death: A Study in Romantic Melancholy.* Albuquerque, N.M., 1952.

INDEX OF AUTHORS

AUTHORS

AUTHORS

AUTHORS F-G

Fone, B. R. S., 1168, 1176
Forbes, Duncan, 1291
Ford, Boris, 62
Ford, Franklin L., 85
Formigari, Lia, 593
Forsgren, Adina, 1356
Forster, E. M., 1260
Forster, Harold, 2899
Foss, Michael, 242
Foster, John W., 456
Fothergill, Brian, 495
Foucault, Michel, 316
Foxon, David F., 6, 2002, 2746
France, Claude A., 2864
Francis, T. R., 2747
Frankena, William, 1627/8
Frantz, Ray W., 357
Fraser, G. S., 1447
Frazer, Catherine S., 1582
Free, William N., 866, 1227
Freehafer, John, 951
Freimarck, Vincent, 877
French, David P., 2160, 2537, 2613
French, Roger, 317
Friedman, Albert B., 405, 910, 1966
Friedman, Arthur, 370, 1436, 2137
Friedman, John B., 2421
Fries, Charles C., 878
Fritz, Paul, 32
Frost, William, 406, 2105
Fry, Roger, 243
Frye, Northrop, 371, 620
Fuller, John, 1357, 2233
Furber, Elizabeth C., 96
Furlong, E. J., 1583
Furst, Lillian R., 338
Fussell, G. E., 138
Fussell, Paul, Jr., 72, 407, 590, 1036, 1670

Gabler, Anthony J., 694
Gagey, Edmond M., 556
Gallon, D. N., 1255
Garrod, H. W., 1193, 1533
Gaskell, Philip, 1918
Gassman, Byron, 1464
Gaunt, William, 245
Gay, Peter, 33, 165, 172, 911
Gazley, John G., 2895
George, M. Dorothy, 139, 246, 247
George, Margaret, 2885/6
Gerber, Helmut E., 1208, 2297
Gibbs, F. W., 2250
Gibson, William A., 2207

Gifford, Henry, 1815, 1824
Gilbert, Jack G., 2566
Gill, F. C., 209
Gilliam, John G., 2251
Gillie, Christopher, 2123
Gillis, William E., 1298
Gilmore, Thomas B., Jr., 573, 803, 811, 814, 1177
Glathe, Alfred B., 1584
Glazier, Lyle, 1534
Godwin, William, 2887
Goggin, L. P., 2106
Golden, James L., 996, 1037, 2456, 2853
Golden, Morris, 1164, 1165, 1228, 1485, 1499
Goldgar, Bertrand A., 812, 2161, 2567, 2656
Goldstein, Harvey D., 2298
Goldstein, Malcolm, 2036, 2309, 2314
Gombrich, E. H., 2299
Goodwin, A., 1078, 2640
Gordon, Ian A., 2379
Gore-Brown, Robert, 496
Graham, Edwin, 1358
Graham, Walter, 705, 706, 745, 895, 2501, 2502
Grant, Douglas, 1157, 2748
Grave, S. A., 173
Gray, Charles H., 621
Gray, James, 1844
Grean, Stanley, 2360/1
Green, Clarence C., 622
Green, David, 248, 280
Green, Richard, 2850
Greene, Donald J., 86, 90, 205, 210, 408, 789, 879, 1642, 1648, 1671–1676, 1797, 1845, 2037, 2422, 2657, 2658, 2689, 2727
Greene, Elvena M., 2503
Greenough, Chester N., 912, 2504
Gregor, Ian, 1782
Greig, J. Y. T., 1568
Grene, Marjorie, 623
Griffith, Philip M., 755, 2817
Griffith, Reginald H., 1976, 1995, 1999, 2038
Grigson, Geoffrey, 2423
Grundy, C. Reginald, 249
Grundy, Isobel, 1934, 2208
Guerinot, Joseph V., 2004, 2010
Guerlac, Henry, 318
Guilhemet, Leon M., 1500
Guite, Harold, 813

AUTHORS

AUTHORS

AUTHORS

165

AUTHORS

AUTHORS

AUTHORS

AUTHORS

INDEX OF SUBJECTS

SUBJECTS

SUBJECTS

Gay, John, 142, 1343–1375, 2233, 2704
Gazette littéraire de l'Europe, 2868/9
Gazetteer, The, 748
General Magazine of Arts and Sciences, The, 749
Genius, 584, 608, 687, 690, 2469; original g., 582, 639
Gentleman's Magazine, The, 692, 750, 751, 754
Geology, 312
George I, 134
George II, 108
George III, 96, 112, 124, 125, 323
Georgic, 453, 455
Gerard, Alexander, 583, 584, 623, 857, 958
Germany: Mrs. Piozzi in, 1983; Pope's reputation in, 2171; romanticism in, 338, 344; visitors from, 502; Edward Young's reputation in, 2913
Gibbon, Edward, 776, 777, 866, 1376–1408
Gibbons, Grinling, 248
Gibbs, James, 260
Gibson, Edmund, 223
Gildon, Charles, 1409–1416
Gilpin, William, 598, 660
Girtin's Sketching Club, 1463
Godwin, William, 1417–1435. *See also* Wollstonecraft, Mary
Goldsmith, Oliver, 74, 416, 541, 1184, 1436–1487, 2268 , 2295
Gothic, 234, 236; drama, 493; novels, 531
Gout, 313
Grainger, James, 1288
Granville, Earl. *See* Carteret
Graves, Richard, 2382
Gray, Thomas, 382, 384, 428, 866, 1184, 1488–1542, 1613, 2206, 2381
Greek: influences, 73; poems of Gray, 1488
Grenvilles, the, 126
Griffiths, Ralph, 762
Grotesque, the, 2152
Grub Street, 153, 1660, 2269, 2807
Grub Street Journal, The, 752, 753

Hailes, David Dalrymple, Lord, 1956
Halifax, Charles Montagu, 1st Earl of, 1409
Handel, G. F., 233, 300–309

Hanmer, Sir Thomas, 568
Harris, James, 652, 657
Harrison, William, 2500
Harte, Walter, 814
Hartley, David, 167, 657
Haslewood, Joseph, 597
Hastings, Warren, 2397, 2398
Hawkesworth, John, 754–756
Hawksmoor, Nicholas, 237
Hayley, William, 585, 2342
Healey, Samuel, 660
Hebrew, 2428
Hell, 205; "News from Hell," 799
Hellenism, 349
Herd, David, 1967
Heroic couplet, 395, 421
Heroic poetry. *See* Epic
Hertford, Frances, Countess of, 1286, 2305, 2306, 2383, 2742, 2750
Hervey, James, 380
Hervey, John, Lord, 108, 2181, 2195
Hill, Aaron, 1543–1550
Hill, John, 319
Hinchcliffe, William, 2743
Historical Background, 96–128
Histories of eighteenth-century literature and general studies, 55–95
History, 9, 96–128, 1095, 1615; writing of, 776–785, 2581. *See also* Bolingbroke, Gibbon, Hume
Hobbes, Thomas, 962, 1012, 2615
Hogarth, William, 233, 245, 247, 266, 608, 1551–1562
Holcroft, Thomas, 1435
Homer, 618, 1803, 2609; Pope's translation, 1990, 2105, 2217–2224
Hooker, Richard, 2607
Horace: imitations of, 398, 1990, 2175–2199; translations, 2438
Humanitarianism, 363, 372, 373, 377, 1229
Hume, David, 75, 167, 608, 975, 1563–1612; and benevolence, 182; and sentiment, 367; and Adam Smith, 2465; Beattie on, 962; Ferguson on, 1292, 1296; historical writing, 776, 777; on imagination and truth, 960
Humor, 586, 848–856, 1787
Hunter, John, 315
Huntington Library, 14, 517, 694
Hurd, Richard, 1613–1621
Husbands, John, 353

SUBJECTS

SUBJECTS

SUBJECTS

SUBJECTS

SUBJECTS

Servant class, 140
Sévigné, Marie de Rabutin-Chantal, marquise de, 2791
Seward, Anna, 1053, 2335–2342
Shadwell, Thomas, 551
Shaftesbury, Anthony Ashley Cooper, 3d Earl of, 657, 938, 1005, 1054, 2156, 2343–2376, 2822
Shakespeare, William, 562–570; and Gray, 1536; and Walpole, 2793; John Dennis on, 568; Richard Farmer on, 568; Garrick's productions, 1329–1339; Sir Thomas Hanmer on, 568; Johnson's edition, 568, 1629, 1825–1838; the Jubilee, 1322, 1328; Mason's notes on, 1922; Maurice Morgann on, 568; Pope's edition, 568, 2225–2230; Rowe's edition, 568, 2316; Warburton on, 568; J. Warton on, 2817
Sharp, John, 211
Shelley, Percy Bysshe, 493
Shenstone, William, 1963, 2377–2388
Sheridan, R. B., 541, 1465, 1470, 2389–2408
Sherlock, Thomas, 196
Shiels, Robert, 898, 2737
Siddons, Mrs. Sarah, 494, 564
Simeon, Charles, 221
Simplicity, 627
Singer, Elizabeth. See Rowe, Elizabeth Singer
Smart, Christopher, 428, 2409–2441
Smith, Adam, 1292, 2442–2465
Smollett, Tobias, 727, 729
Social and cultural background, 129–163
Sociology, beginnings of, 1295
Sonnet, the, 410
South Sea Bubble, 103, 1178
Spain, Richard Cumberland in, 1269
Spanish plays, 512
Spectator, The. See Addison
Spence, Joseph, 2466–2471
Spenser, Edmund, 611, 1736, 2108
Spinoza, Benedict de, 198
Stanhope, Philip, 1150
Steele, Sir Richard, 553, 894, 1415, 2139, 2472–2525, 2567. See also Addison
Sterne, Laurence, 79, 208, 2460, 2611
Stevens, Wallace, 2703
Stoicism, 1703, 1769
Stourhead, 290

Stowe, 289
Stubbs, George, 270
Stylistics, 872–891, 1706, 1759
Sublime, the, 420, 578, 628, 658, 691, 803, 1059, 1079, 1087, 1096
Supernatural, the, 427
Surrey, Henry Howard, Earl of, 1960
Swedish literature, 2751
Sacheverell, Rev. Henry, 212, 952
Salons, 156
Swift, Jonathan, 72, 79, 184, 821, 2526–2730; and The Examiner, 740; and Godwin, 1433; and William Harrison, 2500; and Steele, 2506; as letter writer, 866; criticism of Descartes, 2595A; Johnson's life of, 1728, 1737; on faction, 1015; on language, 883; Swift-Pope Miscellanies, 1995
Swift, Thomas, 2603
Switzerland, Gibbon in, 1380, 1381

Taste: and the Wartons, 2811; essays on, 573, 579, 583, 589, 998, 999, 1566, 1579, 1609; in criticism, 596, 599, 600, 604, 606, 630, 644; in fine arts, 234, 461; in letter writing, 869; in music, 295; in poetry, 626, 692, 2340, 2388
Tatler, The. See Steele
Temple, Sir William, 2613
Tenison, Thomas, 197
Theatre, the, 16, 358, 473–570, 2036, 2039, 2757. See also Criticism
Theobald, Lewis, 568, 2030, 2230
Thomson, James, 428, 468, 2731–2772
Thornton, Bonnell, 756
Thrale, Henry, 1669
Tinker Library, 8
Tofts, Mrs. Catherine, 527
Toland, John, 2773–2776
Toleration, 194
Topographical poetry, 451, 456, 1266
Tory party, 107, 1257; and satire, 801; propaganda, 2719; prose style, 879; view of Roman history, 783
Touch-Stone, The, 558, 2276
Travel, 346, 357, 1682, 2803
Triplet, the, 390
Trumbull, Sir William, 1996
Turner, J. M. W., 245
Twining, Thomas, 653
Tyrwhitt, Thomas, 1142

SUBJECTS U-Z

NOTES

Goldentree
Bibliographies
in Language
& Literature

Under the series
editorship of
O.B. Hardison, Jr.

Afro-American Writers • Darwin T. Turner
The Age of Dryden • Donald F. Bond
American Drama from its Beginnings to the Present • E. Hudson Long
American Literature: Poe Through Garland • Harry Hayden Clark
American Literature Through Bryant • Richard Beale Davis
The American Novel: Sinclair Lewis to the Present • Blake Nevius
The American Novel Through Henry James • C. Hugh Holman
The British Novel: Conrad to the Present • Paul J. Wiley
The British Novel: Scott Through Hardy • Ian Watt
Chaucer • Albert C. Baugh
The Eighteenth Century • Donald F. Bond
Linguistics and English Linguistics • Harold B. Allen
Literary Criticism: Plato Through Johnson • Vernon Hall
Milton • James Holly Hanford
Old and Middle English Literature • William Matthews
Romantic Poets and Prose Writers • Richard Harter Fogle
The Sixteenth Century: Skelton Through Hooker • John L. Lievsay
Tudor and Stuart Drama • Irving Ribner
Victorian Poets and Prose Writers • Jerome H. Buckley

FORTHCOMING TITLES:
The American Indian: Language and Literature • Jack W. Marken
The British Novel Through Jane Austen • Wayne C. Booth & Gwin J. Kolb
Modern Poetry • Charles F. Altieri
The Seventeenth Century: Bacon Through Marvell • Arthur E. Barker
Women Writers in Britain and the United States • Florence Howe & Deborah S. Rosenfelt

AHM Publishing Corporation